Competing
Against Time

Competing Against Time

How Time-based Competition
Is Reshaping Global Markets

George Stalk, Jr.
Thomas M. Hout

THE FREE PRESS
A Division of Macmillan, Inc.
NEW YORK

Collier Macmillan Publishers
LONDON

FREE PRESS
Rockefeller Center
1230 Avenue of the Americas
New York, NY 10020

FREE PRESS and colophon are trademarks of Macmillan Library Research USA, Inc. under license by Simon & Schuster, the publisher of this work.

Designed by
Manufactured in the United States of America

10 9 8 7 6 5 4 3 2 1

Library of Congress Cataloging-In-Publication Data

Stalk, George.
    Competing against time : how time-based competition is reshaping
global markets / George Stalk, Jr. (and) Thomas M. Hout.
        p.   cm.
    Includes bibliographical references.
    ISBN | 978-0-7432-5341-3
    1. Time management.   2. Delivery of goods.   3. Competition,
International.   4. Comparative advantage (International trade)
I. Hout, Thomas M.   II. Title
HD69.T54S73 1990
658.5'6—dc20   89-23735
                                                        CIP

For information regarding the special discounts for bulk purchases, please contact Simon & Schuster Special Sales at 1-800-456-6798 or business@simonandschuster.com

We dedicate this book to the past, current, and future clients and staff of The Boston Consulting Group

Contents

Preface

The search for what has become time-based competition began in 1979. In that year, many of us were startled by some data shared with us by a client. The client had benchmarked the performance of his key factories in the United States and in Europe with those of a Japanese affiliate. The differences included substantially higher productivity, better quality, significantly less inventory, less space, and much faster throughput times for the Japanese affiliate compared to what were generally regarded as well-run factories by the client. The better performance of the Japanese affiliate was achieved despite the fact that the company had much lower production volumes and greater variety than did the client factories. As Bruce Henderson said at the time, "Until the causes of these differences can be explained much of the conceptual underpinnings of corporate strategy are suspect."

Over the next years many more examples of companies able to establish similar performance gaps were found. Many of these companies are Japanese but increasingly the list includes American, European, and now Korean, Taiwanese, and Hong Kong companies. Two years were needed to establish cause and effect and the search carried us beyond Japan, the United States, and Europe to the rest of Asia and Australia. Two more years were needed to relate time itself to the many changes being made to factories and the organizations that need and manage factories. Another year was required to demonstrate that time is as important in non-manufacturing businesses as it clearly is to manufacturing businesses.

During these investigations many closely held assumptions as to how costs and customers behave have been altered. Instead of costs going up as run-lengths are reduced, they decline. Instead of costs going up with greater investment in quality, they decrease. And, finally, instead of costs going up with increasing variety and decreasing response time, they go down. Further, instead of customer demand being only marginally affected by expanded choice and better responsiveness, it is astoundingly sensitive to this better service—with the company that is able to set customers' expectations for choice and response very quickly dominating the most profitable segments of demand.

Many people are responsible for the development of this thinking. Most of them are members of client organizations. Any list would be incomplete because The Boston Consulting Group's policy of confidential client relationships prevents identifying many of the most important contributors. In fact, the authors have adhered to this policy throughout. In no case does this book contain data that have not been obtained from public sources or modified to prevent identification with a client of The Boston Consulting Group. None of the extended examples in which the company is identified are clients.

Many staff members of The Boston Consulting Group contributed early, especially Rene Abate, Barbara Berke, Len Friedel, Thia von Ghyczy, Shikar Ghosh, Richard Hermon-Taylor, Rud Istvan, Gilbert Milan, Anthony Miles, Sy Tilles, and Tom Wurster. Later, we were joined by Jim Andrews, Jeanette Besharat, Mark Blaxill, Dana Cain, Phil Catchings, John Clarkeson, Simon Cornwell, Mark Delfino, Jeannie Duck, Jeri Eckhart, Erin Esparza, Philip Evans, Brad Fauvre, Myron Feld, John Frantz, Steve Gunby, Ranch Kimball, Barbara McLagan, Bob Malchione, Mike Marcus, Bob Morette, Klaus Nadler, Dean Nelson, Michael Norkus, Art Peck, Gary Reiner, Wayne Robinson, Heiner Rutt, Simon Sherwood, Larry Shulman, Ashok Siddhanti, Mike Silverstein, Hal Sirkin, Carl Stern, Roger Walcott, Iain Watson, Richard Winger, and Alan Zakon, and many others who made such a difference to their clients by helping them become time-based competitors.

We deeply appreciate the support and long hours of all these people. This is a book about their work and their companies. We also thank our skillful and wise editor, Nan Stone, Senior Editor of the *Harvard Business Review,* our copy editor, Marilyn Shepherd, and Professor Joseph Bower of the Harvard Business School. Finally, we are indebted to Jim Abegglen and Bruce Henderson for lighting the way these many years.

1

◇◇◇◇

The Dawn of a New Competitive Age

I n the competitive environment of the latter twentieth century, innovations in competitive strategy have life cycles of ten to fifteen years. Each innovation is followed by major shifts in competitive positions and in corporate fortunes. As these shifts occur, concerned managements struggle to understand the nature of their competitors' newfound advantage. However, like a military secret the new source of advantage soon becomes understood by all and is thus no longer an exploitable innovation. A new innovation must be found.

Today's innovation is time-based competition. Demanding executives at aggressive companies are altering their measures of performance from competitive costs and quality to competitive costs, quality, *and* responsiveness. Give customers what they want when they want it. This refocusing of attention is enabling early innovators to become time-based competitors. Time-based competitors are offering greater varieties of products and services, at lower costs and in less time than are their more pedestrian competitors. In so doing they are literally running circles around their slower competition.

Companies are obtaining remarkable results by focusing their organization on responsiveness. Each of the companies in Table 1–1 uses its response advantage to grow at least three times faster than other companies in the industry and with profitabilities that are more than twice the industry average.

TABLE 1–1 Time-based Competitors (Estimated Performance)

Company	Business Advantage	Response Difference	Growth	Profit
Wal-Mart	Discount stores	80%	36 vs. 12%	19 vs. 9% ROCE[a]
Atlas Door	Industrial doors	66%	15 vs. 5%	10 vs. 2% ROS[a]
Ralph Wilson Plastics	Decorative laminates	75%	9 vs. 3%	40 vs. 10% RONA[a]
Thomasville	Furniture	70%	12 vs. 3%	21 vs. 11% ROA[a]
Citicorp	Mortgages	85%	100 vs. 3%	N/A

[a] ROCE = return on capital employed; ROS = return on sales; RONA = return on net assets; ROA = return on assets.

TIME-BASED COMPETITORS OUTPERFORM THEIR INDUSTRY

The five examples in Table 1–1 illustrate the competitive force of timely responsiveness to customer needs.

Wal-Mart is one of the fastest growing retailers in the United States. Its stores move nearly $20 billion of merchandise a year. Only K Mart and the floundering giant, Sears, are larger. Wal-Mart's success is due to many factors not the least of which is responsiveness. Wal-Mart replenishes the stock in its stores on average twice a week. Many stores receive deliveries daily. The typical competitor—K Mart, Sears, or Zayre—replenishes its stock every two weeks. Compared to these competitors, Wal-Mart can

- Maintain the same service levels with one-fourth the inventory investment
- Offer its customers four times the choice of stock for the same investment in inventory
- Do some of both

Wal-Mart is growing three times faster than the retail discount industry as a whole and has a return on capital that is more than twice as high as the industry average.

Atlas Door is now the leading supplier of industrial overhead doors in the United States. In concept, these doors are simple. They are just very wide and high. However, the variations of width and height are almost endless. Consequently, unless the buyer is lucky and requests a door that is in stock, he or she might have to wait several months until the desired door can be designed and manufactured—that is, unless they order from Atlas Door. Atlas can fill an order for an out-of-stock door in three to four weeks, one-third the industry average.

Customers are rewarding Atlas Door's responsiveness by buying most of their doors from them, often at 20 percent price premiums. Atlas Door's leading competitor, the Overhead Door Corporation (a division of the Dallas Corporation) has slipped into second place and continues to lose share. Atlas Door is growing three times faster than the industry, and it is five times more profitable than the average firm in the industry.

WilsonArt is the brand name for a line of decorative laminates manufactured by Ralph Wilson Plastics, a unit of Premark. Decorative laminates were pioneered by Formica, a company whose early success made its name a household word. Today, WilsonArt is the leading brand of decorative laminates, and Formica is a struggling company. Wilson Plastics is successful because, compared to its competitors, it is much more responsive. If a user's desired laminate is not available through a local distributor or at Wilson's regional distribution center, Wilson promises to manufacture and deliver the desired product in eight days or less. Competitors typically need more than 30 days to respond to an out-of-stock situation. Demand for WilsonArt decorative laminates is growing three times faster than overall demand, and the profitability of Ralph Wilson Plastics is four times greater than that of the average competitor.

Thomasville Furniture is a new breed of competitor in an industry plagued by slow and unreliable suppliers. Thomasville has a quick-ship program. A buyer is promised 30-day delivery if the article desired is not in stock at the company stores. The average industry response to a similar out-of-stock situation is longer than three months. Thomasville is growing four times faster than the industry, and the company is twice as profitable as the industry average.

Citicorp introduced MortgagePower three years ago. It promised the buyer and the realtor a loan commitment in fifteen days or less. The typical loan originator requires 30 to 60 days to make a commitment. Demand for Citicorp's mortgage loans is growing more than 100 percent per year in an industry with an average growth of 3 percent per year. In the second year of the program, Citicorp was the largest mortgage loan originator in the United States, and management is looking to triple its share in less than five years. Astonishingly, on February 8, 1989, Citicorp announced that henceforth mortgage commitments would be made in fifteen *minutes*.

Clearly, the time advantage is enabling time-based competitors to upset the traditional leaders of their industries and to claim the number one competitive and profitability positions. When a time-based competitor can open up a response advantage with turnaround times three to four times faster than its competitors, it will almost always grow three times faster than the average for the industry and will be twice as profitable as the average for all competitors. Moreover, these estimates are "floors." Many time-based competitors grow faster and earn even higher profits relative to their competitors.

When a company capitalizes on a strategy innovation, its competitors must change. In times of change, executives have two basic choices: Sit out the change until its utility becomes clear or seize the initiative and take action before other competitors do. Generally, companies that actively seek and promptly exploit the newest strategy innovation grow faster and more profitably than do more slowly reacting companies. The challenge to executives is to recognize and act upon the new sources of advantage in their industry before competitors do and to be willing to adapt again when the current source of advantage is exhausted. To do so requires an appreciation of the shifts that have occurred and are occurring.

STRATEGY INNOVATIONS: A RETROSPECTIVE

Until recently, innovations in business strategy were episodic. A major discovery, usually technology based, would upset the balance of an industry, and corporate fortunes would shift. For example, in transportation the railroads drew hoards of customers from river boats and horse-drawn overland transportation companies in the 1880s only to lose customers in the midtwentieth century to trucking firms. Similarly, coal companies replaced wood companies in the market and were themselves upstaged by oil companies.

Historically, the risk of an episodic change has required that management always be prepared for the unexpected, though it seldom was. Today, episodic changes in business strategy are fewer and they are being supplanted by evolutionary change—a continuum of change, not only in physical technologies but in managerial technologies as well.

Time-based competitive advantage is the most recent in a succession of the managerial innovations that have had impact on business outcomes in the last 40 years. The others include experience curve strategies, portfolio strategies, the strategic use of debt, de-averaging of costs, restructuring for advantage, and time-based competition.

EXPERIENCE CURVE STRATEGIES

One of the innovations in strategic thinking, implemented in the 1960s, was the use of cost behavior insights as a cornerstone for corporate strategy. An example of an early insight is experience-curve cost behavior. The theory of the experience curve is that the costs of complex products and services, when corrected for the effects of inflation and arbitrary accounting standards, typically decline about 20 to 30 percent with each doubling of accumulated experience.

The fact that costs decline with accumulated volume has been recognized for a long time. In 1925, officers in the U.S. Army observed that as accumulated production volume of airframes increased, per-unit costs declined. In later investigations, the Army more specifically described the nature of this dynamic: They calculated that the fourth plane assembled required only 80 percent as much direct labor as the second, the eighth plane only 80 percent as much direct labor as the fourth, the sixtieth plane required only 80 percent as much direct labor as the thirtieth, and so on.

During World War II, the understanding of this cost behavior was critical for planning resource requirements in the aircraft industry. After the war, the aircraft industry continued to plot learning curves. For example, the learning phenomena for the Martin-Marietta B-29, the Boeing B-17, and the Douglas Aircraft B-24, as described in a 1957 article, are shown in Exhibit 1-1. Learning curves continue to be used to predict program costs, to set schedules, to evaluate management performance, and to justify contract pricings. Moreover, the concept has been disseminated beyond the aircraft industry.

By the mid-1960s, experience effects were becoming well known and integrated into the strategies of companies. Examples of the decline in costs and in prices with experience are shown in Exhibits 1-2 and 1-3. In Japan the price of beer in constant yen has declined a little less than 20 percent with each doubling of accumulated experience. Electric power generation costs in the United States decline about 20 percent with each doubling, in part be-

Exhibit 1–1 Airframe Manufacturing Exhibits Strong Learning Effects

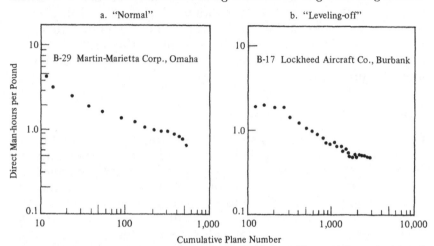

SOURCE: Miguel A. Reguero, "An Economic Study of the Military Airframe Industry," (Ohio: Wright-Patterson Air Force Base, Department of the Air Force, October 1957), pp. 231–235.

cause the direct cost per megawatt of electrical generating capacity declines to about 20 percent with each turbine manufacturer's cumulative megawatts of turbine capacity.

Such price declines reflect underlying cost declines. Costs decline with accumulated experience because

- Workers and management learn to perform their tasks more efficiently
- Better operational methods are adopted such as improved scheduling and work organization
- New materials and process technologies become available that enable costs to be reduced
- Products are redesigned for more efficient manufacturing

Costs have been found to decline continually for extended periods (Exhibit 1–3). Some costs go down in a steady fashion. Others decline slowly, then very fast and then again slowly as innovations in design and production technologies are exploited.

Being able to predict next year's prices is enormously important to management. Being able to predict prices in five and ten years hence is a major strategic advantage. The managements of certain aggressive companies have realized that well-documented cost behavior could be factored into their pricing strategies. They set pricing and investment strategies as a function of volume-driven

Exhibit 1–2 Examples of the Experience Curve

a. Japanese Beer

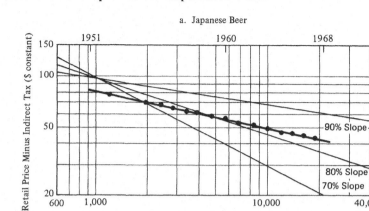

b. U.S. Electric Power

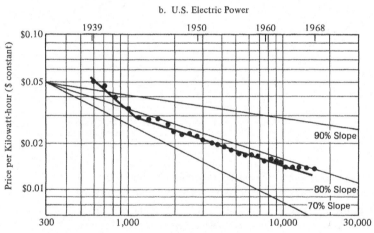

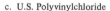

c. U.S. Polyvinylchloride

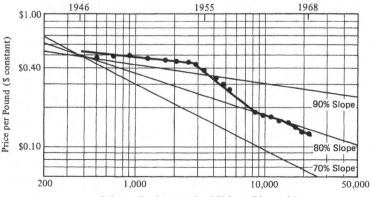

SOURCE: *Perspectives on Experience*. Staff of The Boston Consulting Group, Inc., copyright © 1968, 1970, 1972.

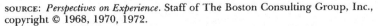

Exhibit 1–3 Direct Costs per Megawatt: Steam Turbine Generators,
1946–1963 *Steam turbine manufacturing exhibits strong experience effects*

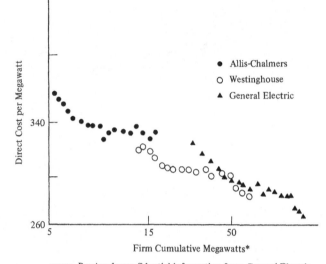

Firm Cumulative Megawatts*

NOTE: Previously confidential information from General Electric,
Westinghouse and Allis-Chalmers was made available in public
records as the result of antitrust litigation.

*Each data point corresponds to a year. The horizontal scale is the
total cumulative output of the specific firm involved to that year.

costs. At times, they reduced prices below current costs in antici-
pation of the decline in costs that they knew would result from expansion of volume. Capacity was added ahead of demand. The
earliest companies to adopt experience-based strategies ran
roughshod over their slower-adapting competitors. They often
preempted their competitors by claiming enough of a growing demand so that when their competitors attempted a response, little
volume remained, and the leaders' costs could not be matched.

Texas Instruments (TI) was an early user of experience-curve
cost dynamics, and they grew rapidly against competitors whose
managements did not understand the phenomenon. TI was an
early technical innovator in silicon transistors and later semiconductors. The company was a management innovator as well. TI's
management observed that with every doubling of accumulative
production volume of a transistor, diode, and eventually a semiconductor, costs declined to 73 percent of their previous level.
They managed a business with an inherent 73 percent learning
curve and relied on this insight to set cost-cutting programs to
ensure the continued decline in costs. In the market, TI slashed

the prices of its products to stimulate demand so as to drive up the accumulated volume of production and drive down costs. TI hammered its competitors in diodes and transistors, moved on to prevail in semiconductors, and ultimately in hand-held calculators and digital watches.

Later, however, the management of TI encountered severe competitive problems in its watch and calculator businesses. Overreliance on experience-curve-based strategies at the expense of market-driven strategies is often cited as the underlying flaw in TI's approach. This is an oversimplification. TI's determined effort to drive costs down allowed no room for product-line proliferation. That single-minded focus created an opening for hardpressed competitors such as Casio and Hewlett-Packard to sell on features rather than on price—a strategy that eventually became the standard for the industry when costs and prices declined to the point that consumers cared more for function and style than for price.

Though other firms may not rely on them so completely as Texas Instruments, strategies exploiting experience cost behaviors are still relevant. In today's semiconductor industry, for example, experience effects continue to drive managements to seek volume. Moreover, in most industries, even when executives do not explicitly base their strategies on managing experience effects, they implicitly recognize experience effects when they set market share targets. Market share is a surrogate for volume—the fundamental driver of experience effects. The company with the greatest market share obtains the most volume on the margin and on the margin increases its accumulated volume faster. For example, the manufacturing costs and profitabilities of the major Japanese tire manufacturers reflect the differences in market share (Exhibit 1–4). Competitors tend to sort out this way until one can break the equilibrium.

PORTFOLIO MANAGEMENT

Just as experience-based strategies were becoming widespread, a new strategic insight emerged. At the time, in the late 1960s and the early 1970s, companies were generally organized into profit centers that could be managed for the most part as independent businesses. This structure enabled corporate management to set performance goals such as profitability for the executives of the operating units and to allocate capital against clear business returns. The General Electric company (GE) and Westinghouse pioneered profit-center management prior to World War II, and

Exhibit 1–4 Tire/Tube Business: Profitability and Relative Market
Shares, 1968–1973

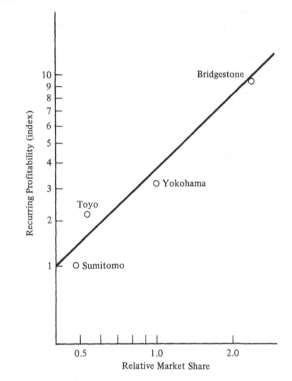

GE became recognized as the leader in the use of this management concept.

The difficulty with the profit center organization structure is
clearly described by business strategy analyst Bruce D. Henderson.

> In large scale, diversified, multiproduct companies it was
> impractical for central management to be familiar in depth
> with each business, each product, each competitive segment,
> and each unit's implied strategy. This led to more and more
> reliance on short-term suboptimization of results. . . . The
> inevitable short-range viewpoint induced by quarterly profit
> measurements as the prime control often confined profit
> center management to tactical resource management only.[1]

In other words, individual businesses are more or less left to
fend for themselves in the profit center structure. For example, in
a profit-center corporate structure, a high-growth operation will

generally receive capital commensurate with the returns it is generating. This can often mean that such a company does not get all the capital it could use because a high-growth operation must invest resources before demand, which increases its expenses and reduces profitability. Conversely, a slow growth operation in a profit-center corporate structure can generate large volumes of excess cash which more often than not, gets reinvested in the operation because it is profitable, whether the operation needs the investment or not. Bruce Henderson went on to write about the profit center structure:

> There . . . was little real management judgment possible at the corporate level with respect to overall strategy except with regard to financial policy. This conflict between strategy and structure may account for a company such as Westinghouse having been the pioneer and technical leader in products that ranged from automobile generators to television tubes to silicon transistors and integrated circuits yet enjoying no success in these products. On the other hand, when the developments were clearly strategic enough to threaten the core business of the company, Westinghouse became a world leader in such developments as alternating current machinery and later atomic power. (Thus, the threat overrode the controlling influence of the profit center structure.)[2]

Innovative competitors came to view their collection of businesses not as profit centers but as members of a portfolio of businesses, each of whose elements have different cash generation potentials as well as different strategic objectives. Some businesses are mature with healthy competitive positions and can generate more cash than needed to sustain their position. Others are growing rapidly and need more cash than they can generate to strengthen and preserve their emerging competitive positions. Thus, a business that needs cash for strategic growth could be fed from another, slower-growing, cash-rich division. In other words, instead of regarding the corporation as a collection of individual businesses where reinvestment is driven by the profit performance of each unit, the collection of businesses is managed as a portfolio of businesses—a portfolio that should contain some stable properties, some high growth/high risk properties, and some properties that are to be disposed of when the opportunity arises.

The use of cash should be proportional to the rate of growth of a business. The rate of cash generation is a function of the profitability of a business, which, because profits are the residual of costs and prices, is itself a function of the competitive position or market share of not only the business but of its competitors. If a business can achieve a two-to-one market share advantage over its largest competitor it should have predictably lower costs for the same value added.

The growth-share matrix was developed as a tool to enable management to visualize the balance of cash use and cash generation of its entire collection of businesses so that trade-offs could be made among the various opportunities to apply cash (Exhibit 1–5). The vertical axis is the rate of growth of demand. The horizontal axis is a measure of cash generation or a proxy for cash generation, such as relative market share. Relative market share is defined as the share held by the business divided by the share held by the largest competitor. Generally the chart is divided into four quadrants by two intersecting lines. The vertical line passes through the point where relative market share is one. To the left of this point, the business should be competitively advantaged and to the right—competitively disadvantaged. The horizontal line passes through the growth rate desired by management. Businesses are then located within the matrix depending on their market growth rates and their relative market share position. Depending on the quadrant they fall in, they are categorized as cash cows, dogs, stars, or question marks:

- Cash cows occupy the lower left quadrant. Companies in this quadrant are growing slowly and, therefore, do not require much cash to sustain their growth. However, because the companies have strong market positions, they should be advantaged in costs and profits and generate much cash.

- Dogs occupy the lower right quadrant. Growth is low but so are relative positions. Because these companies are competitively disadvantaged, they are unlikely to be generating much excess cash and may, if severely disadvantaged, actually consume cash even when profits are reported. As such they are cash traps and can eventually even create negative value.

- Question marks appear in the upper-right quadrant. These businesses are in fast-growing markets but have not yet achieved competitive advantage. As such they are not generating cash and are in need of much cash to enable management to enhance advantage and move the business to the left as far as is possible. Without the needed cash for growth, it will slow, and the business will slip into the lower-right quadrant to become a dog.

- Stars are the upper left quadrant. These businesses are growing rapidly and therefore need much cash. But because these

Exhibit 1–5 Use of Cash Is Proportional to Rate of Growth

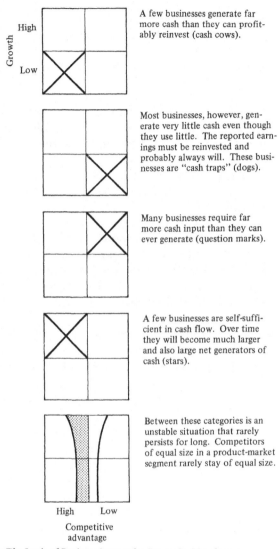

A few businesses generate far more cash than they can profitably reinvest (cash cows).

Most businesses, however, generate very little cash even though they use little. The reported earnings must be reinvested and probably always will. These businesses are "cash traps" (dogs).

Many businesses require far more cash input than they can ever generate (question marks).

A few businesses are self-sufficient in cash flow. Over time they will become much larger and also large net generators of cash (stars).

Between these categories is an unstable situation that rarely persists for long. Competitors of equal size in a product-market segment rarely stay of equal size.

businesses are competitive leaders they are also generating a substantial portion if not all of the cash they need.

The trick was to have a portfolio rich with cash generators and with high opportunity cash users while maintaining a positive cash balance (Exhibit 1–6). Surprisingly, this is not much of a trick in the long run. Most companies develop balanced portfolios over time by default as severely disadvantaged businesses are closed or sold off under the continual pressure for profits and cash. The real challenge is to consciously manage the movement of businesses within the portfolio. Management must allocate the corporation's resources to move question-marked businesses into the star position before the growth slows, to keep the stars advantaged so that when growth slows the stars become cash cows, and to manage the cash cows for cash. The dogs need to be worked out of the portfolio.

Strategic advantage can be achieved against a competitor—often a profit-center-oriented competitor—who is not coordinating its collection of businesses as a portfolio. Such a competitor will tend to underinvest in a high-growth business and overinvest both in a low-growth business and in businesses having poor competitive situations. Thus if a portfolio-oriented competitor has a high-growth question mark or star, it can out-invest a profit-center–oriented competitor, not because it necessarily has more money but because it is not constrained by internal resource allocation schemes from pushing its question marks and stars.

Exhibit 1–6 The Portfolio of a Typical Successfully Diversified Company

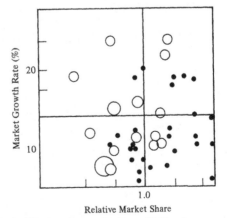

Relative Market Share

source: From *The Logic of Business Strategy* by Bruce D. Henderson, copyright © 1984 by The Boston Consulting Group. Used by permission of Ballinger Division, Harper & Row Publishers, Inc.

In the 1960s and early 1970s, a classic portfolio battle was waged by Dow Chemical against Monsanto. In this battle, Dow actively managed its portfolio for advantage, and Monsanto did not. While Monsanto's management was not afraid to move into businesses with good growth potential, they had a tendency to underinvest in their growth businesses as can be seen in the growth/growth chart in Exhibit 1–7a. In this chart, the various businesses of Monsanto are located on one axis according to growth in overall demand, and on the other axis, by their rate of expansion. Monsanto was expanding its businesses, but beyond this, no pattern seems to exist at first glance. However, if all businesses with market demand growing at a rate less than 15 percent are ignored, a different picture emerges. In 11 of the 14 businesses with market demand growing at a rate faster than 15 percent, Monsanto was expanding only three businesses faster than demand. The other 11 were growing slower than demand and, therefore, losing share.

Thus, for businesses with slow-growing markets, Monsanto's management was gaining share in more than twice as many businesses as it was losing share. But in Monsanto's fast-growing businesses, resources were not forthcoming at a rate sufficient to meet

Exhibit 1–7a Monsanto's Growth in Capacity (circa 1970)

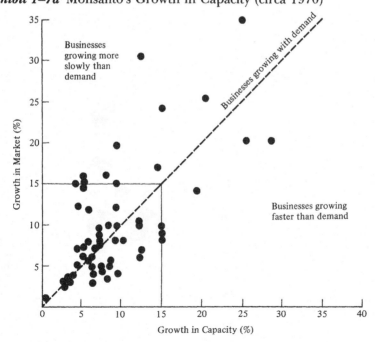

the growth of demand. Slower-growing businesses continued to receive resources for growth in excess of what was needed to hold position and generate profits, which could have been used to fund the fast-growth businesses. These growth patterns are characteristics of managements that seek near-term profits and allocate resources according to profit-center methods. Monsanto's portfolio at the time of this battle with Dow is shown in Exhibit 1–7b. As might be expected, the mix of businesses was heavily skewed towards question marks and dogs. This skew reflects the pattern discussed previously of losing share in high-growth businesses. The portfolio was not very profitable.

In the early 1970s, Dow was much more aggressive than Monsanto in pursuing growth businesses. Dow's businesses are shown in the growth/growth chart in Exhibit 1–7c. Note that, compared with Monsanto in Exhibit 1–7a, Dow did not have as many high-growth business opportunities as did Monsanto. Monsanto had seven businesses whose growth in demand exceeded 20 percent, while Dow had only two. Dow was growing overall, but its mix of

Exhibit 1–7b Monsanto's Portfolio (circa 1970)

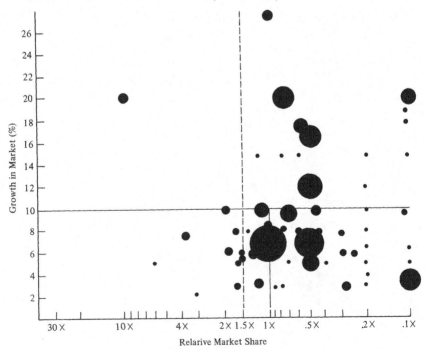

Exhibit 1–7c Dow's Growth in Capacity (circa 1970)

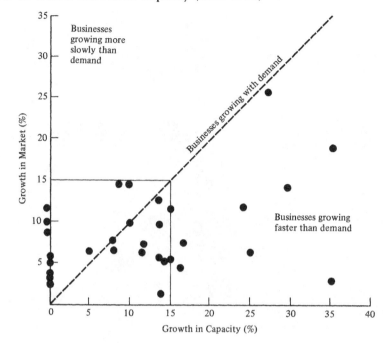

businesses included many with moderate growth, and some that were stopped dead. In fact, eight businesses were not growing at all despite reasonable market growth. However, of the 23 growing businesses, 20 were growing as fast or faster than demand. These patterns are characteristics of managements driven by market share. Their theory is go for dominance or get out.

Dow's portfolio is shown in Exhibit 1–7d. The portfolio was much stronger than Monsanto's with the weight of the businesses to the left of the competitive parity line. The underlying profitability of this portfolio is good and the effect of the aggressive growth policies of Dow's management can be clearly seen.

THE STRATEGIC USE OF DEBT

As the experience curve and the portfolio were becoming widely understood and used for developing management strategies in the late 1960s and early 1970s, some companies began to use debt aggressively to fund investments in their competitive positions. Often these companies were smaller than the leading competitors

Exhibit 1–7d Dow's Portfolio (circa 1970)

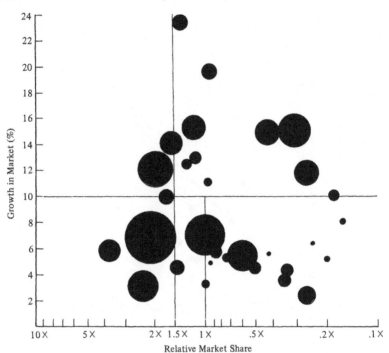

of their industry, and their managements found that the judicious use of debt could offset structural competitive disadvantages, enabling them to grow faster than their leading competitors despite the fact that they generated less profit per dollar of revenue.

Corporations grow when they have good products, competitive prices, and growing demand. Cash is needed to grow a business. The cash available for growth is a function of the profits generated by the business and the financial policies chosen for the use of that cash. Pricing, debt policies, and dividend policies are the key financial policies influencing growth. Differential financial policies are often an important element of the strategy employed by one competitor in outperforming another. Differing financial policies can enable one competitor to grow faster than another even if the faster-growing competitor is fundamentally disadvantaged.

The impact of differing financial policies on the competitiveness of companies can be shown with an example. One company, Company A, is the leader, and the other company, Company B, is the follower. The leader has much greater total sales and is much more profitable than the follower. However, despite having lower profits, Company B is pricing under the leader and growing much faster than the leader and the market.

Company B can accomplish this because its management has chosen more aggressive financial policies than the management of Company A. The management of Company A is very conservative in its financial strategy. Management likes high profits, the good debt quality ratings that come with high profits and no debt and high dividends per share. Company B, as a follower, wants high growth and has chosen financial policies—high debt-to-equity ratios and no dividends—that fund this growth in the face of the lower profits created by price cutting and comparatively high costs of production.

Company B, the follower, is growing more than twice as fast as the leader and is undercutting the prices of the leader by 15 percent, even though its costs are 25 percent higher. The effects of the financial policies of Company B that make this possible are shown in Table 1–2.

Company A wants to grow 10 percent per year. To meet this target, Company A must increase its asset base by 10 percent, or by $6 million, per year; it finances this increase entirely with retained earnings. Its prices and costs yield operating profits of $36 million. After taxes and dividends, $6 million is left for growth.

Company B's financial policies enable it to grow at 25 percent per year. Because of low prices and higher costs, Company B's operating margin is 37 percent, or less than two-thirds the operating margin of the leader. After interest payments and taxes, Company B has only $1.25 million of profits available for growth. Since this is not enough to meet management's growth targets, no dividends are paid and an additional $2.5 million is borrowed from the banks to obtain the $3.75 million needed to grow the asset base at 25 percent per year.

For now, Company B is strategically using debt to fund its attempt to gain share over Company A. If the management of Company A does not cut prices, increase customer value, which is effectively a price cut, or change its financial and investment policies to check the growth of Company B, it could find itself slipping into the follower position with higher costs, lower profits, and a poor business position.

Dow funded its attack on Monsanto's businesses with debt (Table 1–3). Dow's absolute debt-to-equity ratio in the early 1970s was 1.1:1 compared to Monsanto's ratio of 0.46:1. On the margin, Dow borrowed 2.2 dollars of debt for every dollar of profit gen-

TABLE 1–2 The Strategic Use of Debt by a Follower to Upset a Leader

	Company A	Company B
Market share (% of units)	60	10
Growth rate per year (%)	10	25
Price per unit sold (indexed)	100	85
Cost per unit produced (indexed)	100	125
Capital structure		
Debt ($ million)	0	10
Equity ($ million)	60	5
Total assets ($ million)	60	15
Debt-to-equity ratio	0:1	2:1
Required reinvestment ($ million)	6.0	3.75
Sales ($ million)	60	8.50
COGS[a] ($ million)	24	5.00
Operating margin ($ million)	36	3.50
(%)	60	37
Less interest ($ million)	0	1.00
	36	2.50
Less taxes ($ million)	18	1.25
Profit ($ million)	18	1.25
Dividends ($ million)	8	0.00
(payout ratio)	0.44	0.00
Retained profit ($ million)	10	1.25
New debt ($ million)	0	2.50
Available for growth ($ million)	10	3.75

[a] COGS stands for "cost of goods sold."

TABLE 1–3 The Strategic Use of Debt by Dow

	Absolute Debt/Equity	Marginal Debt/Equity
Monsanto	0.46:1	0.30:1
Dow	1.1:1	2.2:1

erated while Monsanto borrowed only 0.3 dollars of debt for each
dollar of profit generated. Thus, in this period of high growth,
Monsanto's management was actually constraining growth with
conservative financial policies that decreased debt risks but increased competitive risks.

Debt as a strategic weapon remains a powerful influence on
competition today. Many North American companies are yielding
an unfair competitive advantage to their Japanese and European
competitors by refusing to remove the "debt umbrella" they hold
over their less-strong competitors. By refusing to match the financial policies of their competitors, these North American companies often negate the other competitive advantages they have
such as costs, technology, market share. As Bruce Henderson has
observed,

> It is important to realize that competitive superiority can be
> converted into either higher return on equity or lower risk
> under extreme conditions. In turn this relationship can be
> converted into either lower prices or higher return for the
> same risk. Where competitive position is price (or investment)
> sensitive, debt can become a major strategic weapon.
>
> Use more debt than your competition or get out of the
> business. Any other policy is self limiting, no-win, or a bet
> that the competition will go bankrupt before they displace
> you.[3]

Needless to say, with increasing debt comes increasing financial
risk. However, increasing financial risk must be weighed against
the risk that a competitor will use debt to fund faster growth to a
leadership position. If management insists on conservative financial policies, it risks losing market position. Later, in the 1980s,
there emerged the risk of losing company control to corporate
raiders who exploited this same debt and portfolio logic at the
expense of "safe" managers.

DE-AVERAGING OF COSTS

The advantages inherent in managing experience effects, the business portfolio, and the strategic use of debt continued to be recognized in the mid-1970s. However, management's attention also
now turned to the quality of its cost-accounting information and
to the impact this might have on its ability to manage its businesses
strategically. In the mid-1970s, a more refined understanding of
how costs are driven by varying levels of complexity in an orga-

nization enabled innovative companies to achieve competitive advantage through both aggressive and defensive strategies. Aggressive companies determined that the economics of their operations were very sensitive to the amount of complexity in their system and that their management information systems, particularly their accounting systems, did not accurately capture this sensitivity. They knew that these information systems hampered their ability to set prices reflecting the value provided. They also recognized that their competitors' information systems usually had the same shortcomings.

The major shortcoming of most cost-accounting systems is that large portions of costs, typically overhead costs, are averaged and added to the costs that can be clearly identified with a specific product or service to obtain the total cost of manufacturing a product or providing a service. Then prices are set on the basis of these average costs, which don't reflect the actual cost of producing the product in question.

When overhead is averaged across all products, high-volume and simpler activities tend to be assigned costs at levels higher than they actually were, while low-volume and more complex activities tend to be credited with costs far lower than their actual ones. This is because higher-volume activities generally require much less management support than lower-volume activities. In fact, low-volume activities are very disruptive to organizations because they disturb the rhythm that can be established when processing high-volume activities. More attention means more costs. Moreover, when overhead is averaged, and prices are based on these averaged costs, the high-volume businesses actually appear to be less profitable than lower-volume businesses at the same price levels. This effect is magnified when the low-volume products carry a price premium, as they are likely to do.

For example, the management of a manufacturer of steel wheels for railroads almost put itself out of business with accounting disinformation. Early in the history of the corporation, the top two high-volume products accounted for 100 percent of the total production volume. With only two products, production costs could easily be identified with each product. After eight years of growth and capacity expansions, the company found itself with excess capacity. To fill the excess capacity, new product designs were developed and sold. Initially the new business was very attractive since the gross margins were higher than those of the old product line. Consequently, more new products were sold. Over time, the proportion of production that the top two products accounted for declined to less than 50 percent (Exhibit 1–8).

Exhibit 1–8 The De-focusing of a Train Wheel Factory

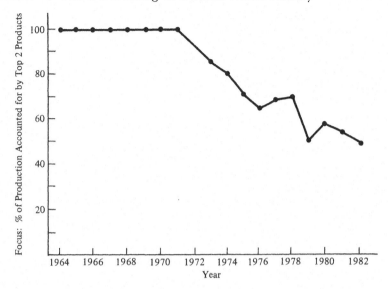

Although the manufacturing process for train wheels is fairly straightforward—molding, casting, machining, then balancing—the addition of new products will increase the complexity of the operations. Products have to be scheduled, processes have to be changed over from one product to another, workers have to be retrained to manufacture to the specifications of the new products. Increasingly, this manufacturer's productive time was consumed by management tasks and waste. One measure of the impact of increasing complexity on the performance of the factory was the decline in production yield.

Yield, expressed as good tons cast divided by total tons cast, is a measure of first-time yield for the manufacturing process. Because of the casting step, train wheel manufacturing is very energy intensive and costly. Therefore the more good tons that can make it through the process, the lower the overall manufacturing costs will be. The process yield had never been very stable, but it had been high—hovering about 91 percent. From 1970, as additional products were added, the process yield declined to 83 percent (Exhibit 1–9). The addition of new products increased the material loss experienced at each changeover of the casting and machining processes. The costs of these losses were captured in aggregate, but the cost system did not properly relate these costs to individual products because it averaged the costs over all prod-

Exhibit 1–9 Casting Yield

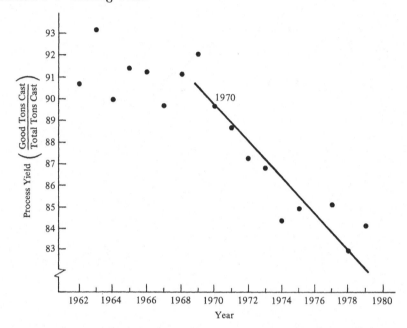

ucts. The profitability of the new products continued to look good even as overall process yields declined and labor productivity deteriorated by 40 percent (Exhibit 1–10).

The deteriorating yields and labor productivities eventually produced losses that forced the company to seek a new strategy. The core effort behind developing strategy options went to de-averaging, to find the true costs of manufacturing. Using the true costs, the individual product lines profitability could be assessed accurately. The assessment found that only 20 percent of the products were profitable. More than 60 percent were not generating profits at all. Another 20 percent could be profitable if prices were raised between 10 and 35 percent. Products were dropped accordingly, prices on many of the remaining products were raised, and the performance of the manufacturing operation improved markedly. The increasing concentration of the product line resulted in improving process yields and an improvement of labor productivity of about 40 percent (Exhibit 1–11).

Clearly, a competitor can, after unraveling accounting misinformation, price very aggressively on high-volume business and raise prices on low-volume activities. If competitors do not re-

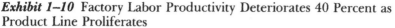

Exhibit 1–10 Factory Labor Productivity Deteriorates 40 Percent as Product Line Proliferates

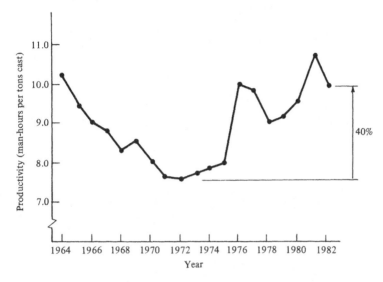

spond, they lose share in the high-volume segments and gain share in the low-volume segments. Eventually, the competitor's market position and profitability will deteriorate and the innovative competitor will prevail.

Another example of the impact of inaccurate costing is that of a large North American manufacturer of circuit breakers, which sought to distinguish itself from its competitors by supplying a full line. Between 1965 and 1975, its product line ranged from the smallest to the largest power circuit breakers available on the market. The number of products it offered increased two and one-half times during this decade.

As with train wheels, the costs of the design and manufacturing processes for power circuit breakers are very sensitive to complexity. The costs that are most sensitive are the management or overhead costs. This dynamic can be seen in Exhibit 1–12. Each dot in the exhibit is a plant. Some plants have as few as four to six products, others as many as thirty or forty. The plants with thirty or forty product families require two to four times more overhead support than do the focused plants and are therefore more costly to run. Generally, the greater the complexity the greater the costs, unless the volumes and prices of the additional units of complexity are enormous. They were not.

This manufacturer had many competitors, none of them as

Exhibit 1–11 The Re-focusing of a Train Wheel Factory

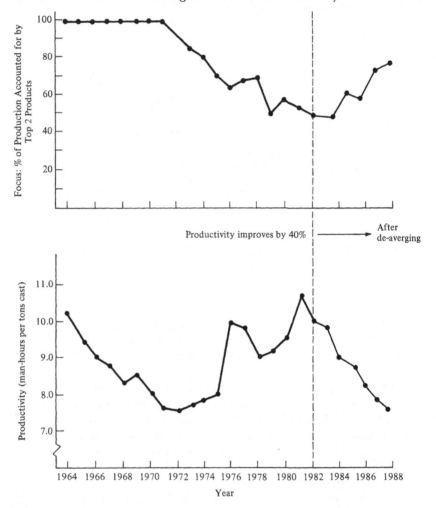

large as it was. However, in each segment of the power circuit business, the company had a competitor that, while smaller in total sales, was larger than the company in that segment. This large unfocused company was competing with many smaller but focused companies—not a sustainable position. As can be seen in Exhibit 1–13, as the company proliferated its product offering in the face of focused competition that was operating at a lower cost, it was not able to recover its higher costs through higher prices. As a result, profits declined. Profits were not to improve until the

Exhibit 1–12 Overhead–Support Burden Increases as Complexity of Product/Plants Increases

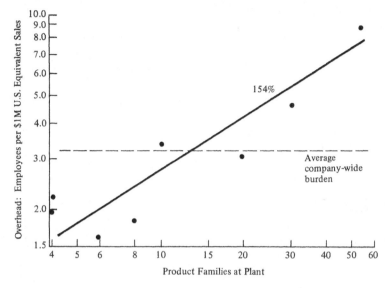

company focused its product line and redesigned its factory to reduce the impact of complexity on the cost of manufacturing.

RESTRUCTURING FOR ADVANTAGE

In the 1980s restructuring became the dominant source of advantage exploited by management. Only now, the advantage management sought was not over its traditional competitors but over a new and, in the short term, more menacing threat—hostile takeovers by corporate raiders. Corporate raiders seek profit opportunities in companies whose managements are not diligent in structuring, managing, and financing their portfolios. Raiders can generate profits by forcing such managements to restructure—dispose of unsuccessful businesses, de-layer managements, match cash generation with debt service, and take other unpleasant but necessary actions to "lean out" and balance a company's portfolio.

Returning to the Monsanto story, since 1981 Dick Mahoney, the CEO, has been cleaning the company's portfolio. Mr. Mahoney and his colleagues have sold businesses with annual sales of almost $4 billion. Most of these businesses were at the core of the company but lacked competitive advantage as part of Monsanto. These businesses included petrochemicals, paper chemicals, ben-

Exhibit 1–13 Complexity and Profitability *As number of models expanded, volume per model declined, which increased costs, decreasing profitability and reducing cash flow*

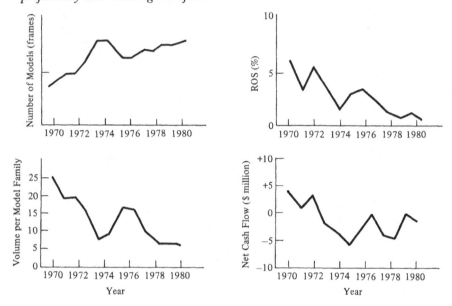

zene, oil and gas, polystyrene and others. This cleaning is helping Monsanto turn in its best return on equity, about 16 percent, since 1974 and a price–earnings ratio that is better than the average of like companies.

Restructuring is a weak competitive innovation, however, because durable competitive advantage is not the objective. Rather, the objective is, at best, to revalue undervalued companies and, at worst, to preserve jobs and status of existing management. Nevertheless, the techniques employed are throwbacks to earlier strategic insights—portfolio management and focus—and thus underscore the fundamental power of these insights.

THE EMERGING NEW SOURCE OF COMPETITIVE ADVANTAGE

In the early 1980s, leading Japanese companies and some small North American and European companies demonstrated the power of two new dimensions of competitive advantage: low-cost variety and fast response time. These leading companies are compressing the time required to manufacture and distribute their products. More importantly, they are also significantly cutting the time required to develop and introduce new products. These newly developed capabilities not only reduce costs, they also enable the Japanese and certain Western companies to offer a broad product line, to cover more market segments, and to rapidly increase the technological sophistication of their products. These innovative companies are becoming *time-based competitors.*

Most of the Japanese companies are developing the new capabilities in response to other Japanese competitors, but in so doing, some are surpassing their Western competitors in product variety and sophistication. These Japanese competitors are using fast response time and increased variety to grow faster and more profitably, thus substantially altering competitive relationships.

The responsiveness gap some Japanese companies have opened over their Western competitors is simply astounding. Basic response times for the fundamental value delivery systems of world class automobile competitors in the West and in Japan are shown in Table 1–4. Japanese companies require between six and eight days to get an order from the field to line set, the point at which managers know the exact time the order will be manufactured. This compares to 16 to 26 days for the better Western automobile companies. Manufacturing itself takes the best Western companies 14 to 30 days per order compared to 2 to 4 days for the fastest Japanese manufacturers. Most important of all is the time required to develop and introduce new automobile designs to the market. The fastest Japanese automobile companies can accomplish this in two and one-half to three years. Western automobile companies require four to over six years to introduce new designs—two to three times longer than the fastest Japanese companies.

TABLE 1–4 The New Pace of Competition: World-Class Automobile Companies

	Representative Cycle Times	
Value Provided	*Western*	*Japanese*
Sales, order and distribution	16–26 days	6–8 days
Vehicle manufacturing	14–30 days	2–4 days
New vehicle design and introduction	4–6 years	2½–3 years
Median age of product offering	5 years	3 years

The implications of being two to three times faster than the best Western companies are fresher product offerings that have a higher degree of technological sophistication. One estimate is that the automobile designs of all Japanese companies in the 1988 model year were about three years old. Using the same estimating procedure, the average age of the designs of the North American products was about five years or almost twice as old. The Japanese are fielding the freshest products to consumers.

The designs are not only fresh but can also be more sophisticated technologically. The key technological differences between a Chevrolet Beretta and a Mazda 626 are compared in Table 1–5. Both cars were introduced in the 1987–1988 model years and have base prices in the $10,000 to $11,000 range. However, the fully optioned Mazda 626 is far more technically advanced. For the Mazda, the consumer has the choice of the technologies offered in the Beretta plus the choice of engines with three or four valves per cylinder, turbocharging or supercharging, four-wheel drive, electronically adjustable transmission and suspension, and electronically controlled four-wheel steering. Some experts believe that the technological leadership in automobiles priced at $30,000 or less is securely held by the Japanese, and these data certainly support such a contention.

Time compression is the fundamental change enabling the Japanese to increase the variety and technological sophistication of

TABLE 1–5 The Change of Technological Leadership: 1988 Automobiles

	Chevrolet Beretta	Mazda 626
Engine	Electronic fuel injection 2 valves	Electronic fuel injection 3 or 4 valves Turbocharger or supercharger
Transmission	4-speed automatic	Electronic automatic 4 wheel drive
Suspension	MacPherson strut	MacPherson strut Automatic adjusting suspension
Steering	Power rack and pinion	Electronic variable assisted power steering Electronic 4-wheel steering

the products and services they offer. Time is the secret weapon of business because advantages in response time lever up all other differences that are basic to overall competitive advantage. Some Western managements know this, others are learning, and the rest will be victims.

Many executives believe that competitive advantage is best achieved by providing the most value for the lowest cost. This is the traditional pattern for corporate success. Providing the most value for the lowest cost in the *least amount of time* is the new pattern for corporate success. An increasing number of companies are achieving success by establishing competitive response advantages.

The strategic implications of compressing time are significant. As time is compressed, the following changes occur:

- Productivity increases
- Prices can be increased
- Risks are reduced
- Share is increased

The impact of compressing time on productivity can be seen in Exhibit 1–14. In most manufacturing facilities, cycle time is inversely proportional to work-in-process turns. As work-in-process turns increase, cycle times decrease. Also, the data show that as work-in-process turns increase, productivity increases (Exhibit 1–15). Generally, for every halving of cycle times and doubling of work-in-process turns, productivity increases 20 to 70 percent!

As the time required to satisfy customer orders is compressed, prices can be increased. The companies shown in Table 1–6 have achieved response advantages over their competitors that range from two-to-one to nine-to-one. With response advantage, these time-based competitors can consistently charge 20 to 100 percent more than the average price. Customers of time-based competitors are willing to pay more for their products and services for both subjective and economic reasons.

As time is compressed, risks are reduced. A cost of business that is rarely made explicit is the cost of over- or under-forecasting demand. The farther into the future demand must be forecast, the greater the probability that the forecast will be wrong at the time of sale. This is apparent in the fashion businesses. Exhibit 1–16 shows the accuracy of forecasts for women's skirts and men's slacks as a function of the lead time required for placing an order. When new fashions are ordered from the Far East, nine-month lead times are sometimes required. A purchase order must then

Exhibit 1–14 As Time Is Compressed, Productivity Increases

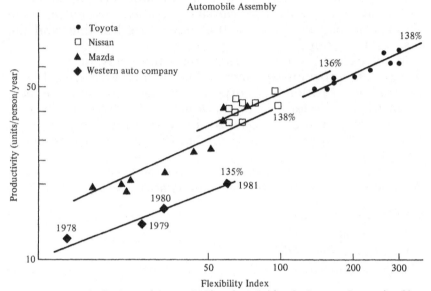

Automobile Assembly

SOURCE: George Stalk, Jr., and James C. Abegglen, *Kaisha, the Japanese Corporation* (New York: Basic Books, 1985), p. 114.

be based on a forecast of demand made nine months before the time of sale. Department store buyers estimate that the actual demand for skirts often ranges from 40 percent more to 40 percent less than forecast. The excess product resulting from a high forecast must be sold at marked-down prices, which is costly. However, a far greater cost results from a low forecast—the opportunity cost of not having goods that could have been sold. Because forecasts made closer to the point of the sale are more accurate, clothing with more volatile demand may be ordered from domestic suppliers; whole lead times are shorter—from two weeks to four months, instead of nine months. Demand for skirts is more volatile than demand for men's slacks because the fashion element is much more important. Similarly, the domestic manufacture of high fashion apparel can be economically justified because of reduced forecasting error, while less fashion-intensive articles remain offshore in low-labor-cost countries.

As time is compressed, share increases. Many successful companies often find themselves unable to grow in their historical markets using traditional approaches such as price cuts. One supplier of a custom industrial product, for example, could not increase its share of customer purchases using traditional means—

Exhibit 1–15 Flexibility and Productivity

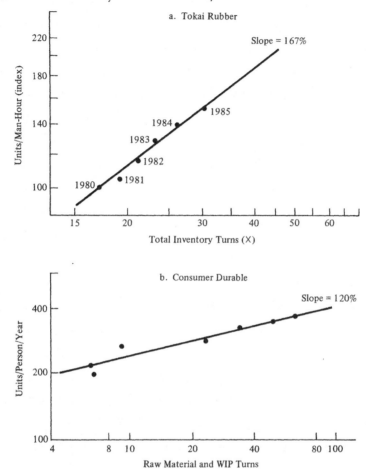

a. Tokai Rubber

b. Consumer Durable

TABLE 1–6 As Time Is Compressed, Prices Can Be Increased

	Time Advantage	Price Premium (%)
Electrical components	2:1	59
Writing papers	5:1	20
Commercial doors	9:1	100

Exhibit 1–16 As Time Is Compressed, Risks Are Reduced: Apparel

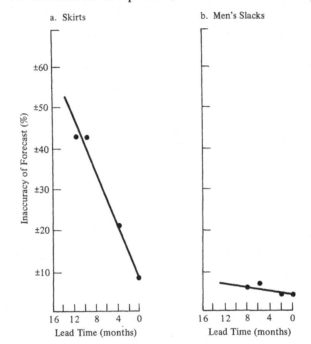

price cuts in one form or another—but did so after improving its response time by 75 percent on every order, including semi-custom fabrication (Table 1–7). As customers became confident that they could rely on this company as a sole supplier, its share of their purchases increased from 30 to 45 percent.

TABLE 1–7 As Time Is Compressed, Share Increases: An Industrial Consumable

	Before Improved Response	After Improved Response	Projection
Delivery lead-time (weeks)	22	8	6
Volume increase (%)	—	16	41
Domestic share (%)	32	37	45

Time-based competitors belong to a new generation of companies that manage and compete in different ways. They are obtaining remarkable results by focusing their organizations on flexibility and responsiveness, using the following methods.

- *Choosing time consumption as the critical management and strategic parameter.* The managements of these companies know precisely how much time is required to give their customers what they want and to perform other vital activities in their companies.

- *Using responsiveness to stay close to their customers, increasing the customers' dependence on them.* In the early 1980s, being close to customers became a popular slogan. However, the necessary metric was not disclosed. This best metric is time—how long must a customer wait from the point he or she asks for a product or service to the time that need is met, whether the need is for a product, service, an answer or a "fix" to a problem. Time-based competitors use their flexible value-delivery systems to expand variety and to enhance their responsiveness to customers' needs. The variety expansion can be in one of, or a combination of, two dimensions—style and/or increased technological sophistication. A comparative advantage in either dimension can propel a competitor to a leadership position in its industry regardless of its responsiveness. When combined with a response advantage, however, fashion and technological advantages can be used to lock up the most attractive channels of distribution to the most profitable customers.

- *Directing their value delivery systems to the most attractive customers, which forces their competitors toward less attractive customers.* The most attractive customers are those who cannot wait for what they want. The least attractive customers are those who will wait because the price they want to pay is low compared to the prices the more impatient customers will pay. Money is made on patient customers only if costs are low, while money is made on impatient customers from higher prices and low costs. Time-based businesses let their competitors have the patient customers while they embrace the impatient ones.

- *Setting the pace of innovation in their industries.* Time-based competitors that have extended their response advantage throughout their organization—including new product development and the introduction process—almost always take the technological and product leadership positions in their industries within about a decade.

- *Growing faster with higher profits than their competitors.* When a time-based business can open up a response advantage that is three to four times faster than its competitors, it almost always grows three times faster than overall demand, at twice the level of profitability of the average competitor. Moreover, these rates are floors since often the differences are greater.
- *Baffling their competitors.* Many time-based competitors are not effectively challenged by their slower brethren. Managements of these companies are by definition slow to change and as such are left behind as faster competitors change their business for them. When the slower managements do respond, they must do so from a disadvantaged position and, as a result, incur all the costs of becoming more responsive without securing many of the benefits.

To become a time-based competitor, three tasks must be accomplished by the management of a company's management.

1. Make the value-delivery systems of the company two to three times more flexible and faster than the value-delivery systems of competitors
2. Determine how its customers value variety and responsiveness, focus on those customers with the greatest sensitivity, and price accordingly
3. Have a strategy for surprising its competitors with the company's time-based advantage

THE IMPORTANCE OF VISION

In approaching the opportunity to use time as a competitive advantage, executives must first determine if an opportunity exists to become a time-based competitor in their industry. Then they must decide whether they are going to lead their competitors by seizing the initiative. The early leader grows in a shrinking window of opportunity, although the first window is always larger than those of the followers. Further, when the windows finally close, the leader almost always holds the most attractive competitive position and earns the highest profits.

The journey to becoming a time-based competitor is demanding. It begins with a vision of what could be. The vision needs to be sufficiently clear and attractive to motivate the organization to rethink the structure and activities of its entire value-delivery system so as to maximize its performance.

Initiating and executing a program that improves the responsiveness of an organization is not easy. Such a program must compete with other programs for attention. Moreover, senior management cannot easily delegate the job to subordinates, because improving responsiveness requires breaking down the organization's resistance to change and reducing across functions well as within them. Finally, sustaining the rate of improvement and the accompanying benefits demands a philosophical change. Senior management must shift its focus from cost to time, and its objectives from control and functional optimization to providing resources to compress time throughout the organization. Senior management, as keeper of the vision, must believe that time is the organization's number-one competitor.

CHAPTER
2

◇◇◇◇

Time and Business

Time is a fundamental business performance variable. Listen to the ways in which managers talk about what is important to the success of their companies: response *time,* lead *time,* up *time,* on *time.* Time may sometimes be a more important performance parameter than money. In fact, as a strategic weapon, time is the equivalent of money, productivity, quality, and even innovation. Yet, until recently management has seldom monitored the consumption of time explicitly and rarely measured time with the same precision with which it measured sales and costs.

Today, time is on the cutting edge of competitive advantage. The ways leading companies manage time—in production, in sales and distribution, in new product development and introduction—are the most powerful new sources of competitive advantage. Although more and more Western companies are pursuing time-based advantage, many of the early developments and leading practices in the use of time as a competitive weapon have been pioneered by leading Japanese companies. The experiences of these Japanese companies are instructive, not because they are necessarily unique, but because they best illustrate the stages through which today's leading companies have evolved—from advantage first based on low wages; next on scale; then on focus; and now on flexibility, variety, speed and innovation.

In the period immediately following World War II, Japanese companies used their low labor costs to enter into a variety of industries whose costs were very much driven by the cost of labor. As wage rates rose and process technology came to have significant impact on the costs of production, leading Japanese companies shifted their sources of competitive advantage first to scale-based strategies and then to focused factories in order to power their growth into export markets. The advent of just-in-time production brought with it a move to flexible factories that enabled leading Japanese companies to achieve low costs and offer greater variety to their customers. Today, cutting edge Japanese companies are capitalizing on time as the critical source of competitive advantage. They manage time as scrupulously as most companies manage costs, quality and inventory. Japanese time-based competitors have not only reduced costs but have broadened product lines, increased market breadth and upgraded the technological sophistication of their products.

FROM LOW WAGES TO FOCUSED FACTORIES

Since 1945 Japanese competitors have shifted their focus for achieving strategic advantage at least four times. The early adaptations—to scale and to focus—were clearly visible to competitors; the shift to time-based competitive advantage has not been nearly so obvious. It does, however, represent a logical evolution from the earlier stages.

In the immediate aftermath of World War II, with their economy devastated and the world around them in shambles, the Japanese concentrated on achieving competitive advantage through low labor costs. Since Japan's workers were still productive and the yen was devalued 98.8 percent against the U.S. dollar, its labor costs were extraordinarily competitive with those of the West's developed economies.

Hungry for foreign exchange, the Japanese government encouraged companies to make the most of their edge by targeting industries with high labor content: textiles, shipbuilding, and steel—businesses where low labor rates more than offset rates of productivity that were low by Western standards. As a result, Japanese companies took share away from their Western competitors.

But this source of advantage was not long-lived. Steadily rising wage rates combined with fixed exchange rates to erode Japan's wage-based advantage. In many industries, manufacturers could not improve their productivity fast enough to offset escalating wage costs. But the early 1960s, for instance, textile companies—comprising the largest industry in Japan—were hard pressed. Having lost the source of the competitive edge in world markets, they spiraled downward, first losing market share, then volume, then profits, and, finally, position and prestige. While the problems created by increasing wage rates were most severe for the textile industry, the rest of Japanese industry suffered as well.

The only course was adaptation. In the early 1960s, the Japanese shifted their strategy and sought competitive advantage based on the use of capital investment to boost work-force productivity. The era of scale-based advantage was inaugurated. Japan companies built the largest and most capital-intensive facilities that were technologically feasible to achieve high labor productivities and low costs. For example, Japanese shipbuilders revolutionized the industry in their effort to raise labor productivity. Adapting fabrication techniques to mass production processes and using automatic and semiautomatic equipment, they efficiently constructed modules and assembled complete vessels from those modules far more rapidly than their competitors could. Their approach had two competitive advantages—it drove up their own productivity and simultaneously erected a high capital-investment barrier to others trying to compete in the business.

In Japan, the search for ways to achieve even higher productivity and lower costs did not end with scale-based advantage. In the mid-1960s, top Japanese companies found a new source of competitive advantage—the focused factory. As focused competitors, these Japanese companies manufactured products either made nowhere else in the world or positioned in the high-volume segment of the overall demand for the product—often in the heart of their Western competitors' product lines. By focusing their production on fewer products, these companies were able to achieve higher productivity, lower costs and substantial strategic advantage over their larger but less-focused Western competitors!

Costs of Variety

The costs of an organization, whether it be a factory or a service business, are very sensitive to the amount of variety or complexity it is attempting to manage. In the case of a factory, costs are very sensitive to the variety of products the plant is producing. Imagine the simplest of organizations—an organization that does only one thing for only one customer. If this organization were a factory, it would be a very simple one to manage. One product would be made day in and day out. Since there would be no change-overs, production time lost to setup would be negligible. Since there would be only one product, each step of the process could have matched capacities and be operated in unison. Quality costs would probably be low, since the process would remain unchanged and the quality problems would have been worked out. Inventories would be very low since purchased items could be brought in regularly, work-in-process kept to a minimum, and finished goods shipped immediately to the customer. Management costs would be very low as well because everything would be almost perfectly predictable.

Unfortunately, this paradise can be destroyed by adding additional products to satisfy additional customers. It's difficult to maintain production of a single product at a constant rate when demand for the others must also be satisfied. Production schedules for each of the products now must be created and managed. Now, there will be changeovers that require both scheduling and people to manage them. Time will be lost to setup. Quality will become more expensive, since with each changeover, the process has to be brought back into tolerance. Since there are additional products, each having its unique process requirement, additional process steps are likely to be required. Because it is much more difficult to match the capacities of each step of the process, it is very unlikely that the steps can be operated in unison.

Inventories, too, will now be more difficult to manage. A greater variety of purchased items will need to be handled—in what is now an irregular pattern—to meet the production schedules. Work-in-process inventories can be expected to increase as inventories are built up to enable the many parts of the process to continue operating. Many other parts of the process will also be down because of changeover, since other parts are being manufactured. Finished goods inventories will increase, because while one product is being manufactured, stocks of other products have to be maintained to satisfy demand for them. Customer priorities must be weighed against the priorities for smooth operation of the factory. Consequently, the process is rarely in balance. In this factory almost nothing is perfectly predictable. So management costs are going to be much, much higher than those of the factory that manufactures only one product for only one customer.

As the complexity of an operation—be it product- or service-oriented—increases, the complexity of the management process increases and thus the cost of management. The corollary is true, too. As the complexity of an operation is simplified, so is the management process and the cost of management is reduced. Moreover, productivity increases with the simplicity of the process.

In the case of discrete manufacturing processes, or processes that have many, distinct steps with idle time between steps, the reduction of product-line variety, for example, results in an increase of productivity by 30%, a reduction in costs by 17% and a substantially lowered break-even (Table 2–1). Cutting the product-line variety

TABLE 2-1 The Variety Barrier: Discrete Manufacturing
Schematic—Constant Production Volume

Variety Index[a]	Productivity[b]	Unit Cost[b]	Break-even Percent of Capacity[b]
100	100	100	80
50	131	83	61
25	172	69	46

[a] Variety is typically a function of the number of product families and degree of vertical integration.
[b] Cost structure: 60% variable labor and material, 40% overhead.

in half again boosts productivity by 75%, slashes costs by 30% and diminishes the break-even point below 50% of total capacity.

JAPAN'S COMPETITIVE EDGE

In industries like anti-friction bearings, where competition was fierce in the late 1960s, the Japanese fielded product lines with one-half to one-quarter the variety of their larger Western competitors. Targeting the high-volume segments of the demand for bearings—bearings for automobile applications, for example—the Japanese used the low costs of their highly productive focused factories to undercut the prices of their Western competitors.

The Swedish firm SKF (Svenska Kullargen Fabrickn) almost became a victim of these attacks. With many small factories scattered throughout Europe, each geared to manufacture a broad product line to service the local demand, the company was a major target of the Japanese competitors with focused factories. SKF's initial reaction to the Japanese attack was to avoid direct competition by adding new products to meet specialized applications that the Japanese could not supply. These products commanded higher prices and appeared to SKF management to be more profitable and therefore more attractive than the products facing direct Japanese competition. However, because SKF did not simultaneously drop its low-margin products, plant operations became more complicated, reducing the firm's productivity and raising its overall costs. In effect, the more SKF sought to avoid competition with the Japanese by adding new, higher-margin products, the more it provided a rising cost umbrella for the Japanese to grow under by expanding their product offering and moving into more varied applications. As long as the

Japanese stayed beneath the umbrella by maintaining a narrower product line than SKF, they could continue to pick off the parts of SKF's business that they wanted, driving SKF into smaller and smaller pockets of demand.

Avoiding price competition by moving into higher-margin products or services is called margin retreat—a common response to stepped up competition and a response that can eventually lead to corporate suicide. As a company retreats, its costs rise along with its prices, thus subsidizing an aggressive competitor's expansion into the vacated position. The retreating company's revenue base stops growing and may eventually shrink to the point where it can no longer support the fixed costs of the operation. Retrenchment, restructuring, and further shrinkage follow in a cycle that leads to inevitable extinction.

SKF avoided this fate by adopting the Japanese strategy. After a review of its factories, the company focused each factory on the products it made most efficiently. If a product did not fit a particular factory, it was either placed in another more suitable plant or dropped altogether. This strategy not only halted SKF's retreat but also beat back the Japanese advance.

The Economics of Focus

The economics of focus are pervasive and not limited to manufacturing alone. As an organization—manufacturing or service-oriented—attempts to expand the variety of products or services it offers the task of management increases exponentially. This increase results in increasing costs and often decreasing response times as management tries to constrain the increase in costs often at the expense of time to maintain service levels. The effect of increasing complexity on nonmanufacturing costs can be seen in Exhibits 2–1, 2–2, and 2–3. For example, as the number of operating divisions in a multinational construction company increased, so did selling and general and administrative expenses (SGA costs) as a percent of sales. Indeed, for every doubling of the number of operating divisions, SGA costs increased 139 percent as a percent of sales! This rate of overhead increase, shown by the slope of the line in the graph, is called the complexity slope. Similar complexity phenomena can be seen at work in the following examples: dairy processors' overheads as a function of the number of delivery routes, design overhead at engineering firms as a function of project size, and medical centers' overheads as a function of the variety of residency programs offered. The range

Exhibit 2–1 Complexity and a Multinational Construction Company

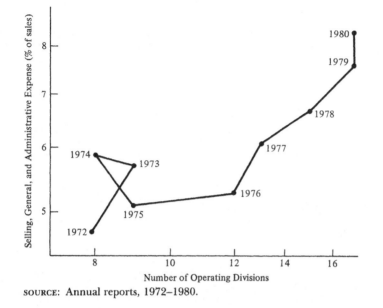

SOURCE: Annual reports, 1972–1980.

of complexity slopes that can be found in a wide variety of businesses is shown in Table 2–2.

In choosing to reduce product variety, however, executives attack the symptoms rather than the root causes of the cost of complexity. Costs go down because complexity has been removed not because the drivers of the cost of complexity have been eliminated. These drivers are hard to identify because they are management rather than activity costs and are therefore less visible. They include the costs of various decision-making processes involving the tasks at hand, as well as the costs of remaking earlier decisions. To support variety and market responsiveness, managers must identify these costs and reduce the complexity of the processes that generate them.

THE FLEXIBLE FACTORY

While many Western executives worked throughout the 1970s and 1980s to reduce their costs by focusing their operations, leading Japanese manufacturers began to move to a new source of competitive advantage—the flexible factory and, later, flexible operations. Two developments drove this move. First, as Japanese

Exhibit 2–2 Complexity and Seven Dairy Processing Firms

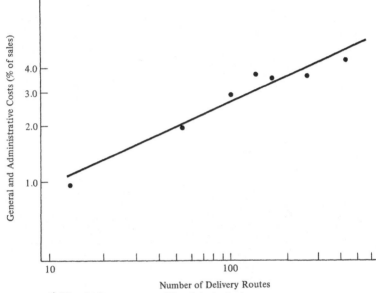

SOURCE: California Department of Food & Agriculture.

companies expanded and penetrated new markets, their narrow product lines began to pinch, limiting their ability to grow. Second, with growth limited, the economics of the focus strategy presented them with an unattractive choice: either reduce variety further or accept the higher costs of broader product lines.

In manufacturing, operating costs traditionally fall into two broad categories: those that respond to increases in volume, or scale-driven costs, and those that are driven by variety (Exhibit 2–4). Scale-driven costs decline 15 percent to 25 percent per unit with every doubling of volume. Variety-driven costs, on the other hand, reflect the costs of complexity in manufacturing. The costs of complexity include machine and activity setup, materials handling, inventory management, and most of the overhead costs of a factory. In traditional factories, as variety doubles, costs increase at a rate of between 20 percent and 35 percent per cost per unit.

The sum of the scale- and variety-driven costs is the total cost of operations for a factory. With effort, managers can determine the optimum mix of volume and variety for their factories to minimize the cost of plant operations. However, when demand is good, managers tend to edge towards increasing variety in search of higher volumes, even when this results in increasing costs. When

Exhibit 2–3 Complexity and Detailed Engineering Design: Typical
Overhead Rates

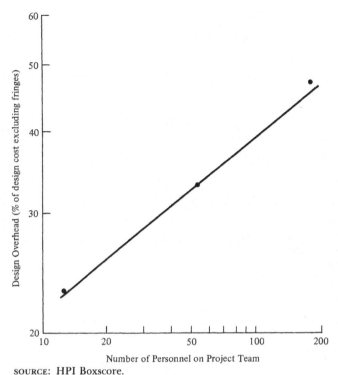

Number of Personnel on Project Team

SOURCE: HPI Boxscore.

times are tough, companies pare their product lines, cutting variety to reduce costs.

In general, flexible manufacturers have policies and practices
that differ from those of traditional manufacturers along three
key dimensions (Table 2–3).

- the length of a typical production run
- the organization of the process components
- the complexity of the scheduling procedures

Traditional factories attempt to maximize the length of their
production runs in an effort to amortize lengthy and costly setups
over the maximum number of pieces. Flexible manufacturers, on
the other hand, try to shorten their production runs as much as is
possible. To prevent the costs of short runs from getting out of
control, management focuses on reducing the complexity and
hence the length and costs of setups and changeovers. The logic

TABLE 2–2 Characteristic Complexity Slopes

Percent Increase in Overhead Cost Per Unit with Each Doubling of Complexity	Complexity Slope (%)
Hand tool manufacturing	154
Multinational construction company	139
Dairy product delivery network	137
Lift truck manufacturing plants	133
Chemical processing	133
Petroleum refining	128
Lift truck manufacturing—time series	128
Detailed engineering design	121
Medical centers	117

Percent Increase in Total Cost Per Unit with Each Doubling of Complexity	Complexity Slope (%)
Computer programming	141
Advertising agencies	117
Custom software programming houses	108

Exhibit 2–4 Breaking the Variety Barrier *Traditional Trade-off*

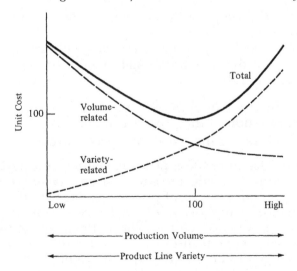

TABLE 2–3 Contrast in Manufacturing Management

	Traditional	*Flexible*
Lot size	Large batches	Small batches
Flow pattern	Move through process technology centers	Organized by product
Scheduling	Centrally scheduled	Locally scheduled
Lead times	100	100
Productivity	100	150–300

behind this approach is as simple as it is fundamental to competitive success: reduced run lengths mean more frequent production of the complete mix of products and faster response to customers' demands.

Factory layout can contribute to reducing production complexity and, thus, time consumption. Traditional factories are organized by process technology centers. For example, metal goods manufacturers often organize their factories into shearing, punching, and braking departments; electronic assemblers have stuffing, wave-soldering, wire harnesses, assembly, testing, and packaging departments. Parts are moved from one process technology center to the next. Each step consumes valuable time: parts sit, wait to be moved, are then moved, then wait to be used by the next step. Amazingly, in traditional manufacturing systems, products usually receive value for only 0.05 percent to 5 percent of the time they are in the system. The rest of the time, products are waiting to receive value.

To increase value-adding time, flexible manufacturers organize their factories by product. To minimize the handling and movement of parts, the manufacturing processes for a component or a product are located as close together as is possible. Parts move from one activity to the next with little or no delay. Because the production process reduces or eliminates the need to pile and re-pile parts, they flow quickly and efficiently through the factory.

In traditional factories, scheduling is another source of delay and waste of time. Most traditional factories use central scheduling that requires sophisticated materials resource planning and shop floor control systems. Even though these systems can be quite sensitive, they are inaccurate and they waste time: work orders usually flow to the factory on a monthly or weekly basis; parts of the process can be scheduled for overtime while other parts are idle; new parts can be produced that are not needed because the same parts are being expedited by humans through the system. All the while, parts sit idle—not receiving value.

In flexible factories, a combination of small run lengths and simplified plant layout makes production scheduling and management operate more smoothly. Since process layouts are product-oriented, they can be directed locally. Local scheduling enables employees to make more production control decisions on the factory floor without time-consuming loop-backs to management for decisions and approvals. Moreover, once a part starts into production, much of its movements between manufacturing steps are purely automatic and require no intermediate scheduling.

The potential absurdity of organizing a factory in a traditional fashion can be illustrated with a simple example. Imagine that you are building cabinets and other wood furniture in your home workshop. Now, imagine that you are to execute your work in batches. All the round pieces are to be lathed together, all the sawing done at once, all the drilling done together, and so on. Further imagine that all your tools have been scattered about the house so that saws are in the basement, clamps are in the dining room, glue is in the living room, sand paper is in a bedroom, and on and on and on. Now you must cart the pieces of the cabinet and the other furniture from one room to another to work on it. You are directed to each step by a process sheet. When you arrive at the sanding room, you must wait until the pieces currently being sanded are completed. You must then wait until all the other pieces that arrived ahead of you or have been designated rush pieces are completed. Using this strategy, an enormous amount of time would be consumed for very little economic value. Who would organize and manage their home workshops in such a fashion?

The differences between traditional and flexible factories add up to competitive advantage for flexible factories in both productivity and time. The labor productivity advantage of a flexible factory can be 50 to 100 percent over a traditional factory. A factory's position on that 50–100 percent range is a function of the complexity of its process. The more complex the process, the greater the productivity advantage can be. For example, since wire drawing is a process with very few steps, a flexible wire drawing factory might only achieve 50 percent greater productivity than a traditional one. Automobile fabrication and assembly is, by comparison, much more complex. Flexible automobile manufacturers can have productivity advantages over most traditional manufacturers of over 100 percent. Flexible automobile factories can respond to demand eight to ten times faster than can traditional factories. Flexible manufacturing means significant improvements in both labor and asset productivity. These, in turn, yield reductions of up to 20 to 30 percent in total costs for products requiring complex manufacturing processes, allowing increased growth for a smaller additional investment.

In a flexible factory, variety-driven costs start lower and increase more slowly as variety expands (Exhibit 2–5). Scale-driven costs remain largely unchanged when a factory becomes flexible. Thus, the optimum operating cost point for a flexible factory occurs at a higher volume and with greater variety than does the optimum for traditional factories. A strategic gap emerges between the capabilities of the flexible and traditional factories. This is the cost/variety gap that represents the essence of the new source of competitive advantage enjoyed by leading Japanese and aggressive Western companies. Very simply, a flexible factory can accommodate more variety at lower costs than can a traditional factory, which must make the trade-off between variety and scale at an earlier point. Compared to a similar traditional factory with only half its product variety, the flexible factory's productivity is often 50 to 150 percent higher and its costs are often 20 to 30 percent lower.

GROWTH THROUGH FLEXIBILITY

Yanmar Diesel illustrates how increased flexibility can be used to support growth. In 1973, with the Japanese economy in recession,

Exhibit 2–5 Breaking the Variety Barrier *Traditional Trade-off vs. Increased Flexibility*

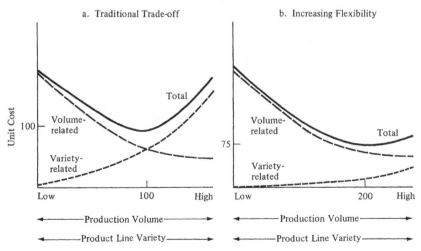

Yanmar Diesel was mired in red ink. Worse, there was no real promise that once the recession had passed, its existing strategies for growth would guarantee real improvement in the company's position.

As a Toyota supplier, Yanmar was familiar with the automaker's flexible manufacturing system. Moreover, Yanmar was impressed with the Toyota's ability to weather the recession without losing money. So Yanmar decided to install the Toyota process in its own factories. The conversion took less than five years and produced dramatic results: total manufacturing productivity improved by more than 100 percent; manufacturing costs declined 40 percent to 60 percent, depending on the product; and factory break-even fell from 80 percent to 50 percent.

Although this growth in productivity and cost efficiency were impressive, it was Yanmar's newfound capability to expand variety that signaled the arrival of a strategic edge. During the restructuring, the company more than quadrupled the breadth of its product line. If Yanmar had maintained focused factories, it would have had to reduce the breadth of its product offering by 75 percent in order to have doubled productivity in such a short time. The Toyota system made Yanmar's factories more flexible, less costly to operate, and able to handle a greatly expanded variety of products.

As its inventor, Taiichi Ohno, said, the Toyota production system was "born of the need to make many types of automobiles, in small quantities with the same manufacturing processes." With its emphasis on just-in-time production, close supplier relations, total quality control, simplified production flows, and a scheduling mechanism that enabled employee decision-making on the factory floor, the Toyota system met this need. It gave the many Japanese manufacturers who adopted it in the mid-1970s a distinct competitive advantage over those companies that chose to stick with traditional forms of manufacturing management.

A comparison of a U.S. company with a Japanese competitor in the manufacture of a particular automotive suspension component illustrates the nature and extent of the advantage of flexible manufacturing (Table 2–4). The U.S. company bases its strategy on economies of scale and focus. It produces 10 million units per year, making it the world's largest producer. The U.S. company is also the most focused producer of this component: it offers only 11 variants on the product. In contrast, the Japanese company's strategy is to exploit flexibility. It is both smaller and less focused than the U.S. company: it manufactures only 3.5 million units per year, but has 38 types of finished products.

TABLE 2–4 Breaking the Variety Barrier: Automobile Suspension Component

	U.S. Competitor	Japanese Competitor
Annual unit volume	10M[a]	3.5M[a]
Finished part numbers	11	38
Units per employee	43,100	61,400
Employees		
Direct	107	50
Indirect	135	7
Total	242	57
Unit cost for comparable part	$ 100	$ 49

[a] M = million; 180 yen = one dollar.

With one-third the scale and more than three times the product variety, the Japanese company also boasts total labor productivity that is half again as that of its American competitor. Moreover, the unit cost of the Japanese manufacturer is less than half that of the U.S. company. But, interestingly, the productivity of the Japanese direct laborers is not as high as that of the comparable U.S. workers, a reflection of the differences in overall scale. The productivity advantage of the Japanese company is entirely in the productivity of its overhead employees. With one-third the volume and three times the variety, the Japanese company has only one-eighteenth the number of overhead employees.

THREE OVERHEAD BEHAVIOR TYPES

Very often, when the productivity of one competitor is so much greater than that of another competitor, the advantage resides in overhead. This is especially apparent in manufacturing businesses. Exhibit 2–6 shows the overhead behaviors of over 75 industrial component manufacturers—American, German, and Japanese. The number of overhead people per million dollars of sales is compared to the overall size of the operation expressed as sales per product family. By expressing size in this fashion the impact of different degrees of product line complexity on overhead costs is neutralized. Three very distinct behaviors of overhead are apparent, reflecting the existence of three distinct operations archetypes, each with its own characteristic overheads. These are large, complex *bureaucratic* operations that require high

Exhibit 2–6 Time-based Management Can Reduce Costs
Example: Industrial Component Suppliers

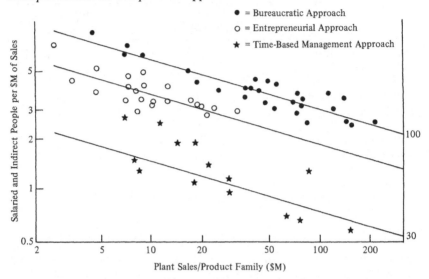

NOTE: "Indirect people" includes all hourly factory support personnel.

overheads; smaller, focused *entrepreneurial* operations that need only moderate overheads; and flexible, balanced *time-compressed* operations that have eliminated a substantial number of the kinds of overheads needed by the other two archetypes. Companies using these different approaches compete with each other to supply the same customers.

The bureaucratic archetype is represented by older, scale-oriented plants that have failed to adapt to today's high variety and short-lead-time world. These companies typically make large capital investments to reduce direct labor, organize work around specialists, and focus on developing product technology far more than process capability or teamwork skills. Their corporate vision may well have been conceived in the 1950s and 1960s when larger centralized operations in manufacturing, engineering, purchasing, and distribution prevailed in the marketplace. They like big plants and often consolidate plants to "spread overheads." They focus on cost position. These companies can often be identified by their large size, age, multiple layers of management and unionized work forces who are managed to the contract.

Over time, these bureaucratic companies have reacted to their changing environment by increasing organizational complexity, thus raising overheads. When the growth of base demand slows, they increase product variety and add new lines to keep volume rising. But very often, these additions to the product offering are not designed around the capability of the process and around process commonalities. So the plant flow is disturbed. More products that marginally add to total demand mean more engineers, more purchasing agents, and more indirect plant intervention. Management negotiates restrictive work practices and additional worker classifications with the unions, reflecting their belief in and the value of specialization in holding direct labor costs down. Functional specialization among the management staffs increases, too, as technology becomes more arcane and financial control strengthens, fragmenting the work flow and reducing the speed of performance information feedback. Key operations managers are rotated frequently to "broaden" them, a process that undermines in-depth understanding of the operations. Standing above all this is corporate management, oriented to planning and finance, believing that rising overhead is the necessary price of increased product complexity and technology input.

A sharp contrast to the bureaucratic archetype is the entrepreneurial archetype. The entrepreneurial archetype is the small company run by a dedicated management group that is close to its processes and customers. Recently, a great deal of attention has been given to the importance of entrepreneurship in the creation of jobs and in the reinvigoration of large corporations. Much statistical evidence shows that small, entrepreneurial companies have grown faster than their bureaucratic counterparts, in part because they are more cost efficient and more responsive to customers and changing technologies than are bureaucratic companies. The data in Exhibit 2–6 confirm at least the cost aspect of this observation. The entrepreneurial company operates with overheads that are approximately 30 percent lower on a per unit basis than are those of bureaucratic companies. And like the overhead costs of bureaucratic companies, these overheads decline 15 percent to 20 percent per unit with every doubling of volume per product category.

Entrepreneurial operations are common in newer companies, which have smaller plants with fewer product lines, have fewer levels of management, and are typically non-union. In the way they define their business and manage their companies accordingly, they seem to be more effective than bureaucratic companies. Markets that demand variety and speed stress complex bureaucratic operations beyond their tolerance. In contrast, entrepreneurial firms can streamline operations to access technology and skills quickly, adapting to market changes.

Entrepreneurial companies strive for simpler organization and focus on fewer product lines, although within a line, they may offer as much variety as their competition. They value focus and teamwork more than scale and technologies. Senior management usually knows the operations well and may even run them. Managers are not rotated. Engineers tend to be collocated at the plant and to stay with a product line. There is less specialization in the white-collar work force—reflecting less functional hierarchy in the organization, and there is seldom a union. Entrepreneurial operations tend to work in teams and to have shorter communication and feedback loops.

All of the above makes it easier for entrepreneurial firms to operate with relatively low overhead. There is less complexity and fragmentation, and more informality and compactness than in bureaucratic organizations. An entrepreneurial manager can "eyeball" an operation and manage by personal influence, while a bureaucratic manager may be limited to managing by policy directives. Although entrepreneurial operations may be financially vulnerable when compared to larger bureaucratic organizations, they are leaner, generally more cost efficient, and are faster growing.

The third overhead behavior archetype is a kind of big company/entrepreneurial hybrid—the time-compressed operation. These are very large companies that have successfully flattened hierarchies and adapted process management to satisfy rapidly changing market needs. They have introduced time-compressed operations that increase the company's ability to produce variety with short lead times and its ability to innovate quickly and consistently to the level their customers want. The organizational cycle times of these firms have been radically compressed, and they are designed not to become unbalanced or stressed when variety and the pace of operation is increased. Managers of these firms keep overheads low by organizing production, engineering, and other management tasks in closed-loop cells with short operating cycles that are expected to be flexible, that is, changing in organization as needed. Closed-loop cells are self-contained, multifunctional, self-scheduling sub-organizations empowered to perform the key activities required to meet explicit objectives. Some examples of closed-loop cells are the following: a JIT manufacturing cell; a product development team focused on a product family; a department in a retail store whose employees take full responsibility for the overall performance of that department—from selecting merchandise, to closing the sale, to managing inventory, to markdowns. Placing all the functions required to meet performance objectives into empowered, focused cells closes the time distances between the employees that must make the system work and shortens the feedback loops required for the cell to react to changing events. This type of organization eliminates the layers of management that previously provided coordination from a distance.

Time-compressed organizations can be very large companies, but they are quick to initiate additional cells when added volume or changes in variety threaten the smooth functioning of existing cells. Close-loop organizations thus avoid the scale, specialization, and centralization of the bureaucratic organization. Yet they are able to pursue volume and the benefits of scale economies as entrepreneurial firms cannot.

While entrepreneurial systems reduce overhead through compactness and focus—thus sacrificing some variety and possibly sacrificing the increased innovation that a desire for greater variety fosters—the closed-loop cell in a time-compressed operation provides focus without specialization. Thus, compressed systems can reduce overheads even further than can entrepreneurial systems (Exhibit 2–6).

To be truly flexible, however, the cells must have short operating and change cycles. They must take less time to get valuable work done, less time from design concept to introduction, less time from receipt of order to start and completion of production, and less time from identification of a problem to its successful resolution. Because compressed operations take less time in production, they waste less time managing the flow of materials. Quality problems are discovered sooner and are rapidly eliminated. Shorter cycles also mean that employees accumulate more experience in less time. In effect, the momentum of compressed organizations is greater than that of either the bureaucratic or focused organizations.

These archetypes illuminate many of the challenges by U.S. and European manufacturing sectors faced today. First, they explain much of Japanese corporations' continuing ability to compete despite the sharp appreciation of the yen. Most of the compressed operations in Exhibit 2–6 are Japanese companies, and the very lowest overhead companies are all Japanese. On average, Japanese overheads are one-third the overheads of U.S. and European competitors. Even though the current yen rates bring Japanese wage rates in line with Western rates, Japanese companies can still be cost-advantaged. In products where overheads are a significant portion of the cost structure—such as operations with high variety, high tolerances, or great engineering/process management intensities—the Japanese compressed system can yield enormous cost advantages.

Transforming bureaucratic organizations into compressed organizations is a two-step process: the first step is downsizing, which takes the organization up to the performance levels of the entrepreneurial system. When downsizing, management sheds product lines, manufacturing processes, and operations that add complexity and therefore costs in an effort to enlarge the organization's focus. Downsizing reduces overhead costs but does not fundamentally make an organization flexible or fast. This step has been or is being accomplished by many U.S. companies including General Electric, Xerox, Chrysler, and Ford. The second step is time-compression, which is more difficult and takes longer. Time-compression means that the basic structure of work in critical processes of the organization is altered to minimize the unproductive consumption of time. Only a few large American firms—Ford, Hewlett-Packard, Xerox, and parts of General Electric—have progressed beyond downsizing to time-compression. Time-compression allows an organization to improve on all dimensions: cost, variety, speed, and innovation.

Japan's Variety Wars

In the late 1970s, Japanese companies exploited the benefits of flexible manufacturing to the point that a new competitive thrust emerged—the variety war. A classic example of the variety war was the battle that erupted between Honda and Yamaha for supremacy in the motorcycle industry, a struggle popularly known in Japanese business circles as the H-Y war. Yamaha ignited the H-Y war in 1981 when it announced the opening of a new factory that when full, would make it the world's largest manufacturer of motorcycles—a position of prestige then held by Honda.

Honda had been watching Yamaha's gradual gain of production share for several years. It had chosen not to respond because it had been concentrating its corporate resources on building its automobile business, and away from its motorcycle operations. Now faced with Yamaha's overt and public challenge, Honda chose to counterattack.

Honda launched its attack with the war cry, "Yamaha wo tsubusu!" This is a rather impolite Japanese phrase that roughly translates as, "We will crush, squash, butcher, slaughter, etc. Yamaha!" In the no-holds-barred battle that ensued, Honda cut prices, flooded the distribution channel with new products, and boosted advertising expenditures.

Most important—and most visible to consumers—Honda also increased the rate of change in its product line rapidly. Honda used expanding variety to bury Yamaha under a flood of new products. At the start of the war, Honda had about 60 models of motorcycles in its product line. Over the next 18 months, Honda introduced or replaced 113 models, effectively turning over its entire product line twice. Yamaha also began the war with about 60 models but was only able to manage 37 changes in its product line during those 18 months.

Honda's massive new product introductions devastated Yamaha. First, Honda succeeded in making motorcycle design a matter of fashion, where newness and freshness are important attributes to customers. Second, Honda increased the technological sophistication of its products, introducing four-valve engines (that would later be the basis for its automobile engines), composites, direct drive, and other new features and technologies. Next to Honda's motorcycles, Yamaha's bikes looked old, out-of-date, and unattractive. Demand for Yamaha motorcycles dried up. In a desperate effort to move them, dealers were forced to price them below cost, but even this did not help. At the most intense point of the H-Y war, Yamaha had more than 12 months of inventory in its dealer network. Finally Yamaha surrendered. In a public statement, Yamaha President Eguchi announced, "We want to end the H-Y war. It is our fault. We cannot match Honda's sales and product strength. Of course there will be competition in the future, but it will be based on a mutual recognition of our respective positions."[2]

Honda did not go unscathed either. The company's sales and service network was severely disrupted, requiring additional investment before it returned to a stable footing. However, so decisive was its victory that Honda effectively had as much time as it wanted to recover. It had emphatically defended its title as the world's largest motorcycle producer and had done so in a way that clearly warned Suzuki and Kawasaki not to challenge that leadership. Variety had won the war.

TIME-BASED COMPETITIVE ADVANTAGE

The strength of the rapid expansion of variety as a competitive weapon raises the question: How could Japanese companies accommodate such rapid rates of change? In Honda's case, there could be only three possible answers

1. Begin development of more than 100 new models 10 to 15 years before the attack
2. Authorize a sudden, massive spending surge to develop and manufacture products on a crash basis
3. Use structurally different methods to develop, introduce, and manufacture new products

In fact, what Honda and other variety-driven companies pioneered was to make structural changes in their operations that enabled them to execute their processes much faster than before. The result is time-based competition—time is their new source of competitive advantage.

Today's new-generation competitors have an expanded pattern for corporate success. The traditional pattern has been to provide the most value for the least cost. The expanded pattern is to provide the most value for the least cost *in the least elapsed amount of time.* These new-generation competitors use flexible factories and operations to respond to their customers' needs rapidly by expanding variety and by increasing the rate of innovation. A company that builds its strategy on this cycle is a more powerful competitor than one with a traditional strategy based on low wages, scale, or focus. These older, cost-based strategies require managers to do whatever is necessary to drive down costs: move production to, or source from, a low-wage country; build new facilities or consolidate old plants to gain economies of scale; or focus operations down to the most economic subset of activities. Such tactics reduce costs but at the expense of responsiveness to customer needs—a dangerous exposure.

In contrast, strategies based on the cycle of flexible manufacturing—rapid response, expanding variety, and increasing innovation—are time based. Factories are close to the customers they serve. Organization structures are designed and managed to enable fast response rather than low costs and control. Time-based competitors concentrate their efforts on reducing and eliminating delays and on using their response advantages to attract the most profitable customers.

Many—but certainly not all—of today's time-based competitors are Japanese. Some of them are Sony, Matsushita, Sharp, Toyota, Hitachi, NEC, Toshiba, Canon, Honda, and Hino. Western time-based competitors include Benetton, The Limited, Federal Express, Domino's Pizza, Ralph Wilson Plastics, Jumping-Jacks

Shoes, Everex Systems, and Sun Microsystems. For these leading competitors, time has become the overarching measurement of performance. By reducing the consumption of time in every aspect of the business, these companies also reduce costs, improve quality, and stay close to their customers. Before they could reduce time consumption, however, each of these companies had to take a long look at its value delivery system.

VALUE-DELIVERY SYSTEM COMPETITION

Underlying the operations of every company—working like its spine or cerebral cortex—is a system. For example, what does it take for an appliance manufacturer to receive an order, process the order, produce the appliance, deliver it and collect? What are all the steps that a bank goes through in processing transactions, coordinating branches, and delivering timely and accurate loan decisions? How does an automobile manufacturer design a new vehicle made up of thousands of different component parts and manage the daily flow of orders and shipments with suppliers and assembly plants? Each business operation is different, but all share one powerful common trait: all are systems for providing value to customers—value delivery systems.

A value delivery system organizes work and guides actions; time connects all the parts of the system. It is a system that develops product, delivers product, and makes decisions. It is a system within a retailing organization that results in orders being placed, goods being manufactured and shipped, and stores being stocked. Whether the system consists of a flow of bits between computers, paper over desks, or parts through a factory, the mandate is the same: A company's performance is the direct result of how effectively the system is structured and managed. Companies that operate more efficiently and responsively than their competitors have better-designed and better-managed systems. Thus, the quality of their systems is often as much or more the basis for their sustainable competitive advantage as are their technologies, products, or services.

A basic test of management's understanding of the systemic nature of its business is whether or not it is caught in the *planning loop*. All businesses must do some sort of planning for the future to be sure they are ready to make the sale. Manufacturers are challenged by the need to order raw material, schedule facilities, add labor, and so on. Traditional manufacturing requires long lead times to resolve conflicts between various jobs or activities that require the same resources. The long lead times, in turn, require sales forecasts to guide planning. But sales forecasts are inevitably wrong; by definition they are guesses, however informed. Naturally, as lead times lengthen, the accuracy of sales forecasts declines. With more forecasting errors, the need for safety stocks at all levels and excess capacity at all levels increases, and inventories balloon. Errors in forecasting also mean more unscheduled jobs that have to be expedited, thereby crowding out scheduled jobs. The need for even longer lead times grows greater, and the planning loop expands—driving up costs, increasing delays, and creating system inefficiencies.

Managers who find themselves trapped in the planning loop often respond by asking for better forecasts and longer lead times. However, this is treating the symptom rather than the problem. The only way to break the planning loop is to reduce the consumption of time throughout the system, thus reducing the need for lead times. After all, if a company could ever drive its lead times all the way to zero, it would have to forecast only the next day's sales. The most powerful competitors understand this concept and are breaking the debilitating loop that strangles much of traditional manufacturing and many nonmanufacturing organizations. While lead times of zero do not occur, successful time-based competitors in Japan and in the West have at a minimum kept their lead times from growing and many have reduced them, thereby diminishing the planning loop's damaging effects.

Thirty years ago, Jay W. Forrester of the Massachusetts Institute of Technology published a pioneering article in the *Harvard Business Review*,[3] which established a model of time's impact on the performance of an organization. Using "industrial dynamics"—a technique originally developed to direct shipboard fire-control systems—Forrester tracked the effects of time delays and decision policies within a simple but representative business system consisting of a factory, its warehouse, a distributor, and a retailer. The numbers in Exhibit 2–7 are the delays measured in weeks in the flow of information and product from one level in the system to another. In this example, the orders accumulate at the retailer for three weeks, are in the mail for one half of a week, are delayed at the distributor for two weeks, go back in the mail for another half week, and need eight weeks for processing at the factory and its warehouse. The finished product then begins its journey back to the retailer. The complete cycle takes 19 weeks.

The customer does not often see a 19-week cycle. That is because inventories are held at various levels—to deceive the customer into thinking that the responsiveness of this system is much

Exhibit 2–7 The Effect of Delays on a Business System *A Schematic of the System*

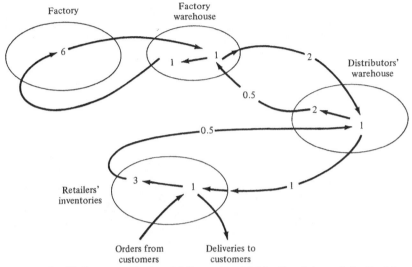

SOURCE: Jay W. Forrester, "Industrial Dynamics: A Major Breakthrough for Decision Makers," *Harvard Business Review*, July-August 1958, p. 43.

faster than 19 weeks. However, the basic cycle of the business is 19 weeks, and all planning must reflect this fact.

The system in this example can be expected to be very stable as long as retail demand is stable, or as long as sales forecasts are perfectly accurate 19 weeks into the future. But if unexpected changes occur the system must respond. The response of the factory to a simple 10 percent increase in retail demand is shown in Exhibit 2–8. Acting on new forecasts and seeking to cut delivery delays, the factory first responds by ramping up production 40 percent. When management realizes—too late—that it has overshot the mark, it cuts production 30 percent. Too late again, it learns that it has overcorrected. This ramping up and cutting back continue for well over a year until the system finally stabilizes at the new level of demand.

What distorts the system so badly is time: the lengthy delay between the event that creates the change of demand and the time when the factory finally responds to this information. The oscillations occur because the factory acts on out-of-date information. Information is bundled and passed on at each step, finally reaching the factory and presenting a delayed and distorted view of reality. The longer the delays, the more distorted is the view of the change in the market. Those distortions rever-

Exhibit 2–8 Response of a Production-Distribution System to a
Sudden Increase in Sales

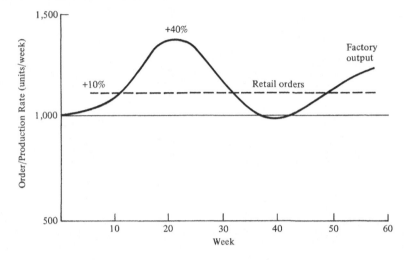

berate throughout the system, producing disruptions, waste, and
inefficiency.

Another, more realistic scenario is that of factory's response to
predictable yearly retail demand with random week-to-week variations. The simulated demand and the factory's response are
shown in Exhibit 2–9. The jagged line is the random demand, and
the smoother line is the factory response over a four-year period.
The factory settles into a periodic response of approximately 56
weeks or about one year. An executive in this company might
believe his business is seasonal, based on the demands on his
factory. However, if he or she attempted to smooth demand by
advertising and promoting in the troughs and raising prices in the
peaks, the oscillations would actually increase.

Exhibit 2–9 Effects of Random Deviations in Retail Sales on Factory
Production

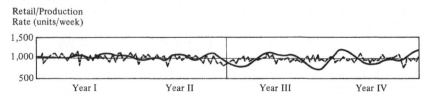

Many companies have seasonal characteristics and must face seasonal oscillations. Sometimes, seasonal businesses cause significant portions of their swings by virtue of their own actions. In such situations management's promotional policies inadvertently aggravate the oscillations that are the natural consequence of the basic delays in the system. Examples of businesses in which significant portions of sales are booked in a narrow period of a few months include luggage, cameras, and automobiles. Often, though, these "seasonal" variations are self-induced. For example, a leading manufacturer of luggage has sharply reduced the production oscillations by first reducing poorly timed seasonal promotions and then by substantially reducing the delays in its value delivery system.

The impact of "seasonal" variations on the operations of the companies can be enormous. Overheads must be increased to enable output to be ramped up and down. Accommodating these oscillations, however, increases the cost of doing business. The cost of accommodation is estimated to increase as the cubic function of the area between the oscillating output curve for the factory and the neutral axis.

The distortions between actual demand and perceived demand plague most businesses today. To escape them, companies have a choice. They can produce to forecast and try to ignore the reverberations that would cause them to do otherwise, or they can reduce the time delays in the flow of information and product through the system. The traditional solution is to produce to forecast. Management knows that the final demand is more predictable than that which their factories experience, so they "level" production and try as hard as they can to ignore the signals to increase or decrease production being sent through their distribution system. Usually, the best that can be expected from this solution is a compromise between submitting to the oscillations and running level.

The new solution is to reduce the consumption of time throughout the system. If the delays in the Forrester model are cut in half across the board, the maximum inventory oscillations resulting from random demand (Exhibit 2–10) are less than 20 percent of their previous levels. Operating costs can be expected to be reduced as well, since the area between the factory output curve and the neutral axis is less than one-twentieth that of the previous simulation.

The flexible production system can produce significant reductions of delays. Flexible factories consume significantly less time than do traditionally managed factories. In fact the improvements in production response time resulting from becoming flexible are

Exhibit 2–10 Effects of Random Deviations in Retail Sales on Factory Production

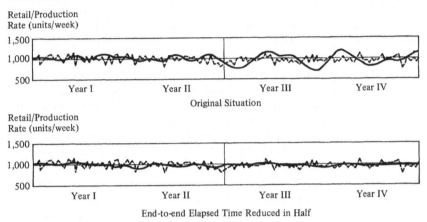

Retail/Production
Rate (units/week)

Original Situation

Retail/Production
Rate (units/week)

End-to-end Elapsed Time Reduced in Half

even more impressive than the improvements in the productivity of labor and of assets.

Toyota offers a dramatic example of the kinds of improvement that time-based competitors are making. One of Toyota's suppliers needed 15 days from the arrival of raw materials at the factory to the shipment of the finished product. Dissatisfied with this level of responsiveness to its changing needs, Toyota went to work. By reducing lot sizes, they cut the supplier's response time to six days. After the factory layout was streamlined to reduce inventory holding points, the required time fell to three days. The elimination of all work-in-process inventories resulted in the supplier being able to respond to Toyota with only a one-day notice. This Japanese supplier improved its manufacturing response time by more than an *order of magnitude.*

Many companies are dramatically improving their manufacturing response times by streamlining their factories and becoming more flexible. Examples of improved responsiveness are shown in Table 2–5. Matsushita reduced the time required to manufacture washing machines from 360 hours to just 2 hours. Harley-Davidson reduced its value delivery time by more than 90 percent. The remaining companies in the table are North American; each has improved its manufacturing response times by approximately 90 percent.

TIME-BASED OPERATIONS

The challenge of becoming a time-based competitor is as much a white-collar task as it is a factory task, because time delays can

TABLE 2–5 Typical Improvements in Production Flow Times

	Before	*After*	*Percent Reduction*
Japan			
Washing machines (Matsushita)	360 hours	2 hours	99
United States			
Motorcycles (Harley-Davidson)	360 days	< 3 days	99
Motor controllers	56 days	7 days	88
Electric components	24 days	1 day	96
Radar detectors	22 days	3 days	86

appear anywhere in the value delivery system. In fact, typically, the majority of time is consumed beyond the factory—by decision makers and by information processors. In the Forrester model, the factory contributed 6 of the 19 weeks of delay. The remaining 13 weeks of delay were consumed by the distribution system. At most companies, factories consume less than 40 percent of the time customers are forced to wait.

In many cases, factories consume even less time than do those in the Forrester model, perhaps less than 10 percent of total value delivery time. This observation is key because in it lies the possibility of time-based competition in service businesses. Ultimately, in both manufacturing and service firms, the *entire* value delivery system must be made flexible to obtain the least time consumption. Truly responsive value delivery systems must have flexible sales, order entry, procurement, and distribution systems as well as flexible factories. By the late 1970s, many leading Japanese companies were discovering this. They were finding that their sales and distribution systems were limiting the effectiveness of their flexible production systems. The factory benefits of being flexible were not making it through the rest of the system to the customer.

For example the Toyota Motor Manufacturing company built cars and then sold and distributed them through the Toyota Motor Sales company. The factories of Toyota Motor Manufacturing had become so flexible that they could build a car in less than two days. But Toyota Motor Sales required an additional 15 to 26 days to close the sale, transmit the order to the factory, and deliver the car to the consumer.

By the late 1970s, the engineers at Toyota Motor Manufacturing company were frustrated because the sales and distribution network was frittering away their reductions in manufacturing time. Twenty to 30 percent of the cost of a car to a consumer, which was more than it cost Toyota to manufacture the car, and more than 90 percent of the time a customer had to wait was consumed by the distribution and sales function. And if ever a company disliked waiting and paying to move product around, that company is Toyota.

In 1981 this frustration led to the merger of Toyota Motor Manufacturing and Toyota Motor Sales. Eighteen months after the merger, all the directors of the sales company had been retired, and their jobs were either abolished or filled by executives from the manufacturing company.

The new Toyota developed and implemented a plan to reduce delays and costs in its sales and distribution system. Toyota found that the existing distribution system handled information in layers, sequentially and in large batches. Information would accumulate at one step of the sales and distribution process before being sent to another level. This accumulation consumed time, generated costs, and distanced the factory from the customers' needs.

To speed the flow of information, the new sales directors wanted to reduce the accumulation batch size. They developed a computer network system to tie the salespeople directly to the factory scheduling function, bypassing several levels of the sales and distribution system and enabling the modified system to operate with very small information batch sizes.

This new approach to handling information was expected to reduce cycle time in the sales and distribution system from four to six weeks to two to three weeks across Japan. The goal in the Tokyo and Osaka regions, which account for about two-thirds of Japan's population, was to reduce cycle time to two days. By the spring of 1987, the responsiveness of the sales and distribution system had improved in the best situations to six days, thus exceeding their first goal and achieving more than a 50 percent reduction in sales and distribution time.

The undertaking was massive in people as well as costs. Yet, at the time of the merger, Toyota executives were publicly very guarded in their explanations about the change—preferring to cite a return to the original organization of the company—the combination of sales and manufacturing that had existed in the 1950s. By 1988 the new network carried information between factories and sales branches connecting 317 wholesalers and 4,200 dependent distributors. A critical head start over competitors had been achieved. Consequently, Toyota executives are now more public in explaining their strategy. The system is being described as a way to change the sales strategy from "sell the customer what we have" to "sell the customer what he wants." With the previous strategy, the "salesperson had to anticipate the mix of sales and order in advance. To reduce risk to the minimum, salespeople tended to order only cars with mass market appeal. However, sales of these cars produced lower profits than did sales of custom-ordered cars. With the introduction of the new network system, dealers can now order more profitable, custom cars with less risk. This leads to high customer satisfaction as well as high profits."[4] One year after the full introduction of the new network, sales have increased by about 5 percent, and dealer profits have increased by over 13 percent.

Toyota's accomplishments can be related to the Forrester example. Using time compressions in factories and in the sales and distribution functions that are comparable to Toyota's achievements, the overall delays in the Forrester model would be reduced from 19 weeks to 6 weeks. This would cut delays by better than the 50 percent that was shown to have such a stabilizing effect on Forrester's factory output oscillations. Thus, the overall shorter cycle time reduces the effects of random demand on Toyota. The company can more accurately forecast sales for a shorter interval of time, their costs are less, and their customers happier. Is it any wonder that Toyota operations appear to run so smoothly to Western executives whose own systems often have very long delays throughout and who experience surging demand?

A few years ago, a major North American manufacturer of central office switch gear for telephone companies* faced a problem similar to Toyota's. Much effort had been expended to make the factories that assembled and tested these switches flexible and responsive. However, even though the factory cycle times had been reduced from months to days, the customers still faced 10- and 12-week lead times.

The process of meeting the customers' needs is, conceptually, straightforward for this manufacturer (Exhibit 2–11). Eight steps are required. Sales takes the order, the order is entered into the

---

* This is a stylized example based on the experiences of another company in an industry with many of the characteristics of the switch gear industry.

Exhibit 2–11 Compressing Time: In the Value Delivery System

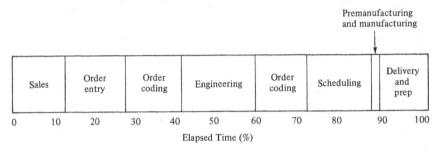

company's scheduling system, any necessary custom engineering is done, the results of the special engineering are then coded and entered into the company's scheduling system, the actual assembly of the switch is scheduled, the switch is assembled and then shipped to the customer. The assembly took less than 10 percent of the total elapsed time. More people outside of the factories were involved in this conceptually simple process than were involved in the factories. Obviously, what is simple in concept is much more complex in reality.

Exhibit 2–12 shows a much more detailed map of the process of getting the switch order from the customer to the point of assembly. The customer's order moves through four phases before the requested switch can be assembled. These are closing the sale, initial order entry, entry of the customized engineering, and finally plant scheduling. These phases break down to 28 steps that are executed as the customer's order is passed from the customer to sales, to sales engineering, back to sales, up to sales administration, back to sales engineering, and so on. The circles in the diagram represent loopbacks that occur when an error is found or clarification is needed. The numbers within the circles represent the point in the process to which the order might have to return. Because of the potential for loopbacks, the typical order required not 28 processing steps but almost 100 processing steps. Some orders required even more. If this information-processing network is thought of as a factory, it must be viewed not as a simple factory but as a very complex factory.

The typical order processing time for each step are shown in Exhibit 2–13. Some steps can be accomplished in a day or less. Other steps require one to 3 days, 3 to 10 days, 10 to 15 days and potentially more than 15 days if loopbacks occur. Since, the capacities and operating rates of these steps are not the same, the

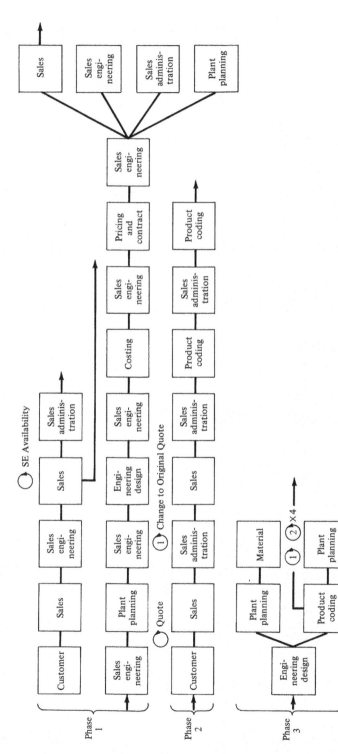

Exhibit 2–12 Order Flow Logistics—Sequencing   28 steps occur from customer request to line set

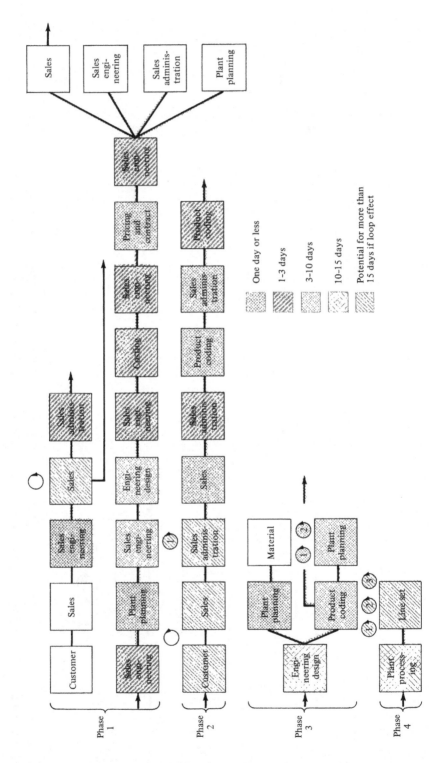

Legend:

- One day or less
- 1-3 days
- 3-10 days
- 10-15 days
- Potential for more than 15 days if loop effect

Exhibit 2-13 Order Flow Logistics—Process Time

process is out of balance and the speed of order processing is erratic with many time-consuming bottlenecks.

Geography complicates the process even further, as shown in Exhibit 2–14. This information-processing network can—in the extreme where a distant field office is involved—be spread over five geographical locations. This is not even counting the variety of buildings, floors of buildings, offices and desks that the complete set of steps occupy. The typical order changes location 22 times—not counting the effects of loopbacks. Because the process is in so many locations, many of the steps are in different time zones. Accounting for different starting and quitting times as well as breaks and lunches, the network is working end-to-end less than four hours of the day. During the other times, a part of the network is not functioning. Consequently, this information-processing network is a complex factory, not only out of balance but spread over God's creation.

The roles of the vice presidents heading departments are highlighted in Exhibit 2–15. A typical order passes through product coding, sales administration, sales engineering, plant planning, engineering design, and sales on three to six separate occasions. It is no wonder that nine times more time is consumed outside the factory than within it.

The management of this company has a commitment to the board of directors to streamline this process, and are well on the way to doing so. The payoff is enormous. A halving of the time customers are forced to wait is expected to save over $50 million dollars in operating costs and to lead to increased market share.

The approach to streamlining this information-processing dynamic is not unlike that required to streamline a factory. If a factory is complex, out of balance, spread over God's creation, and reports to many supervisors, then it must be made simple, balanced, collocated and organized, so that its management can see the process for which it is being held accountable. Of course accomplishing this can be difficult. Appropriate methods for such streamlining are discussed in more detail in later chapters. For now suffice it to say that simplification must be done in ways that reduce risks and still provide the needed values. Some of the questions that must be answered are: What capacities are needed by what step? Collocation, but where? What should the design of the organization be? How should its performance be measured and rewarded? Who should report to whom?

When these questions have been asked, then the real work begins. This is the task of moving an organization from where it is to where it wants to be. Tasks of this nature—whether they are

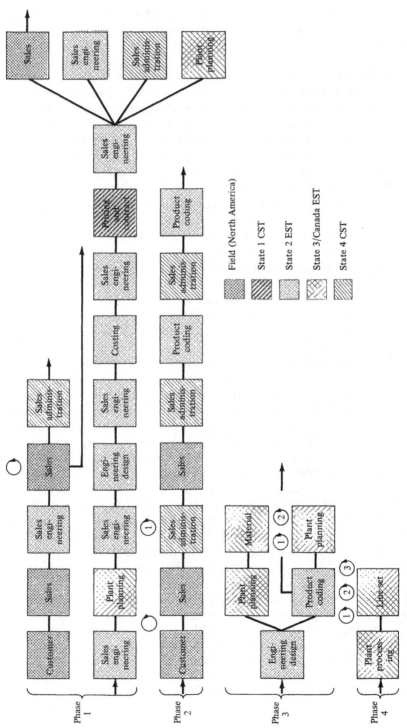

Exhibit 2–14 Order Flow Logistics—Location of Departments   *The order processing location changes 22 times*

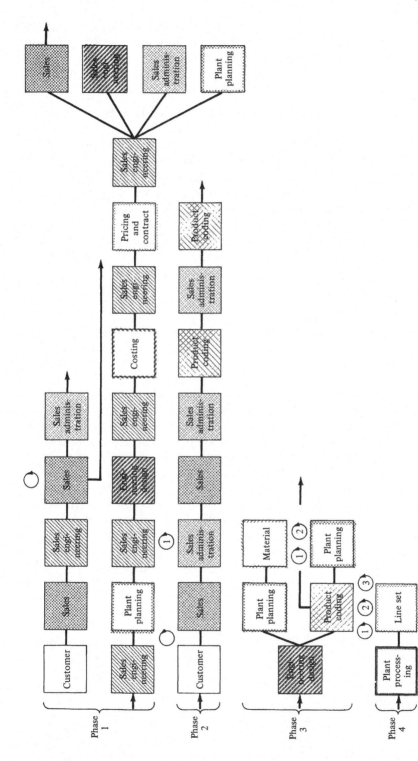

Exhibit 2–15 Order Flow Logistics—Departments *Product Coding, Sales Administration, and Sales Engineering work on an* order on 3 to 6 separate occasions from start to finish

time-based or not—are seldom easy to accomplish. When hundreds of people must execute their work differently, education and patience are needed to help them find their way.

STRATEGIC IMPLICATIONS

The refocusing of attention from cost to time is enabling the early innovators to become time-based competitors who can, literally, run circles around their slower competition. Time-based competitors are offering greater varieties of products at lower costs and in less time than their more pedestrian competitors.

A set of empirical rules is emerging as more and more companies become time-based competitors. These are the *Rules of Response.*[5]

- the 0.05 to 5 rule
- the 3/3 rule
- the 1/4-2-20 rule
- the 3 × 2 rule

THE 0.05 TO 5 RULE

Across a spectrum of businesses, the amount of time required to execute a service or an order, manufacture and deliver a product is far less than the actual time the service or product spends in the value-delivery system. For example, a manufacturer of heavy vehicles takes 45 days to prepare an order for assembly, but only 16 hours to assemble each vehicle. The vehicle is actually receiving value for less than 1 percent of the time it spends in the system.

The 0.05 to 5 rule highlights the poor "time productivity" of most organizations since most products and many services are actually receiving value for only 0.05 to 5 percent of the time they are in the value delivery systems of their companies.

THE 3/3 RULE

During the 95 to 99.95 percent of the time a product or service is not receiving value while in the value-delivery system, the product or service is waiting.

The waiting time has three components, which are the amounts of time lost while waiting for

- Completion of the batch a particular product or service is a part of as well as the completion of the batch *ahead* of the batch a particular product or service is a part of
- Physical and intellectual rework to be completed
- Management to get around to making and executing the decision to send the batch on to the next step of the value-adding process

Generally the 95 to 99.95 percent of the time lost divides almost equally among these three categories.

The amount of time lost is affected very little by working harder. But working smarter has a tremendous impact. Companies that reduce the size of the batches they process—whether the batches are physical goods or packets of information—streamline the work flows and significantly reduce the time lost in their value-delivery systems. For example, when a manufacturer of hospital equipment reduced standard production lot sizes by half, the time required to manufacture the product declined by 65 percent. After the production flow was streamlined to reduce material handling and the number of intermediate events requiring scheduling was reduced, the total time was reduced by another 65 percent for a total reduction of 58 percent.

While these improvements were dramatic, this company barely escaped the 0.05 to 5 rule. Its time productivity increased over 200 percent from 3 percent to 7 percent.

THE 1/4-2-20 RULE

Companies that attack the consumption of time in their value-delivery system experience remarkable performance improvements. For every quartering of the time interval required to provide a service or product, the productivity of labor and of working capital can often double. These productivity gains result in as much as a 20 percent reduction in costs.

A North American manufacturer of a consumer durable has reduced its time interval from five weeks to slightly more than one week. Labor and asset productivities have more than doubled, and profits are approaching extraordinary levels.

THE 3 × 2 RULE

Companies that cut their time consumption of their value-delivery systems turn the basis of competitive advantage to their favor.

Growth rates of three times the average of their industry with two times the industry profit margins are exciting and achievable targets.

A manufacturer of prefinished building materials reduced the time required to meet any and all customer orders to less than ten days. Most orders can be on the customer's site one to three days from when their order was placed. The other competitors required 30 to 45 days to fill any and all orders.

This time-based competitor has grown over 10 percent a year for the last ten years, to become the market leader. The industry average growth rate has been less than 3 percent per year over the same period. The pretax return on net assets of this time-based competitor is 80 percent—more than double the average of the industry.

Western companies are obtaining remarkable results by focusing their organizations on responsiveness. Consistent with the 3 × 2 rule discussed above, each of the companies in Table 2–6 uses its response advantage to grow at least three times faster than the growth of its industry and with profitabilities that are more than twice the average of others in its industries.

Consider the remarkable example of Atlas Door, a ten-year-old U.S. company. It has grown at an annual rate of 15 percent per year in an industry with an annual growth of 5 percent. In recent years, after-tax earnings were in excess of 10 percent of sales, about five times the industry average. Atlas is debt free. In its tenth year of existence, it achieved the number one leadership position in the industry.

TABLE 2–6 Time-based Competitors Lead the Performance of Their Industries

Company	Business	Response Difference	Profit Advantage	Profit
Wal-Mart	Discount stores	80%	36 vs. 12%	19 vs. 9% ROCE[a]
Atlas Door	Industrial doors	66%	15 vs. 5%	10 vs. 2% ROS[a]
Ralph Wilson Plastics	Decorative laminates	75%	9 vs. 3%	40 vs. 10% RONA[a]
Thomasville	Furniture	70%	12 vs. 3%	21 vs. 11% ROA[a]

[a] ROCE is return on capital employed; ROS is return on sales; RONA is return on net assets; ROA is return on assets.

The company's product: industrial doors. These doors involve considerable variety, with many possible choices of width, height dimensions and material. This variety limits the effectiveness of responding to customers through inventory. Most doors must be manufactured to order.

Historically, the industry has needed on average 12 to 15 weeks to respond to an order for a customized or out-of-stock door. Atlas' strategic advantage is time. It can reliably respond in three to four weeks because it has structured its order entry, engineering factories, and logistics to move information and product quickly and reliably.

First, Atlas built just-in-time factories. These are fairly simple in concept: extra tooling and machinery to substantially reduce changeover times; and a fabrication process organized by product and scheduled so that most all of the parts needed to fulfill an order for a door can be started and completed at about the same time. However, the performance of the factory, while critical to the company's overall responsiveness, consumes only about two-and-a-half weeks of the complete cycle.

Second, Atlas compressed time at the front end of the system, where the order is received and entered into the process. Traditionally, when a customer, distributor, or salesperson called a door manufacturer with a request for price and delivery, he or she might have to wait a week or more for a response. If the door was not in stock, not in the schedule, or not engineered, then the request had to be kicked around the supplier's organization before the answers were known. Atlas automated its entire order entry, engineering, pricing, and scheduling processes. Today 80 percent of all incoming orders can be priced and scheduled while the caller is still on the telephone. Special orders can be engineered quickly because the amount of re-engineering has been substantially reduced by preserving the design and production data of all previous special orders.

Third, Atlas controls logistics tightly so that a complete order can always be shipped to construction sites. An order requires many components. Getting them together at the factory and making sure they are with the correct order can be a time-consuming task. Getting the correct parts to the job site if they missed the initial shipment is even more time consuming. Atlas developed a system to track the parts in production and the purchased parts for each order to ensure that all parts arrive at the shipping dock in time and at the customer site at the same time.

Early in the company's life, Atlas' salespeople were often rebuffed when they approached new distributors. The large, established, and attractive distributors already carried the door line of a larger competitor and saw no reason short of major price concessions to switch suppliers. As a startup company, Atlas was too small to compete on price alone. Instead, the company positioned itself as the door supplier of last resort. It was the company people came to if the established supplier could not deliver or missed a key date.

Of course, with industry lead times averaging 12 to 14 weeks, the company was likely to receive some calls. When the company did get a call, it was able to command a higher price because of its faster delivery. Not only was its price realization high, but its streamlined and effective processes were lower cost. The company had the best of both worlds. In the short span of ten years, Atlas replaced the established door suppliers for 80 percent of the distributors in the country. Now the company could be selective when asked to become the house supplier and could acquire the stronger distributors.

Atlas's competitors are not responding at all effectively. The conventional view at one major competitor is that the company is a "garage shop operator" that cannot sustain its growth. In other words, the competitors expect the company's performance to degrade to the industry average as it grows larger. But this response—or nonresponse—only reflects a fundamental lack of understanding time as a source of competitive advantage in business. The competitors' delay in responding often allows the time-based competitor to build a lead that is insurmountable or at least very expensive to close.

Much of this chapter's discussion of time and business has been manufacturing oriented. Manufacturing companies seem to consume more time than service companies. The issue, though, is time consumption relative to competitors. As will be shown in the next chapter, if Company A, a provider of mortgage money, requires 45 days to approve a mortgage application and Citicorp can provide the same value in 15 days or less, Company A is dangerously exposed.

Time as a source of competitive advantage is applicable whenever customers have to wait to receive the value they have decided they want. This leads to new ways of thinking about business. A business is a collection of systems for providing value to customers. The company's resources should be organized to support the value-adding process.

Time-based organizations often look very different from the traditional functional- and control-oriented organizations of traditional companies. For example, at one defense contractor instead of contracts, systems engineering, operations, procurement, and program management departments, there is simply a proposal factory. Instead of separate and often conflicting functional goals, measures, and rewards—as well as frustrated customers who are waiting to learn if a project can be done, when it can be done, and for how much—there are integrated goals, measures, and rewards, such as proposal backlogs, completion times, win/loss rates, cost-estimating accuracy and satisfied customers. While traditional companies track costs and size, the new competitor derives advantage from time, staying on the cutting edge and leaving its rivals behind.

Also, much of the discussion in the West about customer-oriented, responsive companies has highlighted the accomplishments of smaller companies. In small companies, thinking in terms of responsiveness—time and variety—is usually second nature. Many smaller companies have no other strategic options. Because they are small, they do not have the competitive cost position associated with their larger competitors. Most small companies that exist despite large competitors do so because they have been able to redefine the business in a way that is attractive to some of the market's customers. These may be customers that represent demand not large enough in aggregate to be worth the larger companies' trouble. In order to find such demand, small companies must be very customer oriented. They can be more responsive to creating value for the customer because everyone works directly on the product or service and with the customer. Policies, procedures, practices, or people that interfere with getting the product out the door or with providing service are easy to see and can be dealt with quickly. The systems of smaller companies, while sometimes crude technologically, are almost always tightly linked and very sensitive to customers' needs and changes in external events.

As companies grow, however, the system-like nature of the core organization often gets distorted. Distances—physical and time—increase as different departments focus on their own needs, administrative activities multiply, specialists are hired, and written reports replace face-to-face conversations. Soon it becomes hard to see clearly what parts of the company directly add value to what the customer is buying and what parts just plan, pass data, intermediate, administrate, or raise questions. When this happens, the company stops functioning as a well-connected system. Of course, senior management thinks it is lubricating the company by adding these support activities, but it is really slowing down the working parts by filtering contact between them. The effect is to frustrate the customer. "I don't care what *your* job is!" the overwhelmed customer finally complains. "When can I get *my* order?"

Time-based performance levels are interesting, however, because large companies like Wal-Mart, Milliken, and Hewlett-Packard are achieving them. Time-based companies are restoring the advantages of scale that large firms with costly, complex operations and management structures have dissipated in the last 20 years. Large, powerful corporations should be able to do things for customers that smaller, less resource-rich companies cannot. And finally, once again they can.

CHAPTER

3

◇◇◇◇

Time and Customers

Customers can be a nuisance. First, they want what they want. Then, they want it when they want it. Finally, they expect the quality of the goods or services purchased to be perfect. Sometimes it seems that they are never satisfied.

Demanding customers disrupt business. When customers demand choice in the form of nonstandard product or service, costs increase. When work schedules must be expedited to satisfy demanding customers, other customers are forced to wait, and this causes aggravation, defections, and more expediting.

Management has three choices when responding to demanding customers:

1. *Fight customers by forcing them to accept standard performance, product, or service.* For example, most car dealerships offer service to their customers on weekdays only, from 7:30 A.M. to 4 P.M. and do not make appointments. Customers must adjust their schedules to meet that of the dealerships.

2. *Insulate its organization from customers by building mounds of inventory or by getting them to do a lot of their own work.* The service managers of these same car dealerships are happiest if their customers drop their cars off the night before after filling out their own work requests and then keep quiet until the service manager calls with the estimate. The service manager then waits for the customer to call or to show up for his repaired vehicle.

3. *Embrace them and be sure that they are more satisfied with the service provided than they could ever have imagined.* The impatient car owner can now get a 10-minute oil change, a 20-minute muffler replacement, a 59-minute tune-up, and a one-hour brake job from the many specialty automotive service retailers that offer fast ser-

vice and guarantees as well as low price. The car dealerships are increasingly being left with warranty work and major repairs, which, while potentially profitable, are not where the volume is.

The most attractive customers are often the most difficult to satisfy. These customers are demanding—wanting exactly what meets their needs. If you can satisfy them they will be reluctant to take their business elsewhere. They become dependent, and dependency can be profitable.

Being responsive to the needs of customers pays in four ways:

1. Customers are more loyal to suppliers who are consistently responsive to their needs.
2. Customers will pay a premium over the typical price to a responsive supplier.
3. Customers will buy more goods and services from a responsive supplier.
4. The supplier becomes strategically advantaged when it secures the demanding customer.

CUSTOMER LOYALTY

Circumstantial evidence that customers are more loyal to consistently responsive suppliers is easy to find in our day-to-day lives. As consumers we avoid stores that are frequently out of stock of the items we want and visit stores that often refresh the variety of their stock. We use convenience stores and fast food outlets to avoid losing time roaming aisles in a supermarket. As frequent flyers, we avoid airlines and airports that are consistently late or backed up. We find a combination of carriers and routes that work and stick with them until performance deteriorates, and we are forced to find alternatives.

Carefully done surveys can underscore quantitatively the importance of being responsive to customers. With this data, managers can make informed judgements about investing in enhanced responsiveness. For example, the *1988 Survey of Consumer Attitudes and the Supermarkets* by the Food Marketing Institute found that "two shoppers in five believe the service at their supermarket has improved over the last year or two, while half believe the service has remained the same. Shopper satisfaction with the service provided is the best indicator of their overall satisfaction with the supermarket."[1] However, among the many expectations consumers have for their supermarkets—quality products, choice, location, and so on—fast checkout is the key aspect of service with which they are dissatisfied. Fast checkout is somewhat or very important to 88 percent of the polled shopping public, but only 70 percent of this public give their supermarkets a good or an excellent rating—a gap between expectations and delivery of 26 percent. The average gap between expectations and delivery for the 16 categories was only 6 percent. Clearly, the profitability of supermarkets will be well served by investing in responsiveness.

Obtaining customer loyalty is a two-edged sword. Customers often "vote with their feet" if they come to believe that their supplier is no longer responsive to their needs. Such behavior is the dark side of customer loyalty. If management is lucky, the walking customer will leave a message as to why he or she is dissatisfied before leaving. Most often though, management is forced to uncover customer dissatisfaction from secondary evidence. In a survey of trends and issues in wholesale banking the researchers at the Bank Administration Institute found that 81 percent of the chief financial officers queried said that in anticipating their future banking needs, they "planned to shop around for the best deals" and that almost half expected to switch their major banking relationship. "An evaluation of the reasons given by the chief financial officers for seeking another (banking relationship) indicates that the quality of service clearly surpasses other factors for companies of all sizes." Quality of service was ranked as the first or second reason for switching by 58 percent of the respondents. The ranking of service surpassed pricing of loans and other products by a margin of almost three to one.[2] The managements of banks that act on these findings are going to be getting the customers of banks whose managements do not. In all likelihood, the managements of the banks losing out are going to believe that the business is being lost because of price cutting rather than improved service.

Silent, dissatisfied customers can hurt a business very quickly. For example, the management of a manufacturer of prefabricated-kit homes experienced falling profits, even as the backlog of the company increased. Unresponsiveness to the needs of its best customers was the root cause of the company's problem.

The company's delivery times averaged about 150 days from the signing of a contract with the customer to the delivery of the product. Most of this waiting time was caused not by the manufacturing process but by the preparation for it—in particular, by a 45- to 60-day credit approval process.

This manufacturer provided bridge financing until the construction of the prefabricated house was complete, and the customer could obtain permanent financing from the traditional sources of home mortgages. Management believed the credit approval process necessary to limit financial risk. However, during this lengthy interval, a fair number of customers would cancel their orders. Worse yet, the more credit-worthy customers usually cancelled their contracts before the less credit-worthy customers did. The poorest credit risks had few alternatives, so they would hang on until the bitter end.

As the lengthy credit approval process reduced and even reversed customer loyalty, the impact on the manufacturer's profit was more negative than just that of a lost sale. Credit-worthy customers defected, and the proportion of attractive customers to all customers declined. Sales marketing and credit-checking expenses increased, because new customers had to be found and qualified; the credit-checking process slowed even more as the mix of customers shifted from those who could readily be qualified to those whose applications required more time. Bridge loans to less credit-worthy customers as a percentage of all loans increased, and, the loan losses mounted.

At first, no one explicitly worked on shortening credit approval process time, and it inevitably lengthened. Eventually, however, management found that by carefully rethinking its loan-approval process, the time consumed could be substantially reduced. Instead of having all loan applicants go through the same review process, whether or not they were obviously good credit risks, a surprisingly simple algorithm was developed to predict applicants' credit worthiness. Data on four characteristics led to a very accurate prediction of a customer's credit worthiness: simple credit check, absolute family income, net worth, and years in current job. Applicants could now be *reliably* divided into high, medium, and low credit risks, and the approval process could be shortened greatly for good credit risks and moderately for medium credit risks. Poor credit risks were avoided altogether. Today, this company's typical customer waits less than a week for credit approval, SG&A (sales, general and administrative) expenses are declining, and the quality of the loan portfolio is improving.

Seeking out demanding but loyal customers is useful for two reasons. First, the supplier who can more consistently give customers what they want when they want it will have customers who will bring not only repeat business but new business as well. The cost of making a sale to a new customer can be as high as ten times the cost of selling to an existing customer. Every satisfied existing customer can mean valuable referrals that cost less to secure than they would for a typical new customer. As Joe Girard, certified by the Guinness Book of Records as the world's greatest automobile salesmen, observed,

> Let me explain to you what I call Girard's Law of 250. (A) Protestant funeral director bought a car from me. After the close, I asked him the average number of people who come to see the body and attend the funeral. He said, "About 250." Then one day, my wife and I were at a wedding, and I met the man who owns the catering place where the reception took place. I asked him what the average number of guests at a wedding was, and he told me, "About 250 from the bride's side, and about 250 from the groom's."
>
> I guess you can figure out what Girard's Law of 250 is, but I'll tell you anyway: Everyone knows 250 people in his or her life important enough to invite to the wedding or funeral— 250![3]

Second, the supplier who focuses on response-sensitive customers may also benefit by weeding out marginal customers. Some customers are willing to compromise their choice and to wait a long time to get the best price. These customers can be difficult to make money on and are seldom loyal. As such they are "marginal customers"—customers who are sought only after the more attractive customers are all taken; as such they are best left to the competition.

The importance of recognizing that customers have different sensitivities to responsiveness should be reflected in the way customers are served. The managements of many companies treat their customers as if they all had the same or similar sensitivity to responsiveness. In the case of the prefabricated home manufacturer, every customer passed through the same credit approval process despite the fact that credit worthiness is almost as variable as the way each customer dresses. The customers who are sensitive to responsiveness have to be identified and served differently if their loyalty is to be obtained and retained.

TIME-BASED COMPETITIVE STRATEGY

The true profit potential of being a time-based competitor can be realized when the improved cost efficiencies of being responsive are matched with the customers' awareness of better service, their desire for choice, and their willingness to pay well for both. For example, some customers, such as the business traveler, are more concerned about flight schedules and airline choice than about price. Others, such as the vacation traveler, are most concerned about price and will accept schedule compromises. The seat cost per mile for both passengers can be equal since very often they end up sitting next to each other! However, the business traveler pays a higher price and is a much more profitable and desirable customer to an airline than is the vacation traveler. Some airlines, such as American Airlines, concentrate their marketing efforts in successfully attracting the business traveler while others, such as Continental, court the vacation traveler. Thus, customers are segmentable by their sensitivities to time and choice.

PRICE PREMIUMS

A company's responsiveness to the needs of its customers sharply influences the price it receives for its goods and services and therefore its profitability. The faster a company can consistently respond better to its customers than can its competitors, the higher its growth, prices and profitability will be. The converse is also true. As a company chooses to or unintentionally becomes less responsive, its growth, prices, and profitability can be expected to diminish.

The willingness of customers to pay higher prices for faster response can be measured by the *time elasticity of price*. Understanding the influence of time elasticity in your business yields strategic insights into your customers' needs. It can also reveal competitors' vulnerabilities and create opportunities for you to substantially out-perform your rivals.

The essence of the time elasticity of price is shown schematically in Exhibit 3–1. Many customers will pay top dollar, or retail, to obtain the product or service they want very close to the time they make the purchase decision. If a supplier can provide the product or service quickly, the supplier's profits can be great. The longer the customer has to wait or chooses to wait to receive the desired product or service, the more likely he or she is to shop around for better prices, and the lower the supplier's potential profit will be.

Let's return to the travel industry as an obvious example of the time elasticity of price or in other words, the sensitivity of profits to customers' willingness to wait. A family planning a vacation next summer will work hard to obtain the best airfare, hotel, and car rental rates. They will negotiate down the profits of each of the travel industry participants, each is likely to be at a loss for the sale on a full-cost basis and on a marginal contribution on a variable cost basis. However, if there is an emergency in that family and they must be in a different city immediately, availability will

Exhibit 3–1 The Time Elasticity of Profitability

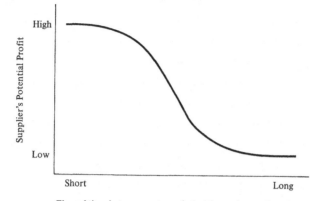

Elapsed time between customer's decision to buy and receipt
of the desired product or service

be more critical than price. There is little or no negotiation, so the
profits of each of the travel industry participants will be high and
will more than cover the full costs of providing the services
needed. Because airline customers vary widely in their price sensitivity, the range in airfares and terms and conditions of purchase is broad. Table 3–1 reflects this breadth.

While airlines typically offer a range of prices to meet varying
customer needs, other industries choose to focus on customers for
whom speed is far more important than price. The Federal Express Corporation created an industry by profitably exploiting the
time elasticity of price. They first promised to deliver a package or
letter by 12 noon the day after it was sent; then, they offered
delivery by 10:30 A.M. the next day. Before Federal Express, the
typical consumer had to wait at least two days or longer for delivery service. Today, customers have many choices for transmitting information and are sometimes willing to pay high prices for
rapid transmission.

Exhibit 3–2 shows the prices for transmitting the information
obtained in a 10-page and a 100-page document from Chicago to

TABLE 3–1 Coach Airfare Prices for DCA–LAX[a] Roundtrip
(December 1988—Indexed)

Full Coach	100	No restrictions
7-Day	72	25% penalty
Discounted	52	Standby

[a] DCA = Washington National Airport; LAX = Los Angeles International Airport.

Exhibit 3–2 Delivery Methods Reveal Value of Time *Chicago to Los Angeles*

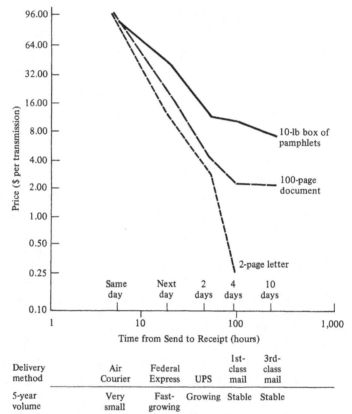

Delivery method	Air Courier	Federal Express	UPS	1st-class mail	3rd-class mail
5-year volume	Very small	Fast-growing	Growing	Stable	Stable

Los Angeles. A consumer willing to wait several days can use the U.S. Postal Service and pay the lowest price per transmission. But someone who needs same-day delivery of documents is going to have to use one of the specialized same-day courier services, such as the National Courier System in Chicago, and will pay $100 to transmit either a 2-page document, a 100-page document, or a 10-pound package. For the 2-page document, the customer is paying 400 times the price of using the U.S. Postal Service. That is, the time elasticity of *price* for document transmittals is about 150 percent—for every halving of the time a customer has to wait for service in this industry, he or she is willing to pay 50 percent more.

Despite the very high premiums consumers must pay for the rapid delivery of information, the demand for fast delivery is growing rapidly, much more rapidly than the growth of the slower services. Today, the fastest growing mode of transmission is the facsimile, known as "fax." A facsimile is a device that enables a user to transmit a page over telephone lines to another facsimile machine that then returns the digital data to its near-original image on a new sheet of paper or computer screen. If customers are really in a hurry and are willing to work with reproductions rather than original documents, they can complete their transmissions in minutes.

Purchases of facsimile machines in the U.S. are increasing at an annual rate of almost 100 percent and for good reason. The price of transmitting a 10-page or a 100-page document by facsimile is substantially less than that of the next fastest modes of transmission and almost as inexpensive as the much slower service provided by the U.S. Postal Service (Exhibit 3–3).

Facsimile machines may eventually be more pervasive than photocopiers. More than 3.4 million of the machines have been installed in Japan, 1.8 million in the U.S. and 1.5 million in Europe. Rock radio stations in California are accepting requests over the "fax," as are "delis" in New York. In Japan, having a car phone in your Mercedes-Benz does not carry much status unless it is a "faxphone."

Service and product companies that offer perishable value products, such as airline seats, hotel rooms, and fresh foods, often exploit the time elasticity of prices in their strategies. Today, the major airlines advertise their ranking for on-time departure—if the ranking is good—to retain their current customers and to attempt to attract away competitors' customers. Domino's Pizza promises that if delivery is not made within 30 minutes, 3 dollars of the price will be refunded to the customer. The Four Seasons hotels, an expensive and successful hotel chain, checks in its best customers before they arrive so that all they need do is pick up their key. In their room they find their favorite amenities including an initialed bath robe!

However, many other companies are not exploiting the phenomenon of the time elasticity of price for at least two reasons: First, their management is not aware of their customers' sensitivities to time and choice. Second, their ability to supply *decreases* as customers' desired waiting time to receive the purchase of choice shortens. Moreover, if they do expedite efforts to increase their responsiveness, their costs may increase while they are cutting price to retain customers, so that their profits may continue to be low.

Companies do not have a single response time for providing the

Exhibit 3–3 Emergence of Fax Easily Understood

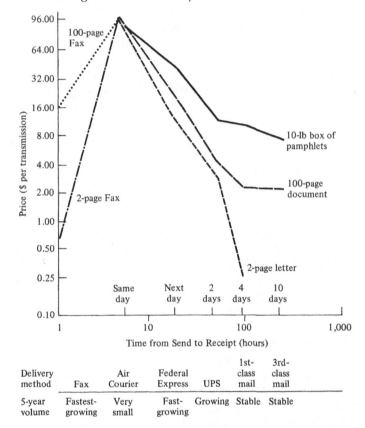

Delivery method	Fax	Air Courier	Federal Express	UPS	1st-class mail	3rd-class mail
5-year volume	Fastest-growing	Very small	Fast-growing	Growing	Stable	Stable

value their customers seek. Some requests for products or services can be processed to completion immediately. These are typically requests for products that are available or very standardized so that they can easily be pushed through the system to the customer. Other requests such as those that entail custom work, seem to require an interminable amount of time. The time required for custom work increases as the product or service is forced through the organization, errors are discovered and reworked, and queues are altered. For example, a truck manufacturer can accept an order for a standard truck, process the order, schedule the manufacture of the order, assemble the truck and deliver it to the customer in about 45 days. In contrast, a moderately customized truck can require 90 days or more.

As Exhibit 3–4 illustrates, the responsiveness of a company to

Exhibit 3–4 Time Elasticity and Supplier Response

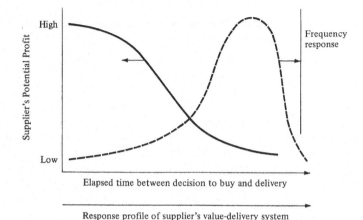

its customers' requests for services or products is actually a distribution of response times, each with its own probability of occur-
rence. The exhibit shows the time elasticity of price compared to
most companies' ability to respond.

If a company's value-delivery system can be altered to exploit
the time elasticity of price, profits can be increased. In terms of
Exhibit 3–4, the company's object would be to move the distribution of response times to the left so that it will more closely match
the shape of the time elasticity of profitability curve.

DETERMINING CUSTOMER'S PRICE SENSITIVITY

Customers can be surprisingly sensitive to time and willing to pay
for responsiveness. For example, small business customers of telephone systems are very sensitive to system down time. Indeed,
along with system expendability, service responsiveness is more
important to users of small business-computer-based systems[*]
than are price, brand name, and technological features, such as
fax mail or data transmission capabilities. The results of a conjoint
investigation[†] revealed the following:

- 85 percent of the users surveyed were willing to pay a 10
  percent price premium for same-day service; 60 percent

---

[*] This is a stylized example based on the experiences of another company in an industry
with many of the characteristics of the small business-computer-based systems industry.
[†] Conjoint or trade-off analysis is a statistical method for assessing the relative customer
response to multiple alternative features of prospective products or service.

would pay 20 percent; 40 percent would pay a 30 percent premium!
- Brand name and distributor reputation were worth only half the premium that same day service was worth
- Technological features were worth only one-fourth the premium that same day service was worth

These are important findings to the manufacturer of small business-computer-based systems. The principal thrust of management has been to invest in technology and to cut price to achieve account penetration. Very little effort was being expended in strengthening the field service responsiveness of the company. But the customers want service more than technology and low prices! As we will see later, investments in field service responsiveness often pay more handsomely than do investments in features or in price cuts.

The best customers of time-based competitors obtain special value from greater choice or from faster service. This value, which can be both economic and subjective, must be identified and used as a lever to capture the sensitive customers' demand. Subjective values can be difficult to price. How much is it worth to a particular group of customers to always be at the front of a line? What is the economic value of flying the Concorde across the Atlantic versus taking a subsonic airliner? Twice the first class fare? The only workable methodology for pricing the subjective value of time is the following:

- Estimate the costs of providing a rapid response or greater choice
- Add the desired profit margin to obtain a price
- If the capacity to add value is oversold, raise the price; if it is undersold, cut the price

When the increased value to a customer is economically measurable, setting prices can be done more rationally. The economic values that are most visible include these:

- The need for the customer to carry less inventory
- The opportunity for the customer to make purchase decisions closer to the time of need, thus decreasing uncertainty and reducing prediction risks
- Reduction of canceled or changed orders by *the customers* of the waiting customers

- Increased special services or customized products to better meet the needs of customers to compete effectively for greater specificity (more observable per lead-in)
- An increase in the velocity of the cash-flow cycle of the customer's businesses

These customer benefits and others positively affect the economics of the customers of time-based competitors, thus creating value. With appropriate strategies, time-based competitors can retain some of the increased value they offer their customers through increased prices and market share.

ECONOMIC VALUE FOR THE CUSTOMER

A ready example of pricing responsiveness to match economic value for the customer is the rapid supply of building hardware products. One hardware manufacturer offers a narrow range of very high quality door and window hardware for high security installations, selling the product at a premium over the lower-quality products of competitors. In the United States, this company derives approximately three-quarters of its demand from institutional buyers—the type of buyers whose sensitivity to security is high enough to justify paying the price premium. The remaining demand is retail consumer based and concentrated in high crime cities, such as Boston and New York.

The manufacturer has a Canadian subsidiary that had been an independent distributor. When the company was independent, management's policy had been to provide same-day service to its customers when the necessary stock was available. They also paid the UPS freight charges if the order was for more than $200 (Canadian). The new owners kept these policies.

About 80 percent of the orders continued to be serviced this rapidly under the new management. Management accomplished this by streamlining the order entry and shipping system and by investing in a great deal of inventory. The Canadian distributor had four times as much inventory as do comparable distributors in the United States. It needed this inventory because delivery lead times from the hardware manufacturer were long and unpredictable.

What is surprising about demand for this company's high quality hardware in Canada, is that consumers account for about 50 percent of the total Canadian sales. On a percent-of-sales basis, penetration of the consumer segment was twice as high in Canada as it was in the United States. On a dollar-of-sales per consumer basis, penetration was actually four times greater. And this is in a country renowned for its comparatively low crime statistics.

THE TURNOVER ADVANTAGE

The explanation lies in the impact of timely response on the economics of this manufacturer's distributors. Retail distributors of this type of product are generally lightly capitalized. What is best for them is to sell a consumer the hardware needed, order the hardware, install it, receive payment and then pay the supplier a month later. The return on capital for such a transaction is infinite. The only problem standing in the way of that return is the customer. Because the customer may not be willing to wait six to eight weeks for the supplier to provide the hardware, the retailer or the supplier is forced to carry large inventories. The pattern in this industry is for the retailers and the suppliers to have approximately equal investments in finished goods inventory. This way, the retailer can meet the customer's need immediately and then reorder from the supplier who then resupplies the retailer on a monthly basis.

The retailer's economics are shown in Table 3–2. The retailer pays $75 for the typical piece of hardware and resells it for $150. This results in a gross margin of $75 or 50 percent of the sales price. This gross margin profit is used to pay the retailer's operating costs including the costs of carrying inventory. The retailer's inventories typically turn three times a year. Therefore gross margin return on inventory investment is 300 percent.

However, if the hardware retailer can receive orders from the supplier a day or so after placing them, the economics are substantially different. As is shown in Table 3–3, the retailer earns a four-times greater margin return on inventory product sourced through the rapid supplier than on product sourced from the slower supplier. When the retailer can be replenished quickly, he can reduce the amount of inventory required to support sales. Because of this turnover differential, retailers in Canada are willing to pay more for product from the faster-response supplier.

TABLE 3–2 Retailer's Economics—Monthly Resupply

Price paid by distributor($)	75
Price paid by consumer($)	150
Gross margin($)	75
Inventory turns	3 ×
Gross margin return on investment	300%

TABLE 3–3 Retailer's Economics—Rapid Resupply

Resupply	Monthly	Rapid
Price paid by distributor($)	75	75
Price paid by consumer($)	150	150
Gross margin($)	75	75
Inventory turns	3 ×	12 ×
Gross margin return on investment(%)	300	1200

Despite the profit potential, few retailers are taking all of the benefits of faster resupply in the form of higher profits, even when they try. In practice, the supplier charges the retailers higher prices—for faster delivery and higher quality than competing products offer—and the retailer is trimming price to induce customers to trade up to the better quality hardware. The typical retailer's economics for the competing product lines is shown in Table 3–4. The supplier charges the retailer a 13 percent price premium for rapid delivery. To move more of the high quality product by inducing the customer to trade up, the retailer then offers a discount of about 7 percent. Still, the retailer's gross margin return on investment from the premium hardware is twice that of the return from competitive products. Indeed, because of faster turnover, the retailer can reduce his price below that of competitive products and still earn a better return.

RECOGNIZING CUSTOMER NEEDS

Clearly, customer loyalty and the prices customers are willing to pay can increase as the supplier becomes more responsive. Customers often purchase more goods and services from their responsive suppliers than they do from their less responsive suppliers even as they are paying higher prices.

TABLE 3–4 Retailer's Economics for Competing Products

Product Supplier	Competitor	High Quality
Frequency of supply	Monthly	Rapid
Price paid by distributor($)	65	85
Price paid by consumer($)	130	140
Gross margin($)	65	55
Inventory turns	3 ×	12 ×
Gross margin return on investment(%)	300	776

The supplier of small business-computer-based systems found that when the company matched the responsiveness of its competitors, its share of business in a city doubled. When the company introduced a new product with the latest features *and* matched competitors' service responsiveness, the company's share increased another 50 percent. This firm found that ensuring competitive service responsiveness was at least as important an investment as investing in technology.

Generally, if a time-based competitor can establish a response three or four times faster than its competitors, it will grow at least three times faster than the market and be at least twice as profitable as the typical industry competitor. Moreover, most time-based competitors have even better performance.

One of the most astoundingly successful time-based competitors today is Citicorp. Citicorp has moved into the lead of the mortgage-lending industry in the United States by exploiting the sensitivities of mortgage applicants to responsiveness and by cleverly pricing its service to attract distribution.

Mortgage originations from Citibank have grown from $756 million in 1983 to $5.5 billion in 1986 and $14.8 billion in 1987—a compounded annual growth rate of over 100 percent per year! By the end of 1987, while accounting for only 3.3 percent of all originations in the United States, Citicorp could claim 37 percent more originations than their largest competitor—H. F. Ahmanson. Seven years ago, Citicorp was not even in the list of the top 100 companies in the mortgage origination business.[4] When asked what was at the core of Citicorp's strategy in mortgage originations, Robert D. Horne, chairman of Citicorp Mortgage, Inc., said, "It's a pretty generic, national market. We thought we could stand out with superior service delivery—high degree of competence and timeliness. We consider the realtor every bit as much a customer as the borrower."[5]

A survey of the borrowers surely did not give a strong indication of the potential for Citicorp's success. In a Gallup Poll consumers appeared to be more interested in a lender's price and reputation than in its service (Table 3–5). Price and reputation were more than 50 percent greater in importance in the surveyed customers' decision processes than the service categories were on average.

However, as Chairman Horne indicated, the borrower is only one of the customers the lender must serve. The real estate agent is also a customer. The borrower very often asks the agent which lending institution in the area has money at the most attractive terms. The larger realtors collect lender data weekly and prepare

TABLE 3–5 Surveyed Consumers Said That the Following
Were "Very Important" Factors in Selecting a Mortgage

Best rates	100[a]
Reputation	91
Knowledgeable staff	87
Quick processing	81
Type of lending institution	65
Single source service	56
Office locations	40

SOURCE: Robert Guenther, "Citicorp Shakes Up the Mortgage Market," *Wall Street Journal,*
November 13, 1988, p. B1.

[a] 100 is most desirable.

price sheets for their buyers. Thus, lenders can think of the point
of sale as not being limited to the lender's desk but as extending
to the desk of the realtor.

Which lending institution is the real estate agent going to recommend? In a survey of what realtors really wanted from lending
institutions conducted by the Mortgage Banking Association,
speed of processing, loan officer responsiveness, and lender reputation were at the top of the respondents' list of needs. "The
broker [real estate agent] is going to help because he wants to
close the deal," says Mary Fruscello, vice president of the finance
division of the National Association of Realtors. The realtor is
looking for a lender with a sense of urgency about closing that is
the same as his or hers.[6] Charles C. Smith, vice president of Real-
Find Mortgage Company of Columbus, Ohio, observes that real
estate agents "prefer the path of least resistance. They'll return to
the funding source they last used successfully. But once an agent
has had a bad experience, he's not likely to forget it."[7]

Buyers do not fare much better than real estate agents. The
purchase of a house is the largest single purchase most consumers
make. Purchases generally begin with the signing of a purchase
and sale agreement that calls for a closing in 60 days. Then the
fun begins, as the buyer wades into the process of arranging mortgage financing for the purchase. The process of applying for and
obtaining approval for mortgage financing has always been
lengthy and, even worse, unpredictable in terms of outcome and
date of decision. Loan application processing times have traditionally taken 45 days, plus or minus two weeks. Many consumers
successfully meet the burden of pulling all their documentation
together and getting it to the mortgage company only to have to
cope with further requests for information at the last minute. As
one realtor said, "Everything the guy [the buyer] owns is on the

line for 45 days of uncertainty. Then, as the closing date nears, some 'flunky' from the mortgage company calls to discuss the need for even more documentation or clarification and everyone has to scramble. It's exhausting."[8]

Realtors were ripe for an alternative approach to funding their buyers when Citicorp created MortgagePower in 1986. The program works this way: real estate agents pay an annual subscription fee of $2,500 to join MortgagePower. The real estate agents then qualify their buyers for Citicorp in return for a half point to a one-and-a-half point discount, "jumbo" financing if needed, and a promise of a loan decision within 15 days. The Realtor can do whatever is allowed by state regualtion with the spread—either, give it all to the buyer or, in some states, keep the spread by charging the buyers a fee for arranging the financing.

As already noted, the results have been astounding. In addition to the sheer volume of loan originations Citicorp has secured, the company "has strung together 3,000 real estate brokers, lawyers, insurance agents and mortgage bankers into a 37-state sales network."[9] The reason for the enormous power of Citicorp's approach is that they have recognized and responded to the buyer. Jack Richardson, a Century 21 real estate agent in Mission Viejo, California explains,

> We control the business, we create the business and we're
> fools not to direct the business. Smart lenders such as
> Citicorp Savings have cut deals with every major power
> broker and have their own reps sitting in our offices. This is
> a controlled business, 52% of our deals go to Citicorp.[10]

Is Citicorp trading risk for speed? Maybe yes, maybe no. It is still too early to tell, but the company does not appear to be doing so. The application process at the originating end does not differ substantially from the traditional process. Much of the speed is the result of doing things smarter. Electronic data transmission enables the real estate agent to get the buyer's data to Citicorp quickly, thus saving perhaps two to six or more days previously consumed by the U.S. Postal Service or by buyers physically taking their applications to their potential lenders. This adds no risk. Increased risks are possible, though, because Citicorp makes "no/low doc" mortgages. Instead of asking for reams of documentation such as employment and deposit verifications and five years of tax returns, the Citicorp application is complete with the applicants last pay stub, most recent bank statement, and a credit check. Further, Citicorp does not ask for mortgage insurance, choosing instead to self-insure its mortgages. Citicorp reduces its risk by only accepting applications with a loan-to-value ratio of 80 percent or less. Most realtors agree that when a buyer defaults on a loan the house is seldom sold at foreclosure for less than 80 percent of its purchase costs except when whole sections of a country become economically depressed. Further, the loan commitment is contingent on an appraisal by a Citicorp-approved appraiser. So while these policies do reduce application time at some increased risks, the actual exposure is not as great as it might seem at first glance.

Moreover, Citicorp probably reduces risks substantially at the back end through its guidelines for choosing realtors. The choice of realtor is a choice of buyer. Jack Blackburn, vice president of Citicorp's Investment Bank, says that Citicorp is planning to repeat its success with MortgagePower in the residential market in the commercial market. Here, too, Citicorp will be very specific about the types of properties and buyers it wants its agents to send to Citicorp. "We are looking for stabilized properties—not quite the cream of the crop, but the best milk right under that and the smaller loans."[11]

Ultimately, the risk that Citicorp is accepting in the residential market and soon in the commercial market is relatively low. Quality customers are directed to Citicorp for quick service, and the higher-risk borrowers are sent to traditional sources of money. As one realtor said, "The buyer who is a professional does not want to be hassled with a long and poorly managed application process. These types of buyers are prime customers for MortgagePower. I *never* take my problem applications to MortgagePower."[12] The buyers who are of questionable quality must go to traditional sources that will require even more time to qualify these buyers, incur more expenses doing so, and accept a greater discount on their packaged securities when going to the secondary market. Thus, Citicorp is not trading risk for speed. The mortgage companies not seeking to use fast response to their customers' needs are making that questionable trade-off.

Buyers' and realtors' sensitivity to time is incredibly strong— stronger than traditional surveys had indicated. Costs of money that are "in the middle of the pack" and responsiveness that is clearly superior to the average is powering Citicorp to the leading position in the loan origination industry of the United States. MortgagePower attractiveness to its customers has led John Reed, Chairman of Citicorp, to claim that Citicorp, "is shooting for 10 percent of the market by 1992,"[13] or, in other words, a tripling of the size of the business in about five years. Such a goal, though, actually requires a slowing of the growth of MortgagePower from over 100 percent per year to about 25 percent per year. The odds are that MortgagePower will grow faster than this. Mortgage-Power accounts for about 20 to 30 percent of member brokers' business. Further, Citicorp announced the 15-minute mortgage approval in February of 1989 and a reduction of the minimum downpayment required from 20 percent to 10 percent—substantially expanding the size of MortgagePower's served customer base.

BECOMING STRATEGICALLY ADVANTAGED

Companies often shorten the response time to their customers by carrying large inventories or by persuading their distributors to do so. While this helps, the potential improvement in profits is usually diluted by the inventory costs and dissipated by the disruptive effects of changing inventories on the company's ability to schedule effectively. Far better gains are possible when companies *attack the consumption of time in their value-delivery system* with the same rigor that they attack costs—thus attacking the causes of the problem rather than the symptoms.

But simply reducing time consumption throughout the value-delivery systems is not adequate. Customers must be segmented and targeted according to their sensitivity to faster response and increased choice. If the customers who are the most sensitive to responsiveness and choice can be locked up, a time-based competitor secures an almost unassailable and profitable advantage.

As discussed in Chapter 1, Ralph Wilson Plastics segments its customers by their sensitivity to time and choice. Ralph Wilson Plastics manufactures, sells, and distributes decorative laminates under the brand name of WilsonArt. Decorative laminates, which were made popular by Formica in the 1950s, are basically a decorative top sheet and layers of kraft paper sheets bonded together with a hard resin. Decorative laminates are popular for kitchen counters, cabinets, furniture, etcetera. Today, Wilson owns the market, and Formica, the household word in laminates during the 1950s, is an "also ran." Ralph Wilson Plastics took the market away from Formica by giving its chosen customers more of what they wanted, closer to the time they wanted it.

The buyers of decorative laminates can be categorized into three segments of about equal volume:

1. The *residential cabinetmaker* who builds cabinets to order. This person usually operates out of a small shop, serves a local area,

and is undercapitalized. When the customer chooses a decorative laminate, the cabinetmaker goes to a distributor to obtain the four-by-eight sheet of laminates needed. The cabinetmaker expects the distributor to stock all the laminates he or she might need and to sell them at a fair price, though not necessarily the lowest price. The cost of the decorative laminate for most jobs is less than 33 percent of the total price of the job with the rest of the costs being for wood, hardware, and labor. Successfully serving this customer means availability first, then good prices.

2. The *commercial specification customer* is an architect or an interior designer. These people chose decorative laminates to enhance the visual appeal of their projects, for example to simulate the look of Italian marble in a hotel bathroom. Choice and merchandising are more important to these designers than is price because the costs of the decorative laminates are a very small portion of the total costs of the projects.

3. The third broad segment is the *OEM direct purchase factory.* This is what the local garage shop cabinetmakers grow up to be. These companies do high-volume production of cabinets, mobile homes, display cases and the like. They buy direct to save money, focusing on limited choice not only to increase their purchase volume from suppliers and to get the best prices but also to keep their own production costs from becoming too great. Successfully serving these companies requires having low costs so that prices can be kept low.

Ralph Wilson Plastics has targeted the residential cabinetmaker and the commercial specification customer. These are the two customer segments most sensitive to time and, in the case of the commercial specification customer, choice. Formica has targeted all segments but dominates the OEM direct purchase segment. To serve the residential cabinetmaker, Ralph Wilson Plastics has an inventory of stock items in regional distribution centers that can be rushed in 24 hours or less to the local distributor. Should the regional distribution center receive an order for a nonstock item that is unavailable, the mill is designed to turn the order around in ten days or less. If the order is for a noncurrent item, the mill will either turn the order in ten or less days, or it will notify the customer otherwise.

Ralph Wilson Plastics' responsiveness to the needs of the distributors who service the residential cabinetmakers enables the distributors to meet the needs of their customers in ten days or less. In contrast, the distributors of Ralph Wilson Plastics' competitors need 25 to 30 days. Because the distributors of WilsonArt can be rapidly replenished, they are more responsive to customers and can also turn their inventory faster. WilsonArt's distributors turn their inventories eight to ten times a year, while their competitors are only able to turn theirs three to five times a year. The consequence is that for the equivalent price and cost of laminate, Ralph Wilson Plastics' distributors are two to three times more profitable than are the competing distributors. Of course, Ralph Wilson Plastics' distributors are not this profitable since they are using their advantage to grow by shaving prices to the end user, increasing the breadth of their inventory offerings and offering better trade terms.

For the commercial specification customer, Ralph Wilson Plastics offers greater variety than do its competitors. To prevent the greater variety from hurting its manufacturing costs, Wilson has streamlined its manufacturing process with carefully considered investments. For example, as the variety of decorative laminates increases, the numbers of resins required increases. Different resins require different cure times. Different cure times complicate the scheduling of the press shops. Ralph Wilson Plastics has worked with its resin supplier to formulate resins that have the same cure times. Wilson pays more for these resins than it would for the traditional resins, but, as a result of the common cure times, the time costs of variety are almost invisible in the firm's manufacturing process.

Ralph Wilson Plastics has secured the dominant share of the residential and commercial specification customers' businesses. It also sells a fair amount to the OEM factory that purchases direct, but Formica has most of this business. Thus, Ralph Wilson Plastics has a more profitable mix of customers where service and variety are more important than price. Formica's sales are skewed toward the price-sensitive OEM customer, so that their profits are substantially less than are Wilson's.

Moreover, the distributors of Ralph Wilson Plastics are very loyal customers. Because they enjoy such high inventory turns, switching to another supplier would mean that their owners would have to reinvest capital to support a new line. Owners of small businesses do not readily do this if they have alternatives. A supplier other than Ralph Wilson Plastics might be able to induce such behavior on the part of a distributor by cutting price. However, given the difference in inventory turns, substantial price cuts—more than any existing competitor can afford—would be required. Thus, not even a price war is an option for displacing Ralph Wilson Plastics at its distributors. The only option for a competitor attempting to displace Wilson would be to exceed the company's responsiveness. This is an option only if Ralph Wilson Plastics allows it to be one.

Customers can be segmented by their sensitivity to responsiveness and choice. The customers who are not very sensitive to time and choice can be very difficult to serve profitably. These customers are willing to wait a long time and to accept a limited choice to get the best price. A supplier's costs must be very low compared to those of its competitors for it to serve these customers profitably. On the other hand, those customers most sensitive to time and choice will often pay more for a product and service to get what they want when they want it and will be more dependent on the supplier who best satisfies these demands. When the customer's desire for choice and responsiveness can be satisfied both subjectively and economically the customer's cost of switching from one supplier to another can be very high.

STRATEGIC IMPLICATIONS OF TIME AND CUSTOMERS

The grand flow of strategic advantage in business is at a turning point. The change originated with companies but is being driven by customers of all types. Competitive advantage based on costs is going through a transition to advantage based on time and choice. Some competitors have evolved their value delivery systems to provide great choice to their customers for reasonable prices without long delivery times. Other competitors cannot do this. Some companies are or have become time-based competitors. Others remain cost-based competitors.

Customers are sorting themselves out into the cost- and time-based segments. The traditional division of customers into specialty and standard segments is blurring because certain suppliers can meet the desires of almost all customers to be special at prices and delivery times approaching the capabilities of those companies able to offer only standard products. Some customers will still be willing to sacrifice choice and speed of delivery for price. Others are not and will not. For example, those customers still willing to wait for the lowest-priced cars are being supplied by companies who buy engine block castings from a company in Korea, ship the casting to Brazil where it is machined and assembled into an engine, ship the vehicle to Spain for assembly, and sell with low prices in West Germany in competition with automobiles assembled in Eastern block countries.

These are the types of customers that companies like Ford,

Toyota, Honda, and most of the other Japanese manufacturers of automobiles are trying to avoid. They are moving factories close to customers, shortening manufacturing and development cycles, and introducing new models quickly with the latest technological and styling features.

Cost-based customers occupy a shrinking segment. Indeed, the boundary between specialty customers who are attracted to time-based suppliers and standard customers who are attracted to cost-based suppliers is an unstable one—thus, the high growth rates of time-based competitors. The boundary existed in the past because the economics of providing fast service and more choice have always been more costly than those of providing a standardized product or service in a reasonable period of time. When faced with paying higher prices for faster service or more choice, most customers made trade-offs—usually buying more of the standard product or service and less of the special product or service. The economics of providing choice and speed are catching up and often surpassing the traditional economics of providing standard products or services. Thus the differences in costs that have been the basis for distinguishing between standard and special products have shrunk. Time-based competitors appeal to customers who have traditionally sought service and choice and to those who have been forced to compromise their natural desires for service and choice because of price. Standard customers are becoming specialty customers.

CHAPTER

4

◇◇◇◇

Time and Innovation

Innovation is key to the long-term vitality of all enterprises. The
Ford Motor Company dramatically improved its fortunes in
the 1980s with four successive new and different products: the
Taurus, the Lincoln, the Thunderbird, and the Probe. Even the
Japanese were caught unprepared by the "aero look" that char-
acterized these new cars. In an explanation for the poor perfor-
mance of Nissan in 1987 and 1988, one Nissan executive admitted,
"Our cars are on the boxy, conservative side."[1]

Innovation means more than just new products; it means new
services and ways of doing business as well. Federal Express has
made the overnight delivery of letters and packages into a multi-
billion dollar service industry. Delta Airlines' basic "hub and
spoke" arrangement of routes became the standard of the airline
industry after deregulation. These are service and business innovations. Innovations along any business dimension can dramatically upset competitive balances by enticing consumers to switch
and by putting competitors on the defensive.

Although the challenge to innovation is in originating new
ideas, time is at the core of an innovation's success. Certainly,
there cannot be innovation without new ideas. But innovation
means change, and change is measured by time. The magnitude
of change is measured as innovations per unit of time. Timely
execution is critical to successful innovation and to high rates of
change. Thus, it is timely execution as much as ideas that is the
challenge to innovation.

Timely execution is very demanding. The process of bringing an innovation to market is complex and harbors many unknowns. An innovation must often successfully defeat a thousand
enemies—inside as well as outside of the enterprise—to become a

reality. Once the innovation is in the market, continued effective execution is critical. The first company to move with the strongest innovation often reaps the greatest reward. But to retain the advantage, the innovator must prevail with the second innovation as well as with the third. Failure to accomplish this means risking all.

The challenge to effective execution is heightened by the discipline imposed by the "outside world." Executives do not innovate in a vacuum. Competitors are also attempting to innovate. Further, customers and suppliers continue to look for new ways to compete and to satisfy themselves: Customers demand new products and services from their suppliers, and suppliers entice their customers to try new products and services. The pace for bringing innovations to market is set as much outside the enterprise as inside.

The pace of innovation is set by and varies by industry as well. Some industries, such as the pharmaceutical industry, have an eight-to-ten year development pace that is largely a function of processes outside the participants' control, including the government and nature itself. At the other extreme is the television news industry. Here product development cycles are measured in hours and are driven by the consumers' desire to know what is news as soon as it is news. Most industries are in the middle where the pace of development is two to four years. In this middle ground, for example, are the automobile industry, the commercial aircraft business, the electric hospital beds industry, and the lodging industry.

Nevertheless, within an industry, competitors can have dramatically different paces of innovation. Ford can conceive and bring new automobiles to market faster than General Motors. Honda is faster than Ford. To maintain or gain position, each has no choice but to speed their pace of innovation.

Companies that allow their pace of innovation to fall significantly behind those of their competitors find themselves being drawn down in a vicious cycle. Because their pace of innovation is comparatively slow, these companies are often surprised by a change in the market or by a competitor's approach. At that point, they have two choices—both distasteful. First, they can proceed as planned and introduce an innovation to meet a need that may no longer exist. Second, they can stop their development effort, redirect it, and then restart it which will cause further delays and risk exposure to additional market and competitive change. For either choice, realized profits will be much less than expected profits. Furthermore, every time the environment changes, the slow company will suffer further.

The only way to break this vicious cycle is to substantially reduce the time required to conceive, develop, and introduce new products and services. Further, matching the pace of competitors is not enough. The new pace must be faster than the competitors', so that they can be caught up and suffer the setbacks of the vicious cycle. To accomplish this, a company must have been innovative, by the standards of the industry, in rethinking and managing its development and introduction processes.

Companies that have significantly reduced their innovation time have distinctly different patterns of innovating and competing than those that have not focused on time. Slower competitors expend their efforts seeking only the major breakthroughs, while fast innovators meter their exposure to risk by incrementally increasing the "newness" of their products or services. For example, General Motors is still trying to bring the Saturn to the market. The Saturn is to be an automobile whose most distinctive features are modular assembly and plastic body panels—features that are more significant to the economics of manufacture than to consumers. However, Honda's Civic CRX, introduced in the early 1980s and steadily improved, already contains almost all of the innovative aspects of the Saturn design that have been made public so far. Further, Honda announced its Acura division at about the same time as Saturn was announced, but Honda will have completed three major model changes by the time Saturn is finally introduced.

Fast innovators can experiment with their customers as they fine-tune innovation. If the executives at a fast innovator are not sure that their new innovation is going to be a hit, they can introduce a version that is their best guess and quickly adjust it to reflect consumers' reactions. One apparel retailer, the Limited, is widely regarded as skilled at spotting consumer trends. When they think they see an item with potential, they order a special lot of the design and test market it for a month. If this lot sells well, they place a subsequent order for 2,000 dozen or more. If the initial order does not sell well, of course there is no subsequent order. Only the winners are pushed; the losers are abandoned. The Limited is able to react so quickly because its apparel acquisition system is four to five times faster than the systems used by most other retailers. The slower systems of the other retailers force them to forecast far into the future and to order all that they hope will sell. In the end, they find that some items would have sold more if they had been available and that others must be marked down to sell at all. In both situations profits are lost.

The toy chain Toys "R" Us also learns rapidly from its customers to alter its behavior. The cash registers of the more than 300 Toys "R" Us outlets in the United States transmit sales data daily to the company's headquarters in Rochelle Park, New Jersey. Every morning management knows what sold and did not sell the previous day. Sales trends can be spotted early and actions taken quickly. New toys can be tried out and can then be reordered in volume if demand looks promising. *Forbes* magazine reported an example of Toys' success with this method: "Toys "R" Us tried out scooters—skateboards with handles—with a trial order of 10,000. They sold out in two days, a trend the computers immediately spotted and jumped on. Last year, Toys sold over a million scooters."[2]

THE PRICE FOR BEING A SLOW INNOVATOR

Fast innovators' patterns of incremental experimentation are enabling them to take the leadership positions in their industries. Honda and Toyota have BMW, Mercedes-Benz, and Volkswagen as well as GM and Chrysler on the defensive. On a wave of rapidly introduced new products, Sun Microsystems, a Silicon Valley company, has motored right on past the former leader in computer work stations, Apollo. These former followers who are time-based innovators are taking leadership positions.

The slower innovators, trapped in the vicious cycle of long development and introduction times, must increasingly depend on the elusive great breakthrough to recapture former glory. Clearly, the price of being a slow innovator is loss of competitive position to the fast innovator. In industry after industry, companies with faster innovation cycles have been able to move from follower positions and to seize leadership in their industries in about ten years.

In 1986, a major U.S. manufacturer of heating and air conditioners began preparing for competition with the Japanese. One of the initial steps was to benchmark the Japanese competitive approaches in their home market. The findings were startling. The Japanese firms' manufacturing costs for the "plain vanilla" air conditioning units were not significantly lower than those of the U.S. manufacturer, despite the very strong dollar. However, the Japanese were not making and selling plain vanilla air conditioners. Rather, they emerged to take this leadership position amid a flurry of new product introductions. The Japanese companies were introducing new products at four times the rate of the U.S. producer. Their product lines were broader, and the average age of their offerings was less than half that of the American firm. Technologically, their air conditioners and heat pumps were the most advanced in the world and are now seven to ten years more advanced than the U.S. products.

The severity of the technological gap that the Japanese have opened can be seen in a comparison between the offerings of Mitsubishi Electric and those of a much larger U.S. manufacturer of air conditioners.

MITSUBISHI

Table 4–1 shows the development history of Mitsubishi's three-horsepower heat pump between 1976 and 1988. The analysis benchmarks the three-horsepower heat pump because it is the mainstream product in the United States. In Japan the mainstream product is the one horsepower heat pump. However, the comparison is still valid, since anything that Mitsubishi did to its

TABLE 4–1 Changes in Features of Melco's[a] Residential Unitary
Melco[a] 3hp Heat Pump

Year	Model Number	Cooling EER[a] (BTU/W.hr)	Added Features or Major Changes in Features
1976	PCH3A	7.4	
1977	PCH3B	7.8	Sheet metal
1979	PCH3C	7.8	Remote control
1980	PCH3D	8.0	IC for control and display
1981	PCH3E	8.0	Microprocessors for 2-wire connection and quick-connect freon lines
1982	PCH3F	8.9	Rotary compressor, louvered fin, inner-fin tube
1983	PCH71AD	9.9	Expanded electronic control of cycle
1984	PCH80AD	7.1–11.5	Inverter
1985	NA[c]	7.1–11.5	Shape memory alloys
1986	NA	8–12.5	Optic sensor control
1987	NA	8–12.5	"Personal Pyramid"
1988	NA	8–14	Learning defrost and setbacks

[a] Melco is Mitsubishi Electric Company.
[b] EER = energy efficient ratio.
[c] NA = not available.

SOURCE: Company product literature.

three-horsepower heat pump has also been done to its smaller units.

From 1975 to 1979, Mitsubishi did not develop this product significantly. They changed the sheet metal work, partly to improve efficiencies but mostly to reduce material costs. At this time, a U.S. company led the industry in the mechanical design of heat pumps. Then, in 1980, Mitsubishi Electric introduced a product that used integrated circuits to control the heat pump cycle. These circuits improved the EER, or the energy efficiency ratio. By 1986, the U.S. company still did not use integrated circuits in any of its residential products.

In 1981, Mitsubishi augmented the integrated circuits with microprocessors. The energy efficiency ratio did not improve—the microprocessors were not intended to improve efficiency. The modification was part of a broader effort to blunt the effects of a decline in Japanese demand for air conditioners by bypassing a level of distribution so that prices to consumers could be lower and the product could be made more widely available. To accomplish the change, the manufacturers had to design a product simple to install and very reliable. Such a product could be sold through white goods outlets and installed and maintained by a local contractor.

Two product innovations facilitated the necessary business innovation. The first was "quick-connect" freon lines. Previously in Japan, and in the U.S. today, freon lines were made from copper tubing which were cut to length, bent, soldered together, purged, and filled with freon. This is a highly skilled operation that must be done by a trained and highly paid installer. The Japanese quick-connect freon lines are precharged flexible hoses that click together, thus requiring almost no skill to install. The second innovation was simplification of the wiring. Previously, and in the U.S. still, a heat pump had a harness of color-coded wires needing proper connections, again by a skilled installer. Because of microprocessors, the color-coded wire connections could be replaced with a two-wire, neutral polarity connection.

As a result of these innovations, the heat pump could be sold through white goods distributors and installed by local contractors—bypassing the traditional and costly heating, ventilating, and air conditioning (HVAC) dealers. The U.S. air conditioning manufacturers, like the U.S. television manufacturers before them, are convinced that their established and well-developed HVAC network is their best line of defense against the Japanese. However, these Japanese products are bypassing the HVAC dealer and the American competitor, much as the

Germans bypassed the Maginot line of the French in World War II.

In 1982, Mitsubishi introduced a new version of its three-horsepower heat pump with a high-efficiency, rotary compressor to replace the very dated reciprocating compressor. The condensing unit of this new product has louvered fins and inner-fin tubes for much better heat transfer in the fan coils and the condensing unit. All the electronics needed changing because the balance of the system changed. However, the EER improved markedly. Then, in 1983, Mitsubishi expanded the electronic control of the cycle by adding sensors and more computing power to the unit, significantly improving EER again.

In 1984, Mitsubishi introduced a version of the product that contained an inverter, which made possible an even higher EER. An inverter converts an alternating current into a direct current and then reconverts the current into a new alternating current with a new wave form. Because the device allows almost infinite control over the speed of an electric motor, the efficiency of an appliance can be improved dramatically. The inverter, however, does require additional electronics for control, thereby requiring another redesign of the unit's electronics.

In 1985, Mitsubishi added shape memory alloys to the unit. Shape memory alloys are used to control the air louvers. When hot air is being blown, the louvers configure themselves to direct the air down so as to establish the appropriate circulation pattern. When cooler air is being blown, the louvers reposition themselves to direct the airstream upward.

In 1986 and 1987, more electronics were employed to improve the products. First, optic sensors were added. Using these sensors, the electronics of the unit can determine if it is day or night and adjust its cycle for greater efficiency. Second, a personal controller was developed. This is a hand-held, remote control device that enables the consumer to set the temperature and humidity for his or her location. The 1988 model uses learning circuitry. With these circuits, the heat pump can learn when to defrost itself. The unit can also follow the patterns of increasing and decreasing temperatures throughout the day, which are unique to each consumer's environment, and mimic these. Finally, in 1989, Mitsubishi added electronic air purifiers to its top-of-the-line products.

This is a lot of change in 13 years. In every year, the product has been improved. Moreover, this pattern is not unique in Japan to Mitsubishi. Matsushita, Toshiba, Sharp, and Hitachi have similar products. They have had to continually upgrade their products to maintain a competitive position in Japan. Note that there have been no great breakthrough inventions. Each change was an application of an existing technology—technologies commonly used in some form or another in other industries. Shepherding new technologies to the marketplace is the hallmark of true innovation. The changes have been accomplished incrementally rather than episodically. But, cumulatively, these changes give Mitsubishi and its Japanese competitors the position of technological leadership among the world's manufacturers of residential air conditioning units.

THE U.S. COMPETITORS

In the mid-1980s, the U.S. company that led the industry was debating whether or not to use integrated circuits in its residential heat pump. The typical four-to-five year new product development and introduction cycle would have meant new product introduction in 1989 or 1990. This "new" product would have been technologically equivalent to the products marketed by the Japanese in 1980. The U.S. company and its U.S. competitors, are at least ten years behind the Japanese in the design of residential air-conditioners. The management of the U.S. leader followed the example of many U.S. companies that have lost technological and innovative leadership. They sourced their advanced air conditioners, heat pumps, and components from their Japanese competitors.

There is much talk today of the "hollowing of America." The phrase refers to the transfer of manufacturing to lower-wage countries while U.S. companies concentrate on the remaining sales and distribution functions. Thus, these companies are hollow shells compared to those that design and manufacture as well as distribute product. But the true "hollowing" of America is the loss of technological and innovative leadership, supposedly America's long-term competitive advantage, because of a stubborn refusal to face up to the core of the problem—long new product development and introduction cycles.

More manufacturing companies will be "hollowed" unless they reduce their new product development and introduction cycles from 36–48 months to 12–18 months or less. This is the basic requirement to be competitive in today's world. In some industries—such as electronics—even faster cycles are required to achieve competitive leadership and to set the pace for technological progress.

THE REQUIREMENTS FOR BEING A FAST
INNOVATOR

The management processes that companies depend on to conceive, develop, and introduce their products and services are more complex than the processes used in their factories or service forces. Yet seldom are these processes, which are critical to making innovations successful, managed with the rigor and discipline to which the factories and service forces are subjected.

According to R. E. Gomory, then senior vice president for science and technology at International Business Machines, and R. W. Schmitt, a retired senior vice president for science and technology at the General Electric Company, in the United States

> The design phase of the cycle of development has traditionally concentrated on the features and performance of the product rather than on the processes by which it is manufactured. We design a product first and then tackle the job of how it is to be made. Yet the eventual cost and quality of the product is inseparable from the way it is made. If a product can be made easily, its costs will be low and, most probably, its quality high.[3] . . .
>
> Much has been said by industry and government leaders about reforming the educational system and strengthening the national scientific base—things that help build a strong foundation. A strong science base supplies a vast storehouse of new ideas, and a good educational system provides engineers and manufacturing workers with knowledge; but strength here cannot make up for inadequacies in the functioning of the development and manufacturing cycle. The United States must learn to succeed, not only in the ladder type of innovation in which a wholly new idea from science creates a wholly new product (the science-dominated process at which we have succeeded in the past), but also at the rapid-cycle, engineer-dominated process of incremental product improvement. Neither process is a substitute for the other; we need both.[4]*

METHODS THAT DON'T WORK

Executives often attempt to accelerate their processes to conceive, develop, and introduce new products and services by turning up

* Excerpts, Vol. 240, Page 1204, 27 May 1988, "Science and Product." Gomory, R. F. Copyright 1988 by the AAAS.

the heat and when that fails by forming "skunk works." Neither does the job over the long term. Turning up the heat is equivalent to plain old expediting. Expediting is a short-term solution—to accelerating a stalled development program—with long-term implications. When the heat is turned up, something else is neglected and inevitably falls behind, so that it, too, must eventually be accelerated, further compounding the ill effects of being late and of expediting.

In contrast to expediting, skunk works do have some dramatic successes. Kelly Johnson, originator of the famous Lockheed Skunk Works, writes in his autobiography,

> For some time I had been pestering (my superiors) to let me set up an experimental department where the designers and shop artisans could work together closely in development of airplanes without the delays and complications of intermediate departments to handle administration, purchasing, and all the other support functions. I wanted a direct relationship between design engineer and mechanic and manufacturing.[5]

The skunk works at Lockheed produced some of the most innovative aircraft of the last 40 years, including XP-80 Shooting Star, the JetStar executive jet, the F-104 Starfighter, the U-2, and the SR-71 Blackbird, as well as many aircraft we probably do not know about. Kelly Johnson further describes the sources of the success of his skunk works:

> The ability to make immediate descisions and put them into rapid effect is basic to our successful operation. Working with a limited number of especially capable and responsible people is another requirement. Reducing reports and other paperwork to a minimum, and including the entire force in the project, stage by stage, for an overall high morale are other basics. With small groups of good people you can work quickly and keep close control over every aspect of the project.

However, skunk works are not contributing on a broad basis to resolving the U.S. innovation crisis described by Gomory and Schmitt. Kelly Johnson explains that the critical shortcoming of the skunk works is that its philosophy is not broadly accepted as a management method:

> I have been trying to convince others to use our principles and practices for years. The basic concept as well as specific

rules have been provided many times. Very seldom has the formula been followed. . . . Most companies, while desiring the benefits, will not pay the price of revised methods and procedures for setting up a Skunk Works-type of operation. They will not delegate the authority to one individual, as Lockheed did in my case from the very first Skunk Works. It requires management confidence and courage.[7]

For at least three reasons, skunk works are not likely to have much effect on the capability of a company to develop and introduce new products rapidly and consistently. First, the very act of isolating a group of development and related support people is an admission that the remaining organization is flawed and not up to the task of innovating. This appears to be expediting on a grand scale. Second, even successful skunk works are renowned for episodic innovation rather than for routine and continuous innovation. Routine and continuous innovation requires the support of the whole organization.

An all-new fighter plane is much more exciting than one whose wing has merely been modified. However, development of an all-new fighter does not generate the organizational structure for retrofitting an installed base of fighters that would also benefit from having a new wing. Such a retrofit program requires the participation of the whole organization if it is to be successful. Third, management needs, as Kelly Johnson admits, "confidence and courage" in the capabilities of the isolated groups. Not many companies have a Kelly Johnson on their payroll, or at least, they probably do not have enough of them.

The fast innovator, unlike the innovator who relies on skunk works, is a company that involves all its departments in the innovation process. When the product development process of a fast innovator is compared to that of a slow innovator, striking differences in approach can be seen. For example, a Western manufacturer of specialty mechanical transmissions learned that its Japanese affiliate could develop and introduce products much faster than it could. The Western company and the Japanese company had been affiliated since the end of the war, and the Western company had played a key role in putting the Japanese company into the business of manufacturing transmissions. By the 1980s, the Japanese company was producing equivalent products at 30 percent lower costs than the Western company. More striking though was the comparative speed of the Japanese company's new product development and introduction cycle. The Western company required 30 to 38 months to complete the development and introduction cycle, while the Japanese affiliate could complete the cycle for equivalent products in 14 to 18 months (Exhibit 4–1). The Japanese company was introducing new products in one-third to one-fourth the time required by its Western affiliate.

More interesting than the fact that the Japanese company was a faster innovator than its Western affiliate was where it achieved its speed advantage. The Japanese did not score a significant advantage in any one step of the development and introduction cycle—design concept, design engineering, design review, detail design, field test, prototype manufacture, or first production. Instead, with the exception of the design review step, the Japanese company outperforms its Western affiliate a half-step every step of the way. Cumulatively, the advantage becomes significant.

The Factory of the Fast Manufacturers

The Japanese transmission manufacturer, like faster innovators everywhere, achieves time advantages by organizing differently than its slower-responding competitors. It uses the organizational techniques that are similar to those employed by flexible manufacturers (Table 4–2); the effects are the same—an increased ability to accommodate variety, an increase in productivity, and a

Exhibit 4–1 Improving Response Time in New Product Development—Mechanical Transmissions

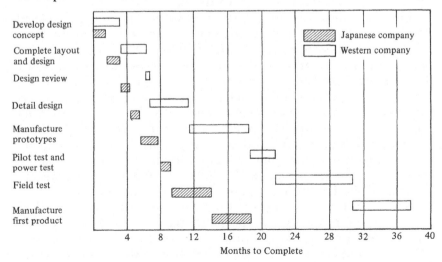

TABLE 4–2 Contrast in Manufacturing Management—An Analogy

Factory Dimension	*Traditional*	*Flexible*
Lot size	Significant improvements planned but fewer projects	Plan for smaller improvements but more of them
Flow pattern	Move through functional centers	Put relevant development resources together
Scheduling	Centrally scheduled	Scheduled within the group
Lead times	100	50
Productivity	100	200
Other	Extensive market research, testing, and deliberation	Market experimentation that, if successful, results in a full roll-out

decrease in response times. In factory management, these techniques revolve around lot size, layout, and scheduling. The ways in which these concepts are used to cut time in manufacturing have a direct impact on new product development cycles.

Lot Size. Traditional factory management in the West attempts to minimize costs by maximizing lot sizes to amortize expensive and time-consuming setups and changeovers and to simplify scheduling. In contrast, flexible manufacturers strive to minimize lot sizes so as to more closely match production with demand and to reduce the importance of long-range forecasting by manufacturing more products more frequently. Indeed, for the most flexible companies, the goal is to achieve lot sizes of one unit. Reduced lot sizes mean that the complete mix of products is more frequently manufactured, allowing faster response to customers.

Layout. The layouts of traditional factories are also different from those of flexible factories. Traditional factories are typically organized by process technology centers. For example, manufacturers of metal goods may organize their factories into shearing, punching, and braking departments; electronic assemblers may separate the stuffing, wave soldering, testing, assembly, and packing departments. Production parts are moved from one process technology center to another. Time is consumed as parts wait to be moved, are moved, and wait to be used in the next step.

Flexible factories are organized by product. The manufacturing functions for a component or a product are brought as close together as possible to minimize the handling and moving of parts.

A part moves from one activity to the next with no, or very short, delays. Rather than being piled and repiled, parts in a product-oriented layout flow quickly through the production process.

Scheduling. The scheduling of traditional factories is compli-cated by the process center organization as well. Traditional fac-tories are often centrally scheduled, requiring sophisticated MRP (material resource planning) and shop floor control systems. These systems direct much of the activity on the floor and feed back to management the results of their decisions. As sophisti-cated as these systems can be, they still consume time. In addition, the floor direction modules may only be exercised monthly or weekly. Between exercises, parts wait.

Flexible factories use more local scheduling. More production control decisions are made on the floor without a loop back to management for approval. Local scheduling does not require more capable employees. Quite the opposite is true. The product-oriented layout of the flexible factory means that when a part is started, many of the movements between manufacturing steps are obvious and do not need intermediate scheduling.

As might be expected, the performance differences between traditional and flexible factories can be significant. Flexible facto-ries are eight to ten times more responsive than are traditional factories. Further, the labor productivity of flexible factories can be 50 to 200 percent higher than that of traditional factories, depending on the complexity of the process.

THE ORGANIZATION OF A FAST INNOVATOR

The structure of an organization that facilitates rapid new prod-uct design and introduction is analogous to the structure of a fast-response factory. Along the dimension of lot size, we have observed that although slow innovators plan significant product improvements for each introduction cycle, they plan less-frequent introductions than do fast innovators. Fast innovators plan for comparatively less improvement with each new product introduc-tion but introduce new products much more frequently. The management approach of the slow innovator is analogous to the factory approach that emphasizes large lot sizes; the fast innova-tor approach is comparable to striving for small lot sizes.

Slow innovators often organize their new product development and introduction programs like traditional factories do—by func-tional centers. There is a group for marketing, for new product design, for product engineering, and for manufacturing. Projects often progress through these functional centers slowly just as products move through process centers on the floor of the traditional factory.

Because of this separation of functions the new product development and introduction programs must be scheduled and actively managed. Product or program managers plot and track the progress of the program through the functional centers. This is analogous to the use of MRP systems in the traditional factories.

In the system structured to introduce new products rapidly, scheduling is done locally, as it is in the flexible factory. Start and milestone dates for the project are set, and the time in between is scheduled by the group members. A company with a rapid new product development cycle functions much like a fast-response factory. It gathers all development resources for one product in one group—including marketing, design, manufacturing, and, in some situations, finance and sales. The participants in these functional areas work together on a full-time basis. Often, they are physically located at the site where the new product is to be manufactured. And as in a factory cell, the development program moves rapidly through each of the functional activities.

The effects of applying these techniques to new product development and introduction are similar to the effects of applying them to the manufacturing process: The amount of time and people required can often be cut in half. Thus, implementing the techniques in both areas allows fast innovators to introduce four times more product than can a traditionally operated company with the same amount of time and people.

As we have said, many of today's fast innovators are Japanese. Japanese manufacturers of residential air conditioning equipment are introducing new products four times faster than are the leading Western manufacturers. Fast Japanese innovators in other industries are Matsushita, Canon, NEC, Toyota, Honda, and Hammamatsu. The capability of introducing new products four times faster than Western competitors is a pretty astounding advantage. It is an advantage seen again and again.

CROSS SECTION OF A SLOW INNOVATOR

In the late 1980s, a major U.S. designer and manufacturer of consumer electronics products was at a turning point. Demanding efforts to revitalize the business had succeeded, and profits were replacing losses. However, compared to its U.S. and Asian competitors, its product line was narrow and aged. Further, because its development and introduction cycle was two to three times slower than its competitors—typically 20 to 30 months—the company was falling ever further behind, and margins were expected to be squeezed.

The company's engineers were regarded as among the best in the industry, yet they were stymied in their efforts to develop and introduce reliable products quickly. Despite high spending on research that generated many new and patentable ideas, the company was consistently slow in introducing new technologies into its products. Even allowing for long development cycles in their planning process, the engineers and managers were continually surprised by missed commitments and constant emergencies.

Contradictory organizational difficulties hampered the company's progress in reducing its development times. The management and staff believed that compared to their competitors, they had too much overhead, but at the same time they all felt overworked and strained to the limit. The temptation to cut back was checked by the fear of error rates even greater than already existed. Management felt little desire to try another improvement program, since the many that had been tried did not seem to budge the company's performance beyond the plateau on which it seemed to be stuck. The company had two alternatives: to succumb to the heat of competition, or to become a fast innovator. Top management's choice was to become a fast innovator.

The first step was to verify that the competitors were indeed faster and to develop hypotheses as to how they obtained their speed. In parallel, the executives began an internal investigation of the workings of their new product and introduction cycle. The external investigation highlighted their own significant shortcomings. Compared to its product offering, the company's best competitors had product lines two to three times broader and products about half the age. Further, the best competitors were introducing products at three to four times the rate of the company.

Discussions with key suppliers and with the competitors themselves revealed that the competitors' design cycles were substantially shorter than were those of the company (Table 4–3). The fastest competitors were designing products in one-third to one-half the time of the company and ramping up production of new designs in one-half to one-eighth the time. The two fastest competitors could design and ramp-up a new product in five to six months compared to the typical twenty-one months required by the company.

Because of these efficiencies, the company's competitors were introducing more new products than it was every year and were more productively using their engineering resources. The best

TABLE 4–3 The World's Fastest New Product Introducers Are Not
Always the Japanese

	Company				
	U.S.—A	U.S.—B	Japan	Hong Kong	Taiwan
Product line breadth	22	33	80	45	110
Average age of product (years)	2.5	2.0	2.0	1.6	1.7
Length of development time (months)	20–30	9.5–11	8.5	5	5

competitors were introducing *twelve and one-half times* as many
products and had more than *ten times* the output per engineer
(Table 4–4).

Naturally, these data were hard to accept. Great care was taken
to ensure comparability. Most of the competitors were coopera-
tive because they were already suppliers of product to the company. In fact, the process of comparing relevant data was
complicated more by the poor form of the company's own data
than of its competitors'. Its own performance records were incomplete, scattered about the organization and used by no one.

Unfortunately, the results of the external investigation were

TABLE 4–4 Competitors Introduce More Models More
Productively[a]

Competitor	New Models/ Year	New Models Designed/ Engineer/Year
Company	100	100
A	100	120
B	120	450
C	120	550
D	140	550
E	200	1,250
F	225	1,500
G	250	1,750
H	300	1,800
I	1,000	2,200
J	525	4,100
K	1,250	3,500

[a] Indexed to the company.

made more believable when augmented by the internal investigation. This investigation highlighted the following:

- Systemic nature of the problem of long design and ramp-up cycles
- Greater influence of management than "nature"—events out of the control of management such as design problems or competitive actions—on the course of development projects
- The possibility of almost any desired change of specification disrupting the development process
- Significance of support functions in delaying development programs
- Impact of the physical separation of the program resources on the ease of execution
- Disruptive influence of reward measurement systems

The internal investigation revealed a very complex process for developing and introducing new products. Typical programs involved 35 to 55 people. These people reported to 8 to 11 functional heads and were scattered over 5 locations and 12 buildings in 3 countries. These people struggled to coordinate over 100 interdependent output points in a constantly changing market.

Of course, many programs had experienced development delays, and a careful review of these delays proved useful (Exhibit 4–2). The study revealed that delays occurred almost everywhere in the process. No one function could be blamed for consistently being the source of problems. Instead, because problems occurred everywhere, the system itself was the root of the problem.

Exhibit 4–2 Delays Can Occur at Virtually Any Point in the Process

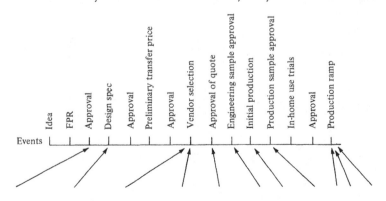

ACTS OF MANAGEMENT

Many believed that problems were to be expected in new product development programs because by definition the task of developing a new product involves doing new things. Therefore, one can never be sure when the unexpected will take its toll. However, a review of the types of difficulties encountered by real programs showed that "acts of management" far outnumbered "acts of nature" (see Exhibit 4–3). "Acts of nature" were limited to the electrical and physical design problems. "Acts of management" included the following:

- Having a development process that is so long as to be exposed to the risks of changes in the market or competitive environment
- Turnover of the program management and design team members
- Continual interruption of the design process
- Being unprepared at the factory for the volume and schedule demands
- Allowing support to block the progress of key sequence activities

The turnover of the program management and design teams at the company resulted in program managers with markedly less

Exhibit 4–3 Mapping the Current System *Initial delays set off a chain reaction*

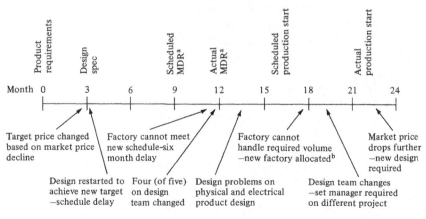

[a]MDR is manufacturing design review.

[b]Slot available due to schedule slip on different product.

experience than those of competitors. At this company, a manager was considered to be unsuccessful if he or she had the same job for more than two years. The program management group as a whole averaged 18 months of experience in their positions. Since development programs often took two years and longer, a program manager seldom saw a program from beginning to end. In contrast, the program managers at the fastest Asian competitors averaged 10 years of experience in their positions. Because their development programs averaged 6 months, these program managers had experience in an average of 20 programs.

An impact of the turnover in program management can be seen in Exhibit 4–2. Note the many approvals required. These were not in place to capture technical risks but to catch error resulting from inexperience. The result was slower programs with more overhead than would have been incurred if the experience levels of participants were greater.

All the development programs reviewed had experienced many disruptions due to the absence of detailed medium- and long-term product planning. Managers with a new idea felt compelled to get their idea into a development program as soon was possible. Thus, the initial specification was never "frozen" and always open for revision. Under these circumstances, programs become vulnerable to a process called "feature creep." Someone with higher authority than the program managers could always change or add a feature. Whenever a cost reduction opportunity became apparent, the design process was interrupted so that the opportunity could be realized.

Further, without detailed product plans, the company's technical managers could not be sure that they were in command of the difficult technologies they were attempting to implement. In the midst of a development program, engineers would often have to halt their work on the program and invent or develop basic technologies.

Another act of management that caused product development delays was the fact that they allowed support functions to "gate" the key sequence activities needing execution. The key sequence activities are shown in Exhibit 4–4. These are critical path activities—those activities that must be executed if a new product is to result. Yet, all along the critical path are points at which several support functions must be brought into the process at once.

Support functions at these points "gate" the key sequence of activities, forcing key activities to wait in queues before the support activity can perform its task. For example, one support func-

Exhibit 4–4 Mapping the Current System—The "Critical" Path
Several functions can delay the process at each stage

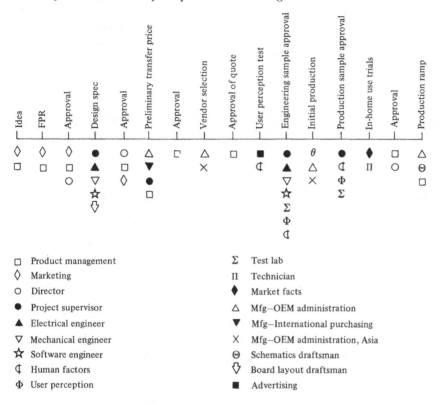

	Product management		Σ	Test lab
◇	Marketing		Π	Technician
○	Director		◆	Market facts
●	Project supervisor		△	Mfg–OEM administration
▲	Electrical engineer		▼	Mfg–International purchasing
▽	Mechanical engineer		X	Mfg–OEM administration, Asia
☆	Software engineer		⊖	Schematics draftsman
₵	Human factors		⇩	Board layout draftsman
Φ	User perception		■	Advertising

tion was UL testing, where the safety of the design was certified. Midway into the development process, support staff would box up a statistically significant sample of prototypes of the new design and ship them to a company lab in another city for testing. At the labs, the lot of prototypes would stay in one of several testing queues until the engineers could perform their tests. A variety of tests, including electrical shock and impact resistance, were performed. After six to eight weeks, the lab sent the results back to the program manager and design engineers—who were usually less than fully employed or were fighting other problems during this interlude.

The internal investigation thus revealed that, while support functions added comparatively little direct monetary costs to the program, they added significant time costs. These time costs, by delaying expensive key sequence resources, added significantly to the overall costs of the program.

In fact, the investigation found that the proportion of time that the product was in a support function and receiving true value was less than 5 percent. Moreover, expediting, without other changes, was of little utility since the unexpedited projects were always slipped to accommodate the expedited projects that later needed to be expedited themselves.

LACK OF COLLOCATION

The lack of collocation of the support functions was a major factor in these delays and costs. Over time as the company had grown, the functions of the company had become geographically spread out. The company had design activities spread through one building and through other buildings in several cities. Styling was done in the East, and human factors analysis was done on the West Coast. Prototypes were constructed in Asia, tested in the U.S., and then handed off to manufacturing facilities both in the United States and in Asian countries. This lack of collocation was an important difference between this company and its fast-innovating competitors (Exhibit 4–5).

Because of the separation of functions, the program resources worked on several projects at once. Progress of these projects was coordinated by computer-based scheduling routines that moved them from formal review to review. Because of the physical separation of activities, program participants had to travel a great deal, even within a building. Program managers themselves, who were highly paid, walked between two and nine miles a day performing their tasks. On average, more than 25 percent of their time was lost walking from one task to another, and another 25 percent was spent in coordinating meetings, leaving less than 50 percent of their time available to add value.

In contrast, fast-innovating competitors concentrate their program resources not only in one city but in one building and on one floor. The manufacturing facility is also in the same building or in one nearby. Communication is almost instantaneous. Problems can be quickly resolved not only because they are more visible to all but also because the feedback loops for information are short.

Moreover the program resources of the fast innovators are organized as a team. Each team is comprised of electrical and mechanical engineers, sales and marketing representatives, technicians and a manager. Each team and its members are focused on one program alone. Between milestone dates, the team guides itself, relying on the visual coordination that is possible by being in

Exhibit 4–5 Competitors Are Faster Because They Have
Fundamentally Different Approaches

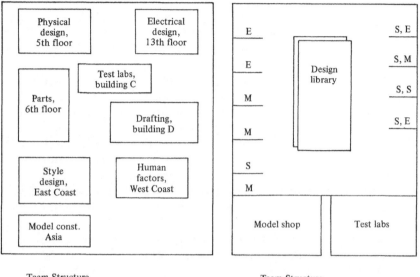

Team Structure

• Multiple projects
• Formal reviews
• Coordinated by computer
• Physically separate locations
• Only includes design

Team Structure

• Focused on one project
• Internal guidance
• Visual coordination
• One large room
• Inlcudes design and manufacturing

one large room. Having the model shop, the test labs, and manufacturing nearby also speeds their work.

CONFLICTING GOALS

The U.S. company was hampered by lack of employee incentive
as well as by operational inefficiencies. The members of the various functions had little incentive to pursue time and cost reductions. Their performance goals and measurements were different
and, as can be expected, so were their behaviors. For example,
members of the marketing group held as their goal the elaborate
specification of the best product using rigorous analysis. Aside
from the ultimate success of the product, no specific performance
measurements existed for them. Their behavior was social with
very little sense of time other than a feeling that it would be nice
to finish the specification so that a new project could be started.
The program manager's goal was to meet the plan, and his per-

formance was measured against the plan. His behavior was very short-term oriented, and he was always under pressure. The design group included engineers of many different specialties. The engineers' goal was to ensure the functionality of their specialty in the design. High-performing engineers were expected to meet or exceed the targets set in the specification. As a group, the engineers tended to be conservative and were primarily oriented to optimizing within their specialty, rather than across the total product design. Thus one engineer could spend a great deal of time altering a design to reduce power consumption in a circuit while, at the same time, another engineer was designing an electromechanical device whose power consumption would overwhelm anything the electrical circuit would consume. The consequences of conservatism and local optimization were long development times and high costs, including the added costs of reworking the individual components and subsystem designs so that the total product performance could be closer to optimum.

The criteria of the support functions were the functional standards of their specialties. Drafting had its drawing practices. The test labs set and held the rest of the organization to its test standards. Consumer documentation had format parameters. Members of each support function measured their performance against their standards and had virtually no incentive to compromise and every incentive to stick to their measurements.

Manufacturing, a function that was so large it behaved as if it were a separate company, used internally generated cost and delivery targets and measured its performance against these targets. Low costs were at the top of the list, and time to market was not even on the list. Consequently, manufacturing seldom felt committed to a delivery date. Indeed, all commitments were off if manufacturing believed that a modification to the design or an alternative manufacturing process or supplier might reduce costs.

In summary, the key functions were characterized by goals that were not internally consistent and measurements that were very narrowly defined and did not reflect the performance of the programs as a whole. Their behaviors reflected the needs of the functional members rather than of the programs.

Across the company many things were not working because fast response and timeliness were too low among the priorities of the organization. One of the major personnel problems was that the functional managers were stronger than the program managers and therefore set the agendas and the pace. In fact, a widely held belief existed that program management was where managers went to get their "tickets punched," or where they ended up because none of the rest of the organization wanted them. Another problem was that inexperienced managers, as a result of turnover, were making mistakes and required considerable direction from their superiors, who themselves had not been in their positions for very long.

Although every attempt was being made to design quality into the product, precious little effort was being expended to design quality into the design process. The same categories of mistakes were being corrected over and over again. The time required to act on an engineering change notice was so long as to virtually eliminate all learning in the organization as well as to dangerously expose the program to additional, related quality problems in the interim.

In summary, the investigations highlighted the critical differences in the structure and management of the organizations of fast and slow innovators. The organizations of fast innovators are structured for ease of coordination and speed of execution. Slow innovators are structured for functional control, cost efficiency, and risk avoidance, a structure that results in a slow and cumbersome development process. With the functional organization come multiple hand-offs that consume time, cause errors to occur and diminish overall accountability. Coordination and control can only be accomplished through elaborate review processes and documentation requirements. Quality seems to decline, not improve. Functions have their firm budgets and manage themselves to their budgets even at the expense of time. To help ensure that budgets are met, performance targets are conservative. Senior management actively participates in program decisions, and, because of their very full schedules, further slow the decision-making processes of the company.

BECOME A FAST INNOVATOR

Before the management of the company just described could become fast innovators, they had to develop and embrace a new philosophy of organizing around time. The new philosophy is embedded in these eleven key principles:

I. Time is the key performance variable to be managed to attain improved cost and quality.
II. Time benchmarks are set by the performance of competitors and, if faster, by what is technologically possible.

III. The support functions necessary to advance the development process are actively managed to be "invisible." Their need is to be anticipated; they are to be invested in and kept up-to-date. They are never to be allowed to slow the development process.

IV. Each program is to be managed and executed by a small, dedicated, decision-empowered, and experienced team. Team members have common goals and are measured and evaluated as part of a team.

V. The development programs are to have four steps, and the company will organize itself around these steps:
1. Planning and preparation
2. Product definition
3. Design development
4. Manufacturing ramp-up
5. Product improvement

VI. The objective of planning and preparation is to avoid having to invent in the middle of the development process—make unknowns be knowns.

VII. After definition, the product specification is frozen. The definition is committed to and not allowed to be changed. The improvement phase is to be used for costs and feature enhancements.

VIII. Functional expertise resides in the development program. Manufacturing and design resources are full-time participants in the definition team. Manufacturing resources are full time participants in the design team.

IX. Team members are collocated.

X. Senior management reviews are few. The role of senior management is to ensure that the program teams have the appropriate resources, incentives and environment to execute their tasks quickly.

XI. New programs are generated continuously, at regular market-driven intervals, and incorporate more incremental advances and fewer "great leaps forward."

Implementing the change to being a fast innovator has been challenging for this firm and has required top level leadership. Much work needed to be done, including the development of comprehensive product plans for the next three, five, and eight years. These plans highlighted the magnitude of the required technology development program. Teams had to be formed and space had to be found where they could be brought together. Specifications had to be "frozen," and key dates made sacrosanct. Critical support functions were "staffed up" to make their time invisible to the key sequence of activities. Road blocks and bottlenecks were met every step of the way and had to be kneaded out like lumps in dough.

Perhaps the most demanding change has been adjusting the compensation and promotion system so that people can remain in their positions long enough to accumulate experience and exercise that experience. This change has been hampered by the basic human emotion of fear of change. Corporate-wide personnel policies have been revised and discussed with almost all employees to be sure that their intent and effects are clear. Multiple tiers within a grade have been created to enable people to stay in a position longer and still enjoy salary increases.

The electronics company's efforts have been successful. Its new product and introduction cycle has been reduced from 20 to 30 months to less than a year. A flurry of new products is bolstering margins, and competitive disadvantage is being reduced. Soon, the target for the development cycle will be six months and less.

THE REWARDS FOR BEING A FAST INNOVATOR

The challenge of becoming a fast innovator is great. Fundamental organizational issues must be addressed, and a wrenching process of change is required. However, the agony of change can be justified simply by the avoidance of the tremendous risks involved in being a slow innovator. Organizations should also want to become fast innovators because the benefits of being fast are so attractive. Companies that become fast innovators benefit from many advantages—both internal and external.

The internal advantages include the following:

- The latest technology can be used closer to the time of introduction
- Faster realization of cost reductions as new products with more cost effective designs displace older, less effective designs
- Dramatically improved quality
- Lower development costs because programs are completed sooner with less money being lost to rework, waiting reviews, etc.

- Improved working environment since employees can more closely identify with their tasks and can enjoy more new product experiences in the same interval of time. When asked how she liked the faster new product development process, this program manager said:

  > With the faster development cycles, no pain lasts too long. In the old approach, problems were resolved so slowly that it was like old bubble gum stuck to your shoe. Eventually you quit trying to clean it off. Today, I don't have to live with a problem so long that I lose the energy I need to fix it.

- A very much improved sense of control of one's destiny since, with faster development times, vicious cycles are broken and customer needs can be forecast over shorter time horizons.

The external benefits include:

- Taking the position as a technological or idea leader
- Higher price realization in the market from having a fresher product or service offering that customers find more desirable
- A position in the minds of customers as an innovator that is reliable and responsive, even while products or services are adjusted through successive introductions to get closer to the optimum definition
- The ability to attract and lock up the most attractive channels of distribution, which like to be able to differentiate themselves by offering the latest innovation
- The ability to set standards by being the first with innovations and to use market response to establish the standard
- Improved market share

Fast innovators have new approaches for marketing new products and services as well. Companies with long product development and introduction cycles depend on extensive market research and testing to define the feature, performance, and cost specifications before marketing a new product or service. Companies with rapid development and introduction cycles can experimentally market new products or services and, if successful, introduce them broadly. The impact on marketing approaches is understandable. If development and introduction lead times are very long, a company must be sure the introduction will be a success because it will have little opportunity to modify the product or service if it misses the mark. When development and introduction lead times are fairly short, a new product can be introduced and then modified quickly as the realities of the market become clearer.

The slower company is under great pressure to make the introduction a success. It is necessarily averse to risk and slow to innovate. The faster company can risk a "near miss," because it can respond to new developments in the market. This company is less averse to risk and can gamble on new technologies or ideas. If successful, the fast innovator often sets the pace of technological innovation in its industry.

SONY'S VICTORY

The executives of the Sony Corporation have employed their capabilities to innovate quickly to build its reputation as an innovator, to set standards in its industries, to take market share and to unbalance its competitors. Sony's most recent success as a fast innovator has been the successful establishment of its compact disc technology as the audio industry standard.

In the early 1970s, three technologies were competing to provide digital audio sound to the consumer. One was the CD (compact disc) technology, initially developed by Sony in 1976 and then jointly improved with Philips beginning in 1979. The other two were Telefunken's MD and Japan Victor's AHD technologies. The participants in the audio industry, manufacturers and recording studios alike, wanted a common standard so as to avoid a replay of the Beta and VHS video cassette debacle. As can be seen in Table 4–5, the decision as to which technology to support was not an obvious one. Each had different merits. An industry conference including more than 30 companies convened in February 1978 to discuss the merits of each technology. Then, in April 1981—almost three years later—they decided not to decide. Both CD and AHD were recognized as viable technologies for the consumer audio market.

The conference participants' inability to decide was incredibly frustrating to Sony and Philips who had been withholding a workable design from the market the whole time. The two chose to make their technology the de facto standard by getting a product to market quickly and driving it to the leadership position with heavy advertising and wide distribution coverage.

Sony introduced its first product in Japan in late 1982. Right up to the introduction, the industry experts and nonexperts debated whether the compact disc would be a luxury item and curiosity, appealing only to the audiophile or a product with mass market

TABLE 4–5 Three Types of Digital Audio Device Methods

	CD	MD	AHD
Audio Specifications			
Number of channels	2 channels	2 channels (4 cl)	2, 3, 4 channels
Frequency characteristics	20–20,000 Hz	20–20,000 Hz	2–20,000 Hz
Dynamic range	90 dB or less	85 dB or higher	90 dB or higher
Distortion coefficient	0.05% or less	0.05% or below	0.05% or less
Wow and flutter	Precision of quartz oscillator	Precision of quartz oscillator	Precision of quartz oscillator
Playing time	One side about 60 min. (max. 75 min.)	One side of 60/50 min. (10 min.)	One side 60 min. (60 min. × 2 is possible)
Codevelopers	Philips, Sony	Telefunken, Teldec	Victor Co. of Japan
Basic System Method	Noncontact optical for audio only	Guided groove plezo electric type for audio use only	Grooveless (static electricity) capacitance common use with video player
Disc Specifications			
External diameter	120 ± 0.3 mm	135 mm (75 mm)	260 mm
Thickness	1.2 ± 0.1 mm (one side) +0.1	1.6 mm (both sides)	1.2 mm (both sides)
Hole diameter	15.0 mm–0.0	8 mm	38.2 mm
Recording port	48–116 mm (program: 50–116 mm)	132–60/72 mm and 72–60 mm	244–98.2 mm
Revolution direction	Anti-clockwise	Clockwise	Clockwise
Track pitch	1.6 ± 0.1 μm	2.4 μm	1.35 μm
Tracking method	Grooveless	Guiding groove	Grooveless
Bit system (not identical but deleted)			
Relative speed	1.2–1.4 m/sec.		
Number of revolutions	About 500–200 rpm	250 rpm Double-sided	900 rpm Double-sided
Double-side specification	Normally single sided, two sides optional (pasted together)		
Disc material	Transparent material	PVC (polyvinylchloride)	Electro conductive PVC
Case size	None	144 × 150 × 8 mm (84 × 120 × 8 mm)	324 × 268 × 7 mm

SOURCE: *Sogo Hoso Shuppan.*

appeal, such as the video cassette recorder/player enjoys. The issue, of course, was not trivial. Potential volume affects many business decisions, including the size of the factory, the intensity of the marketing effort, the choice of channels, and the initial pricing strategies, to name just a few. Sony had to decide whether to conduct extensive market research to try to fathom potential consumer response, thus losing valuable time needed to establish competitive position, or to move into the market as early as possible.

Sony decided against extensive market research and introduced a compact disc player priced at 165,000 yen. Several months later, the company introduced four more products—two priced higher and two lower. The subsequent product introductions tell the story (Exhibit 4–6). The market was very sensitive to price. New products were introduced at lower-price points, and sales swelled. Sony, alone, introduced eight new lower-priced products in less than 24 months. The higher-priced models in the product line were left unchanged for most of the growth period.

The Japanese demand for the players exploded, growing at over 200 percent per year. In less than 3 years, the number of participants grew to more than 30 companies, which introduced

Exhibit 4–6 CDP Product Offerings and Life Expectancy—Sony

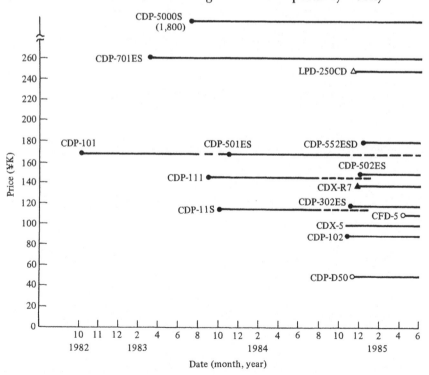

Note: (¥K) indicated prices are in thousands of yen.

more than 100 models while retiring only 30 (see Exhibit 4–7). Many models have been replaced with new models. Today the average life cycle of a compact disc player is nine months. The player is a product appealing to the mass market and is expected by many experts to pass the VCR as the most popular consumer electronics product ever introduced.

As for Sony, for the first time in its corporate history, it has been able to hold onto a leading market share position initially established by its own product innovation. Until the compact disc player, Sony's pattern of competition had been to innovate and then to be beaten into a number two position by Matsushita—the fastest of the fast followers. With its flurry of new product introductions, Sony held onto the leading market position and, in 1988, had 45 percent share of production compared to Matsushita's 12 percent.

Exhibit 4–7 CDP Product Offerings and Price Trends

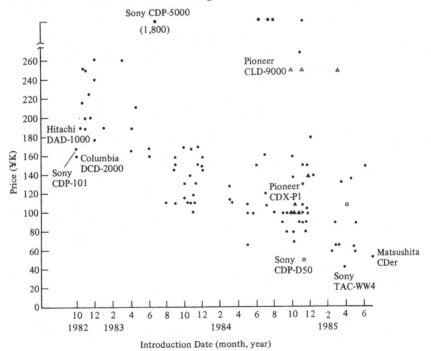

Note: (¥K) indicates prices are in thousands of yen.

FOUR PATTERNS OF COMPETITION

As in Sony's case, other fast innovators are altering the patterns of competition in their industry. Today, four distinct patterns of competition are being exploited either entirely or in part by time-based innovators.

1. *Directly* applying competitive advantage by using the reduced cost of development to provide more value for less cost to the consumer than competitors can provide

2. *Flanking* competitors either by obsoleting their previous product or service design with a new design, or by using innovations to quickly draw customers en masse away from their competitors' offering and toward their own

3. *Breathing new life into mature businesses* by increasing the technological or fashion content of a business so as to reinvigorate consumers' interest in the product or service.

4. *Changing the shape* of a company to escape an industry where the future may be irreversibly bleak

Directly applying reduced development and product or service costs to provide more value for less cost than competitors can is intuitively obvious and is practiced by all time-based innovators. Using time-based innovation to flank competitors' positions, to breathe life into mature businesses, and to change the shape of companies are less obvious and worthy of some examples and explanation.

Flanking Competitors. A company is flanked when a competitor hits it from a direction or with an approach that it is not prepared to defend. A time-based company can flank a competitor in one of two ways: (1) The time-based firm can render obsolete its competitors' previous investment in a product or service design with new designs; or (2) It can use innovation to quickly move customers from the competitors' offering to its own. By successfully flanking its competitors, a time-based innovator can eventually break the will of its competition.

As described in Chapter 2, Yamaha, the motorcycle manufacturer, was not prepared to defend itself against the variety war waged by Honda in the early 1980s. The flurry of new products Honda introduced virtually made obsolete Yamaha's entire product line and field inventories. Not only did Yamaha's sales decline as a result of Honda's strategy, but the company lost money on each sale it did make as it was forced to cut prices to move out-of-fashion motorcycles. Losses mounted, and debt soared. Yamaha's will was clearly broken as evidenced in their public surrender:

"We cannot match Honda's product development strength. . . . I would like to end the Honda-Yamaha War. . . . From now on I want to move cautiously and ensure Yamaha's relative position [as second to Honda]."[8]

However, the Harley-Davidson Corporation may be more successful than was Yamaha in using time-based innovation to flank Honda and escape the clutches of the world's largest motorcycle manufacturer. The mindset at Harley is shifting from "We make Hogs!#@*" to "We make jewelry!" Harley has revamped its procurement and assembly operations and is revamping its marketing and design organization to offer fashion to an expanding customer base. Honda thus far appears unwilling to follow its lead.

Today, in Japan, many companies base their growth on flanking strategies—intending to roll up their competition in a wave of new product introductions. Consider the hot competition to dominate the exploding market for air cleaners for the home. This product first appeared on the market around 1985 and is offered to cleanse the air of dust, pollen, cigarette smoke, and tobacco fumes. Demand was only 450,000 units in 1988, but its growth rate is 15 percent per year and is expected to accelerate. Highlights from the front look like this:

- Matsushita's original entry and main model is the MS–R550 for medium-size rooms. Other models are available for rooms of different size
- In February 1988, Matsushita introduced the Car Air Cleaner that starts automatically when it senses smoke or dust in the car and shuts itself off when the polluted air is removed
- A short while later, Matsushita offered a product line for the office, the Reflora. These are disguised as artificial flowers in pots and have been such a success that home versions are soon to be offered
- Sanyo has countered with the ABC–202SH, a product that can sense the presence of humans, turn itself on, and then shut itself down 30 minutes after the polluting humans have left the room
- Hitachi and Toshiba have been caught flat-footed and are aggressively pushing the low prices of their currently very limited line of cleaners

The second way a company can flank competitors is to use fast innovation to move the customer base en masse away from competitors' offerings. Sun Microsystems has used and is using fast innovation to flank the former leader in engineering work stations, Apollo Computer. Apollo pioneered demand for engineering work stations beginning in 1980 and grew to over $600 million in sales in 1988. Sun started a year-and-a-half later and has grown to over $1 billion in sales. Although for both companies revenues have increased from nothing to a lot in a very short period of time, Sun's growth has far outstripped Apollo's. In the last four years, the annual growth of Sun's revenues has been in excess of 100 percent per year compared to about 35 percent growth at Apollo.

Explanations for the differing growth rates are varied and sometimes acrimonious. In the 1988 annual report for Sun Microsystems, time is prominently featured. "Sun's policies, strategies, and investments all point to a concerted effort to uncover opportunities, increase market visibility, develop new solutions—in short,—to create growth ... *to gain market share* ... Sun's avowed intention [is] doubling the performance of its high-end work stations about every 18 months, on average" (emphasis added). This strategy is in stark contrast to those of most major computer vendors, who typically plan for 3- to 5-year product life cycles. Apollo's annual report has no similar claim.

In an interview with *Fortune* magazine, Bill Joy, one of Sun's founders, said that Sun's strength is in the "recognition of a central truth: Technological change in the computer industry is continually accelerating. No single company can be at the forefront of every important breakthrough, and those that try doing it all themselves—the classical vertical integration route—inevitably fall behind." Sun will use any off-the-shelf technology if the performance of its work stations can be enhanced. Each new Sun system is said to offer twice the performance of its predecessor for nearly the same price.[9]

Apollo has moved slowly from defending its proprietary operating system, the Aegis. The Aegis is a system that management was convinced was technologically superior to the off-the-shelf operating systems available in the early 1980s. Sun has developed systems that use the widely available, though perhaps less capable, Unix operating system.

Pinning its strategy on the use of off-the-shelf technology has opened Sun to criticism from almost everyone but its customers—who like tried and proved technologies and standards more than promises from a startup company. A central criticism of Sun's strategy is that its products can eventually be cloned by lower-cost producers since the technology is generally available to all.

However, if Sun's systems are to be cloned, the follower is going to have to be awfully fast. Bernard Lacroute, Sun's executive vice president observes, "Copying something that moves faster than you can copy it isn't a good business to be in."[10] Manufacturers of mainframe computers are generally expected to upgrade their product lines every four to five years, and personal computer manufacturers usually replace their models every two years or so. Sun introduces new products every 12 months. Says Vice President Carol Bartz, "We wouldn't hesitate to bring out a new product at a price and performance level that absolutely destroyed an existing line. Why should we wait for the competition to do it? That's a brand new concept in this business, and we've proved you can make money doing it."[11]

Apollo gives Sun only limited credit: "[They] do well in certain areas [while continuing] to integrate commodity technology and low price [with] very little added value."[12] In its annual report to the shareholders, the management of Sun views the situation much differently, "Sun . . . may have several generations of new products under development simultaneously, introducing great complexity into the product design and compatibility matrix. At any time, Sun may have dozens of widely varying R&D projects underway, occupying well over a thousand engineers."[13] In absolute terms, Sun is outspending Apollo by about two to one.

Compared to Sun, Apollo is having much difficulty getting its new products to market. The Series 1000 high-end work station has been long in coming, and its full capabilities will not be available to customers until some time after its introduction. Says Vicki Brown, an analyst with IDC, "Apollo is just much more conservative as a company. It takes longer to develop a product and it goes through many more levels of bureaucracy. Innovation may not come as fast there as at Sun."[14]

Meanwhile, Sun may have succeeded in syphoning off Apollo's base. Sun's share of demand has increased from 21 percent in 1985 to 27 percent in 1987 and is expected to reach 33 percent in 1988. Apollo's share has shrunk from 41 percent in 1985 to 21 percent in 1987. Mark Miller, director of marketing for Caeco, a vendor of computer-aided engineering systems observes, "[both] are real good performers for us. Apollo's machines sell into the existing base from the early 80s, but if anybody is interested in replacing complete system families within their design departments, we're finding that they're almost universally buying Sun's at that point. Sun is expected to have a greater installed base than Apollo by the end of 1988."[15]

For whatever reasons, Apollo's after-tax profits were 3.9 percent of sales in fiscal 1987 compared to Sun's 6.8 percent.

Breathing New Life into Mature Businesses. Perhaps the two greatest challenges to executives are breathing new life into mature businesses and changing the "shape" of their corporation. When growth slows, management is faced with three basic choices: live with the fact, diversify, or try to grow what they have through innovation. Few managements do the first, most do the second, and, occasionally, some do the third. Those that choose to breathe new life into their businessses must change the business and, ultimately, this may mean changing the company's shape. They must innovate quickly for maximum effectiveness.

The ability to breathe new life into a business by product innovation is rarely seen in Western companies. When growth slowed for U.S. steel, oil, and automobile companies they diversified into oil, retailing, financial services, and so on. Recently, Ford has found growth through product innovation only to see that growth constrained by its policy of limiting capacity expansion to maximize margin and to minimize the financial risk of an industry downturn.

Japanese companies are more prone to seek growth in their base businesses than Western companies seem to be. In large part this is true because slow-growing Japanese companies have virtually no opportunity to buy someone else's growth business. Growth businesses in Japan are not for sale until they have started to decline. So Japanese management must make do with what it has. One example of such perseverance is Toto, Japan's leading manufacturer of toilet fixtures. Toto is in a classic low-growth business—tied to the boom and bust cycle of the construction industry. But the supplier is growing and has become a darling of the Tokyo stock market thanks to its product innovations.

Toto's first success was the shampoo sink. Japanese women consume shampoo at twice the per capita rate of Western women. To make washing easier for Japanese women, Toto has designed a special sink so the women do not have to get in the bath every time they wish to wash their hair. This sink is a runaway best seller and accounts for over 10 percent of all sinks sold in Japan.

Toto has followed the shampoo sink with the Washlet. This is a toilet equipped with a warm water rinsing nozzle, a dryer, and a heated seat that has been highly appealing to consumers. Now, Toto has entered a joint venture with Omron Tateishi Electronics and Nippon Telegraph and Telephone to design, manufacture, and sell an intelligent toilet. This toilet will measure protein and sugar levels in urine as well as blood pressure, temperature, pulse, and weight. These data are captured and eventually sent via telephone lines for analysis at a medical center. The target price for this product is 300,000 yen (about $2,500).[16]

Another low-growth industry revived by the Japanese is television—especially black & white television. Most of the focus in this industry has been on inducing consumers to buy additional televisions or to buy large screen televisions, but although these have created pockets of growth they have done little to stimulate overall demand. Many observers feel that growth will have to wait for high definition television (HDTV), which promises markedly better picture quality and will ultimately replace all of the older technology television.

But some companies are not waiting for HDTV. These are companies that design and manufacture miniature televisions with screens that are two inches and smaller. They are mostly black and white, but color sets have recently appeared. The sets are offered in male and female versions as well as in designer versions. At this point, overall demand in Japan for miniature televisions is growing at 40 percent per year, with the demand for the color versions exceeding 100 percent per year.

The real payoff to the designers and manufacturers of miniature televisions will come when the sets are installed in the back of airliner seats, in taxis, in trains, in the arms of waiting room chairs, and so on. To achieve this widespread use, costs must come down, and picture quality must be improved. "A new product is released every few months, but it is usually a loss maker. We see this as a big potential market," says Hiroyasu Tatsumi, a manager in Matsushita Electric's television section. "We think if we can increase output, we can make a go of it, but we can't say when it will be profitable. It's hard to say if it will be profitable as long as the only product are pocket TVs."[17]

Western companies can also breath life into mature businesses by innovating. Black & Decker (B&D), the hand tool and small appliance company, is finding growth through the fast introduction of new products. Until recently the only fast-growing company in the hand tool business had been Makita, the dominant Japanese competitor, which had been growing by taking share from Western suppliers. B&D is now growing at twice the industry rate of 9 percent per year.

B&D's growth is the result of an aggressive new product development and introduction program. In the last 18 months, B&D has introduced more than 60 new products, including a low-price, cordless screwdriver, long-life drill bits, a space-saving kitchen appliance that combines a coffee maker, a light, a can opener and a knife sharpener, an automatic shut-off iron, and a new charging system for cordless tools that eliminates the need for different chargers for different devices. About 15 percent of 1988 sales at B&D came from products less than three years old. That is, new products are generating over three-quarters of B&D's growth. Several years ago the percentage was near zero. By the end of this decade, the percentage is expected to be 35 percent.

B&D has been able to generate this onslaught of new products because it has significantly compressed its new product development and introduction times. By reorganizing the design staffs and developing a computer-aided design system that links the company worldwide, B&D has been able to halve its design cycle. For small appliances, the design cycle is down to nine to twelve months.

B&D's share of the worldwide power-tool market is estimated to be 30 percent, up from 25 percent a few years ago. Revenues in the last two years have grown 27 percent and pretax profits have grown 25 percent. Return on equity is up from 6.7 percent in 1986 to 14 percent in 1988.[18]

Changing the Shape of a Company. Fast innovation can enable management to change the shape of its business. Sometimes certain products or services cannot be developed, and an organization has to find something else to do with its resources. The best examples of changing shape not by acquisition or divestiture but through internally focused efforts are Japanese. The list of companies that have made these transitions is long and includes,

- Fujitsu, changing from a machine tool controller manufacturer to a computer company
- Honda, changing from the manufacturer of small motors to motorcycles to cars
- Brother, changing from a sewing machine manufacturer to a manufacturer of typewriters, then of printers, and then of small computers
- Nikon, changing from a manufacturer of high-end cameras sold to consumers to the leading supplier of wafer-steppers, which are sold to semiconductor manufacturers.

Canon, Inc. is an instructive example of the use of innovation to change shape as well as sustain growth in mature markets. Canon used to be just a camera manufacturer. Cameras are a product that seems to mature, then grow and then mature again. In the second-to-the-last maturing cycle, in the mid–1970s, Canon launched itself into the plain paper copier business in search of growth. Canon found growth, but it was not long lived. By the early 1980s, Canon found itself in two slow growth businesses—cameras and copiers—deriving over 80% of its revenues from these two lines of products. The remaining 20% included calculators and portable typewriters.

By 1988, sales of cameras and copiers were less than 60% of total Canon revenues. Virtually all of Canon's growth came from products other than cameras and copiers. These new products include high-speed and resolution facsimile machines and laser computer printers. Both these products have double digit growth rates that if continue to grow as expected will eventually propel Canon out of the camera and copier business for all intents and purpose.

As Fujio Mitari, president of Canon U.S.A. says, "Saturated markets don't matter because innovation can break through to new markets." Canon commits over 10 percent of its almost $8 billion of revenues to research and development—a high ratio by anybody's standard. In the pipeline are the following:

- The Navi, which is a combination personal computer, calculator, Japanese language word processor, a facsimile machine, and a telephone
- A color laser copier that can also shrink, expand, and move images on the page
- A high-speed, G-4 standard facsimile machine for high-volume users of facsimile
- A still video camera for the consumer that can capture 50 images on a 2-inch disc for viewing on television.[19]

TIME-BASED INNOVATION AND OUR NATIONAL WEALTH

Effective methods for research and development are on the minds of executives today—be they Japanese, American, or European. But the sense of urgency varies considerably. A poll of Japanese, U.S., and West German executives conducted by The Wall Street Journal and The Boston Consulting Group found that while 95 percent of the Japanese executives strongly believed that a big push had to be made in R&D over the next five years, only 60 percent of U.S. executives felt as strongly. In terms of the source of technologically based competition, the Japanese were most concerned with competitors in West Germany and in Japan. Both U.S. and West German executives were mostly worried about domestic competitors, despite the fact that Japanese companies are dominating many technology-based industries. Five years ago, U.S. companies secured 64 percent of all the U.S. patents granted the top five companies. Last year, Japanese companies, were granted 63 percent of all the U.S. patents granted the top five companies (Table 4–6). According to the Office of Technology Assessment, "Business-funded R&D in Japan totals 2.1 percent of gross national product, compared to 1.4 percent (in the U.S.)."

Our national wealth is at stake today—whether we are American, European, or Japanese. If our companies cannot hold the edge as time-based innovators, our citizenry will become poorer. Pure invention is not the issue. The issue is the steady and sustained process of developing products and services—and doing so rapidly. From a competitive standpoint, speed is everything. If one company has a four-year development cycle, and its competitor has a two-year cycle, the slower company is done for. The competitor will be in the market two years ahead of the company. When the company's product or service does make it to the market, the faster competitor will already have been able to use its two-year lead to introduce an improved version. Although for virtually all technologies, companies are working from the same storehouse, the faster company will appear to have the newer products or services with the most advanced technologies. The slower company can only compete on price or not compete at all.

TABLE 4–6 Top Five Companies Granted U.S. Patents

Company	Patents Granted
1987	
Canon	847
Hitachi	845
Toshiba	823
General Electric	779
U.S. Philips	687
1982	
General Electric	739
Hitachi	476
RCA	465
IBM	435
Siemens	434

SOURCES: "Missed Opportunities," *Wall Street Journal*, November 14, 1988, special section, pp. 21 and 23; U.S. Congress Office of Technology Assessment, "Commercializing High-Temperature Superconductivity" (Washington, D.C.: U.S. Government Printing Office, June 1988), p. 11, OTA–ITE–338.

An executive of a major, technology-oriented, Western company chose to cut and run. The executive was the product champion for a new electronic imaging technology. The products utilizing this technology would almost certainly at some point face major Japanese competitors. When confronted with the pace of product change in the compact disc business, his reaction was, "At our company, we take four years to develop a product, another year getting it to work after it is in the market, rest two years and then try it again. There is no way we can compete with those companies!" The project was terminated, and the executive was transferred to a marketing job in South America.

The will of this executive and his colleagues was broken before a fight had even taken place. A new technology and a product segment were surrendered to the Japanese. If we are lucky, maybe they will put the factory in the United States. Then we will have to make sure that we have some government program to fund trips by state governors to Japan to try to sell their states as sites for Japanese facilities.

The executive was wrong when he said that companies cannot compete with the Japanese. They can if they do not cede the time-based innovation advantage to them. Compaq Computer and Sun Microsystems are holding well against Japanese competitive pressure because they are as fast or faster than the Japanese in developing new products. Companies that have traditionally been slow to bring new products to market are becoming fast. These companies include Ford, AT&T, and Black & Decker. Their managements are attacking the consumption of time in their new product development and introduction cycle. And they are doing so in a hurry.

5

◇◇◇◇

Time and Money

Time and money are inextricably linked in business. One of the earliest and best-known slogans of commerce is Ben Franklin's, "Time is money!" Well, if time is money why don't more managers talk and act as if it were? Almost none of the Fortune 500 companies' annual reports emphasize the importance of time to the corporation's shareholders. Generally, the only reference to time in these annual reports begins with the phrase, "Compared to last year, this year we . . ." Rarely does the management of a product-oriented company mention its efforts to speed new product development programs, and even service-oriented companies seldom associate time with profitability. Yet money is made by providing the most output per unit of input and that includes the input of time.

As a case in point, consider the earliest industrial time-based competitor—the Ford Motor Company. In his book, *Today and Tomorrow,* Henry Ford describes his philosophy and his company in 1921:

- Ordinarily, money put into raw materials or into finished stocks is thought of as live money. It is money in the business, it is true, but having a stock of raw material or finished goods in excess of requirements is waste—which, like every other waste, turns up in high prices and low wages.
- The time element in manufacturing stretches from the moment the raw material is separated from the earth to the moment when the finished product is delivered to the ultimate consumer. [Time] involves all forms of transportation and has to be considered in every national scheme of service.

[Time] is a method of saving and serving which ranks with the application of power and the division of labor.

- Time waste differs from material waste in that there can be no salvage. The easiest of all wastes, and the hardest to correct, is the waste of time, because wasted time does not litter the floor like wasted material. In our industries, we think of time as human energy. If we buy more material than we need for production, then we are storing human energy—and probably depreciating its value.

- Having on hand twice the material as is needed—is precisely the same as hiring two men to do the job that one man ought to do. Hiring two men to do the job of one is a crime against society.

- Our production cycle is about *eighty hours* (italics added) from the mine to the finished machine in the freight car, or three days and nine hours instead of the fourteen days which we used to think was record breaking.[1]

In this chapter, we will discuss some of the same time-based competitors that have appeared in previous pages of the book, as well as some that have not yet appeared. The focus here, though, will be on determining the specific financial impact of time-based competition for these comparies—in terms of such measures as pretax income, free cash flow, and net asset productivity.

The first group of companies that we will describe were actually the first generation of time-based competitors to follow Henry Ford—that is, the Japanese business leaders of the 1970s. In the mid-1970s, the Japanese economy sank into a severe recession exacerbated by the first shocks of rapidly escalating oil prices. Many Japanese companies lost money, but a few did not, because they streamlined production. Most notable among the success stories was that of Toyota Motor Manufacturing Company.

Over the previous 20 years, Toyota had invested enormous efforts to develop its own proprietary production system. The Toyota production system was the first firm-wide application of flexible manufacturing by a large industrial corporation, and its basic strategy was the following: to limit the volume of scheduled fabrication and assembly jobs to from one-eighth to one-twentieth the traditional lot size. With this production system, Toyota opened up significant productivity advantages over its tradition-bound competitors. Not so surprising, though, the originator of the Toyota production systems credits Henry Ford and his River Rouge facility for the insights driving the development of the system.

The Toyota production system eventually gave Toyota substantial operating advantages over the company's Western competitors. A comparison of plant productivities by a Western automobile manufacturer in the late 1970s found that Toyota had opened up a 200 percent to almost a 500 percent productivity advantage over its Western competitors (Table 5–1)!

In the depths of the 1976 recession, many Japanese companies recognized that Toyota's production system could be their salvation and embarked on crash programs to quickly become much more flexible. Some of the results they were able to achieve, such as doubling net asset productivity over a four-to-five-year period, are shown in Table 5–2.

Yanmar, a leading manufacturer in Japan of agricultural machinery, was one of Toyota's early "disciples." In the recession of 1976, Yanmar knew that they faced losses in their core businesses if they did not initiate an intense turnaround effort to return to profitability. Their efforts were guided by engineers from the Toyota Motor Manufacturing Company—in part because Toyota was making money when many other usually successful Japanese companies were not, and in part because Yanmar was a subcontractor to Toyota.

Toyota lent a team of engineers to Yanmar to help them execute a change in manufacturing strategy, and in about five years, Yanmar and Toyota engineers together developed what came to be called the Yanmar Production System (YPS) modeled after the Toyota Production System (TPS). The results are impressive. The productivity of all employees improved by 90 percent while quality improved by 50 percent. Surprisingly, as Yanmar executed these improvements, they also expanded their product line about 3.7 times. Of course, Yanmar's ability to broaden its product line so rapidly must in part be attributed to the fact that the majority of its new products were added from export markets, including private-label business from well-known companies such as Deere & Company.

TABLE 5–1 Advantages of the Toyota Production System

	Toyota Tsutsumi	*Western A*	*Western B*
Employees	1,800	3,400	5,000
Daily auto production	1,800	1,140	816
Output per employee	1.00	0.34	0.16

TABLE 5–2 Summary of Performance Improvements (5-yr period)

Company	Product	Factory Labor Productivity	Net Asset Productivity	Product Line Variety
Yanmar	Diesel engines	1.9×	2.0×	3.7×
Hitachi	Refrigeration equipment	1.8	1.7	1.3
Komatsu	Construction equipment	1.8	1.7	1.8
Toyo Kogyo	Cars, trucks	2.4	1.5	1.6
Isuzu	Cars, trucks	2.5	1.5	n.a.
Jidosha Kiki	Brakes, etc.	1.9	n.a.	n.a.
Simple average		2.0	1.8	2.1

Beginning in about 1978, a third Japanese manufacturer, Hitachi, began to install its version of Toyota's production system throughout its factories in Japan, calling it the Hitachi MST (minimum-stock-minimum-standard time) system. They too, were able to boast substantial gains—80 percent in labor productivity and 70 percent in net asset productivity.* Another Japanese manufacturer, Komatsu, improved its labor and net asset productivity by these same percentages for construction equipment and diesel engines. Komatsu was second in size only to Caterpillar, and in the mid-1970s, Komatsu's management also made an intensive effort to become more flexible with very successful results.

As successive Japanese companies followed Toyota's lead, each seemed to improve on the one before. Toyo Kogyo, known today as Mazda, was driven to the brink of bankruptcy by the recession in the mid-1970s, as well as by its failed attempt to interest the market in a model with a rotary engine. In a bid for survival, the management of Toyo Kogyo made a crash effort to streamline the company and to cut costs drastically, by installing their version of the Toyota Production System. Labor productivity at the company increased by 140 percent, and net asset productivity increased by 50 percent.

---

* Net assets for Western companies are defined as total assets minus current liabilities. For Japanese companies, net assets are defined as total assets minus current liabilities plus short-term debt. In the case of Japanese companies, most have short-term debt that is treated as long-term debt, i.e., not having to be repaid within a year.

The Japanese truck manufacturer Isuzu did even better than Mazda in terms of productivity increase, with labor productivity up 150 percent, and net asset productivity, up 50 percent. Second in size only to Hino Motors—a sister company of Toyota—Isuzu too had been forced into becoming more flexible. Although management at Isuzu are quick to admit that much more needs to be done, their results to date have been impressive.

Our final Japanese example here is a supplier of Toyota, Jidosha Kiki, which manufactures suspension components. In 1978, the company was achieving work-in-progress turns of about 78 times per year, but Toyota management thought its affiliate could improve performance. As in the case of Yanmar, Toyota assembled a team of engineers and sent them to Jidosha Kiki to improve the company's flexibility. The results were impressive. Work-in-progress turns increased to 312 times a year, and management was committed to doing even better.

TIME COMPRESSION FACTORS INFLUENCING PROFITABILITY

Clearly, a doubling of labor and net asset productivities can be the basis for pretty significant strategic advantages over competitors who are not optimizing their business through time compression. Labor productivity improvement means that costs are lower and therefore prices can be reduced. Higher net asset productivity means that flexible companies can grow faster with less capital than their traditional competitors. As the Japanese firms proved in high-growth businesses, not much time is required for a flexibly advantaged company to outgrow its traditional competitors.

However, more intriguing than either the dramatic improvements in labor or in net asset productivity was the fact that as these companies became more productive they could also *expand* the variety of the product line they offered their customers. They grew by giving their customers more choice. Variety expansion is far more important to growth than is the cutting of price facilitated by improved labor and net asset productivity. After prices are cut, customers have little more to look for, while expanding choice enables companies to become increasingly relevant to their customers. On average, these companies expanded their product lines by 30 to 270 percent. In the case of Komatsu, the company transformed itself in four years from being a short-line producer—a firm whose distributors could not obtain a full product line from the company and that, therefore, had to carry the products of competitors—to a full-line producer with 50 percent more products variety than any of its principal Western competitors.

Time-based competitors know the value of time in their businesses, just as Henry Ford knew it in 1921. They know that as they increase their abilities to give their customers what they want faster than their competitors can, their profitability grows. The managements of these companies know that when their responsiveness exceeds that of their competitors, they can charge consistently higher prices, their costs to provide value and to serve their customers are reduced, the costs of their product development resources decrease, and as a result of these advantages, the productivity of their assets improves.

ABILITY TO CHARGE CONSISTENTLY HIGHER PRICES

As has been discussed in earlier chapters, time-based competitors are attractive to their customers. They are attractive because their responsiveness can substantially impact their customers' economics or because, for whatever subjective reasons, their customers do not want to wait. Therefore, time-based competitors can ask and obtain price premiums over their slower competitors. The price premiums generally range from a low of 10 percent to a high of 100 percent with 20 percent being about average.

COST REDUCTION OPPORTUNITIES

Time-based competitors are more productive. When time consumption in a value-delivery system is reduced by half, or even more, costs decrease substantially. If an order for a semi-custom-made product can be processed in 35 instead of 70 days with the same number of people, then the cost per order processed is reduced by half. In actuality, though, the number of man-hours needed in the faster processing system is probably less than half the number needed in the slower one. In many manufacturing-based businesses, this additional reduction in the costs of goods sold can be expected to be at least 20 to 25 percent as time consumption is reduced by 50 to 75 percent. And for people-intensive businesses such as the processing of insurance claims, the additional cost reduction can be even higher—between 35 and 50 percent.

Cost Effectiveness in New Product Development

Time-based competitors also get more bang for their product development buck. The cost productivities of their development resources can be at least twice as great as those of slow innovators, and their time productivities, more than twice as fast. In fact, as was described in Chapter 4, while the improvements in time productivities (or the previous time required to perform a specific task divided by the improved time required to perform the task) can be two to three times, the improvement in engineering time productivities can range even beyond this.

Seldom do time-based competitors allow all of their cost productivities to flow to their bottom lines, however. Almost always, time-based competitors invest the savings in more new products and services. As a result, they typically introduce new products at rates three to four times greater than those of slower innovators.

In addition to the intrinsic advantage of having a fresher product or service offering for its customers, time-based competitors reap financial benefits through pricing. New products and services seldom require the discounting needed to move dated and late introductions and can often command a price premium until a follower can get its imitation into the market. Further, when a new product or service is a hit in the market, the share of demand earned by the first supplier to the market can be a large multiple of the followers' share.

Sun Microsystems designs, develops, and introduces new computer work stations significantly faster than does its competitor in the business, Apollo Computer. The differences in the financial performances of the two firms is dramatic (Table 5–3). Sun, which actually came into the work station market about two years after Apollo, is now a larger, faster-growing, and more profitable firm because its new product development system is faster and more flexible.

Table 5–3 Sun Dramatically Outperforms Its Rival, Apollo

	Apollo	Sun Microsystems
Approximate 1988 sales (M)[a]	650	1,000
1985 to 1988 growth	2×	9×
Pretax operating profit (%)	4	12

[a] "M" stands for millions of revenue dollars.

MEASURING THE EFFECTIVENESS OF TIME COMPRESSION

The benefits of time-based competition can be measured in various ways. One clear performance indicator is net asset productivity.

NET ASSET PRODUCTIVITY

Time-based competitors are more productive in their use of assets than are their slower competitors. The Japanese companies that were described earlier enjoyed average increases in net asset productivities—or increases in the ratio of sales per net asset investment—of 80 percent. Thus, they need 45 percent less cash to grow at the same pace as before. Also, these companies can grow 80 percent faster than a competitor with the old net asset productivity.

The Sun Microsystems–Apollo battle dramatically illustrates the significance of the net asset productivity advantage (Table 5–4). Sun Microsystems turned its net assets about 16 percent faster than Apollo did. Thus, because Sun earns 28 percent on assets compared to Apollo's 7 percent, Sun, with the same tax and capital structures, can grow about four times faster than Apollo—which Sun did and, is doing.

On April 12, 1989, Hewlett-Packard agreed to purchase Apollo Computer, and in the *Wall Street Journal* article describing the proposed transaction, Vicki Brown, an analyst with International Data Corporation, commented, "This is a cash-hungry business with product life cycles just 12 months long. Apollo needed help in terms of cash."[2] Apollo certainly needs cash, but more importantly it needs faster product development cycles and value delivery systems so that its cash be used more productively.

TABLE 5–4 Sun Dramatically Outperforms Its Rival, Apollo

	Apollo	Sun Microsystems
Approximate 1988 sales (M)	650	1,000
1985 to 1988 growth	2×	9×
Pretax operating profit (%)	4	12
Average net assets (M)	335	475
Net asset turns	1.8×	2.1×
Pretax operating return on net assets (%)	7	28

In another competitive arena, discount department stores, a time-based competitor is steadily gaining on the slower industry leader. Wal-Mart, with sales of $15.9 billion and growing at 37 percent a year, is chasing K Mart the leader with $25.6 billion of sales but growing at only 8 percent per year. If the growth rates do not change Wal-Mart will lead the industry by 1990.

Wal-Mart is a very fast competitor. Its buyers continuously monitor sales data, enabling them to alter the mix of products being ordered and shipped to its stores at least once daily and often more. Wal-Mart also connects its suppliers to this information network. This data link with suppliers is one factor in Wal-Mart's speed and flexibility.

Wal-Mart's financial statements illustrate the economic impact of speed. The firm turns its inventory 50 percent faster than its rival, K Mart does—5.25 times a year compared to 3.46 times. Wal-Mart also turns net assets 50 percent faster than K Mart, despite the fact that Wal-Mart pays its suppliers faster. K Mart's days payable is 44, versus 30 at Wal-Mart. Nevertheless, every dollar Wal-Mart invests in its business generates 50 percent more sales than a dollar invested by K Mart.

Wal-Mart earns preinterest/pretax (EBIT) return on average inventory of 51 percent, compared to K Mart's return of only 28 percent. And Wal-Mart's preinterest/pretax return on net assets is 35 percent as opposed to 19 percent at K Mart.

Table 5–5 presents a graphic summary of the financial differentials between time- and non-time-based competitors.

Clearly, time compression can increase growth and return on investment for firms. The next question becomes, How soon can these benefits be achieved? In the following section, we will examine the results of time-based competition for three companies in the furniture manufacturing industry. The salient points here

TABLE 5–5 Typical Financial Advantages of Time-based Competitors

Income statement
- Prices 10 to 100% higher
- Manufacturing and service costs 10 to 20% lower
- Product and service development cost 30 to 50% less[a]

Balance sheet
- Inventory turns 2 to 4× higher
- Sales-to-plant-and-equipment investment ratios that are about a 50% greater
- Net asset turns about 2× higher

[a] These firms seldom reduce development spending. Most time-based competitors use more new products as a competitive weapon.

are the following: first, although these companies are only beginning the process of compressing time in their value-delivery system, they are already reaping significant benefits; second, with information about available technology and with data from other industries, it is possible to project the longer-term benefits of time compression for these furniture companies if they continue to implement time efficiency improvements.

ESTIMATING POTENTIAL

Planning a strategy for time-based competition and speculating on its financial implications can be a refreshing process, particularly in an industry filled with pedestrian competitors. One such industry, whose participants have certainly tormented all of us at one time or another is the furniture industry. Plagued with long lead times and unreliable delivery schedules, the furniture industry has proved to be a fertile ground for exploiting time-based advantage.

Traditionally, furniture retailers try to protect themselves from stockouts by investing in inventory, but in so doing they take the risk that if an item doesn't sell quickly, its price will have to be reduced until it does sell. Retailers weigh this risk against the risk that the customer will buy elsewhere if their store does not have the desired merchandise. For popularly priced styles that move in great volumes, the retailer may be willing to take the inventory risk because it is a limited one. But for high-priced, stylish, and slower-moving items such as custom-made, high-end furniture, the inventory risks are high. Consequently, retailers rarely carry this inventory and routinely expose their best customers to the industry's legendary delivery practices.

Frustrated furniture retailers know that they could increase their sales and profitabilities if they could get faster and more reliable deliveries from their suppliers. Imagining their response to a fast and reliable supplier, retailers made the following enthusiastic statements:

> The impact on my sales would be phenomenal. The first one to do it will kick the competition in the pants.
>
> —*Colby's in Chicago*

> It would be of enormous value. If a manufacturer makes it easy for me, his share of my business will go up.
>
> —*Macy's in Washington*

The expected growth in furniture demand is with the baby boomers. These are people who are used to getting things pretty fast.

—Colby's in Chicago

The consistent, quick delivery will become like an addiction to the sales force.

—Marshall Field in Chicago

Sales people would love to make their commissions faster.

—Kittles in Chicago

Undoubtedly, a fast and reliable supplier would substantially improve the economics of retailers along a number of dimensions. It would reduce the retailer's inventory risk. Because they could order closer in time to the potential sale, retailers could more accurately predict demand.

A fast supplier would also improve the retailer's cash flow. The retailer usually receives 20 to 50 percent of the purchase price from the consumer as a down payment on an ordered item. The remaining payment is made on delivery. As the interval between order and receipt diminishes, the cash flows faster. In the United States, furniture retailers turn their inventory on average 2.7 times a year and turn their average working capital 5.8 times a year. This means valuable cash is held captive both by inventory itself and by expensive space to store it.

As might be expected, a few, fast suppliers have seized the competitive opportunity in this industry. Stanley, Norwalk, and Thomasville offer "quick ship" programs to their retail customers. Stanley, with sales of about $160 million, is a full-line manufacturer of dining room, bedroom, and occasional furniture whose management recently set a goal of 30-day delivery—an improvement over the traditional 90- to 120-day delivery.

Norwalk, with sales of about $60 million, manufactures upholstered goods at the midrange price points. In addition to offering its retail customers 30-day delivery with 98 percent reliability, Norwalk also provides variety—about 400 frames and 800 fabric choices.

Thomasville, with approximate sales of $315 million, manufactures a full line of case goods. In 1985, Thomasville management instituted a quick-ship program, whereby if the retailer did not have the desired SKU (stock keeping unit), Thomasville would ship it in 30 days or less. Retailers are responding very positively to Thomasville's program, paying a 10 percent premium for the quick delivery.

The performance of these three companies already outstrips the performance of the industry as a whole by far (Table 5–6). On average, the quick shippers are growing about five times faster than the industry, pretax return on sales is three-to-four times greater than the industry average and their pretax return on net assets is two- to-three times greater than the average for the industry as a whole. All in all, these quick shippers are fast growing and profitable in an industry that typically grows slowly and produces anemic profits.

The only measure against which quick shippers do not particularly shine is net asset turns, where their turns are about equal to the average of the industry. This is understandable, though, because at this point in their process of becoming time-based competitors, these companies are reducing delivery times more by carrying inventory than by fundamentally altering the philosophy of their operations. For example, because the fabric industry in the United States has even longer lead times than the furniture industry, Norwalk is forced to hold tremendous inventories of fabric to be able to meet its shipping commitments. Thomasville meets its 30-day commitment to its retailers by stocking 80 percent of its SKUs in finished inventory. At this time, the management of Stanley appears to be the only competitor directly attacking consumption of time in its operation. Although Stan-

TABLE 5–6 Quick Shippers' Performance Outstrips the Industry Average (5-yr period)

Company	Real Sales Growth (%)	Pretax ROS[a] (%)	Pretax RONA[b] (%)	Net Asset Turns
Stanley	9.5	8.2	15.6	1.9×
Norwalk	21.7	7.2	23.4	3.3×
Thomasville	12.3	10.3	21.6	2.1×
Quick ship averages	14.5	8.6	23.5	2.4×
Industry Averages				
Upholstery	2.7	2.4	9.3	2.4×
Case goods	2.7	2.1	8.0	2.4×

[a] ROS = return on sales.
[b] RONA = return on net assets.

ley's inventories are high, its management is changing its operation philosophy. The manufacturer has reduced its cutting rotations—the time between an SKU's last manufacture and its next scheduled round—from 90 days down to 30 to 60 days.

The lesson that these quick shippers provide is that the market and the retailers are very sensitive to supplier responsiveness. The retailer rewards a responsive supplier with higher prices and with growth above the inherent growth of the industry. Furthermore, when the quick shippers alter their operating philosophy from relying on inventories for speed to reducing time consumption throughout their value delivery-systems, they will realize even greater benefits.

A graphic analysis of the furniture value delivery system emphasizes the opportunity for time compression (see Exhibit 5–1). The manufacturing process itself actually consumes very little time relative to shipping and order processing—one week for case goods and one-to-three weeks for upholstered goods. Even these times are overstated because out on the factory floor, the product receives value for less than 5 percent of the time the product is on the floor. The product sits for the remainder of the time waiting to progress to and through the next processing step. Thus, the vast majority of the 13 weeks that the customer is typically forced to wait for merchandise is consumed by the "people factory" side of the system. Order processing and material acquisition consume six weeks; shipping and prep consume another three weeks.

Yet the technologies available to reduce the consumption of time in his value-delivery system are well developed today:

• Facsimile and electronic data transmission to speed the flow of information between parts of the system

Exhibit 5–1 Most of the Time Is Spent Procuring Materials and Scheduling *Same steps also cause variation in delivery times*

Step:	Retailer order processing.	Manufacturing order processing	Manufacturing	Ship to retailer.	Ship to customer	Total
Time (weeks):	1	5	4	1	2	13
Description:	Customer orders. Retailer checks with warehouse, places order with manufacturer	Schedule order. Order materials.	Wait for materials. Production time: • 1-3 weeks upholstered • 1 week case goods	Ship to retailer's warehouse.	Prep item. Schedule customer delivery.	

- Streamlined and, if appropriate, computerized order entry systems to reduce the time required to get an order into the manufacturing system
- Leveled purchasing schedules and electronic information networks to enable suppliers to be more closely linked to the manufacturer
- Quick-ship suppliers, such as Milliken & Company, which are providing fabric to their customers in a week or less
- Flexible factory techniques, including streamlined production flows and quick set-up equipment to reduce the consumption of time in the factory
- Modularized product designs incorporating new materials, such as structural plastics that can be built up more quickly than can the typical unique wood frame
- Direct shipments of "prepped" products to consumers to avoid the time lost to double handling at the retailer

Along with building on the experiences in other industries, one can expect the use of these techniques to reduce value-delivery time from four weeks to one week at the retailer, from nine to three weeks at the factory, and from thirteen weeks overall to four weeks overall.

Obviously, the furniture manufacturer could improve its economics substantially. Tables 5–7 and 5–8 show the typical cost and asset structures for a high-end manufacturer of upholstered goods. As the manufacturer reduces time consumption, these economics should change roughly as follows:

TABLE 5–7 Typical Income Statement Structure of a High-End Upholstery Manufacturer (indexed to revenues)

Revenues		100.00
Cost of goods sold		
Raw materials	33.0	73.55
Direct labor	26.0	
Factory overhead	14.5	
Gross margin		26.5
Below-the-line expenses[a]		20.0
Pretax income		6.5
Taxes[b]		2.2
Net income		4.3

[a] These include general management and sales and marketing costs.
[b] Average industry tax rate.

TABLE 5–8 Typical Balance Sheet Structure of a High-End Upholstery Manufacturer (percent of revenues)

Working capital	12.0
Plant and equipment	33.3
Total net assets	45.3
Sales per net assets	2.2×

- Raw material inventory will likely increase 15 percent to reduce the effect of suppliers who are not or cannot be more flexible
- As the production process is streamlined and the cutting rotations improve, work-in-process inventory will fall by at least 40 percent, direct labor costs by 30 percent, and factory overheads by 20 percent
- Capital expenditures in plant and equipment will increase to the rate that will support a sustained five-year replacement cycle
- As volume doubles, below-the-line expenses will follow an 80 percent scale slope[*]
- The manufacturer can raise prices to the retailer by 10 percent to reflect the value to the retailer of being on a three-week cycle, rather than a nine-week cycle
- Revenues growth will improve from the industry average of about 3 percent to the average of 15 percent experienced by quick shippers

Of course, the supplier will not realize these improvements in economics instantaneously. As will be discussed in following chapters, the process of becoming a time-based competitor can be long and arduous. For the purpose of this example, let us assume that the improvements will occur within three years. Three years is the typical time required to transform most companies, although extremely complex companies may require much more time. Therefore, the company's ability to obtain price premiums will improve steadily over a three-year period. Growth will slowly accelerate from 0 percent per year to 15 percent by year three. After three years, the firm can expect a 30 percent improvement in labor productivity, a 20 percent improvement in overhead productivity, and a 40 percent reduction in work-in-process inventories.

[*] An 80 percent scale slope implies that for every doubling of volume the cost per unit declines to 80 percent of what it was.

TABLE 5–9 Implementing Time-based Competition at a $30 Million Furniture Manufacturer Would Result in a Financially Attractive Company

	Year 0		Year 1		Year 2		Year 3		Year 4		Year 5	
	$M[a]	%	$M	%	$M	%	$M	%	$M	%	$M	%
Revenues	30.00	100.0	35.65	100.0	42.32	100.0	50.19	100.0	57.72	100.0	66.37	100.0
Raw materials	9.90	33.0	11.39	31.9	13.09	30.9	15.06	30.0	17.32	30.0	19.91	30.0
Direct labor	7.80	26.0	8.07	22.6	8.25	19.5	8.30	16.5	9.55	16.5	10.98	16.5
Factory	4.35	14.5	4.67	13.1	4.99	11.8	5.29	10.5	6.09	10.5	7.00	10.5
COGS	22.05	73.5	24.13	67.7	26.33	62.2	28.65	57.1	32.95	57.1	37.89	57.1
Gross margin	7.95	26.5	11.52	32.3	15.99	37.8	21.54	42.9	24.77	42.9	28.48	42.9
Below-the-line expenditures	6.00	20.0	6.85	19.2	7.81	18.4	8.90	17.7	9.90	17.2	11.02	16.6
Pretax income	1.95	6.5	4.68	13.1	8.18	19.3	12.64	25.2	14.86	25.8	17.46	26.3
Taxes	0.66	2.2	1.59	4.5	2.78	6.6	4.30	8.6	5.05	8.8	5.94	8.9
Net income	1.29	4.3	3.09	8.7	5.40	12.8	8.34	16.6	9.81	17.0	11.52	17.4
Depreciation	—		1.00		1.18		1.41		1.62		1.86	
Free cash flow	—		4.09		6.58		10.75		11.43		13.38	
Change in working capital	—		−0.68		−0.80		−0.94		−0.90		−1.06	
Change in work in progress	—		−0.03		−0.01		0.03		−0.17		−0.19	
Change in raw material inventory	—		−0.51		−0.62		−0.76		−0.59		−0.68	
Capital expenditures	—		−2.76		−3.27		−3.87		−3.99		−4.59	
Net cash flow	—		0.10		1.89		4.21		5.78		6.88	
Net present value of cash flow	—											
Working capital	3.6		4.3		5.1		6.0		6.9		8.0	
Plant and equipment	10.0		11.8		13.9		16.3		18.7		21.5	
Total net assets	13.6		16.1		19.0		22.4		25.6		29.4	
Sales/net assets	2.2		2.2		2.2		2.2		2.3		2.3	
Pretax RONA	14.3		29.1		43.1		56.5		58.0		59.4	

[a] $M = million dollars

Table 5–9 shows the impact on this hypothetical furniture company of the transition to time-based competition. While revenues increased 2.2 times, pretax profits increased almost 9 times, and free cash flow, more than 3 times. The pretax return on net assets increased from 14 percent to almost 60 percent. The only profit measure that does not show improvement in this example are net asset turns. However, this measure reflects the fact that the investment in raw material inventories had been stepped up to insulate the furniture manufacturing company from the often unreliable and long lead time of suppliers.

Though these results may seem too good to be true, they are bounded on either side by what real time-based competitors are achieving. Sun Microsystems' performance exceeded the projected performance of this company, and Wal-Mart's results were only slightly less spectacular.

This marked improvement in profitability can be attributed to several sources (Table 5–10). Enhanced price realization and improved effectiveness of the operations each contribute about 35 percent to increased profitability for time-based competitors. Because of growth, below-the-line expenses are reduced as a percent of sales, and this reduction contributes another 15 percent of the improvement. Overall the benefits of being a time-based competitor account for over 85 percent of the improvement of pretax profits. Placing a value on the renovated company is difficult. But ultimately the value is what someone is willing to pay for the transformed company, and the increase in value can be bounded. For example,

- Assuming no debt, the increase in book value is from $13 million to $26 million, or an increase of $13 million
- Valuing free cash flow at 15 percent, the value increases from

TABLE 5–10 Factors Contributing to Increased Profitability *Contribution as Percent of Total Improvement*

Time-based competition—related improvements	
Price premium	39
Reduction in direct labor	34
Reduction of factory overhead	13
Subtotal	86
Growth-related improvement	
Below-the-line savings	14
Total	100

about $13 million to $46 million, or an increase of $33 million

• Valuing pretax earnings at five times, the value increases from about $10 million to $87 million, or an increase of $77 million.

Of course, the use of leverage can amplify these returns as well as the risks.

IMPACT OF TIME-BASED COMPETITION ON EMPLOYEES

The level of financial performance improvements achieved by companies as they become time-based competitors is difficult to match with conventional cost-cutting techniques. For example, the improvements are completely out of the range of what is achievable by the following methods:

• Cutting direct labor wages through renegotiation or going offshore

• Reducing overheads by de-layering management structures and/or narrowing the line of products and services offered

• Automation short of the "peopleless" factory

• Obtaining superior economies of scale

In short, the only way to achieve this degree of performance improvement is by transforming the company into a time-based competitor. Furthermore, the transformation must be made before a competitor makes it—as can be so clearly seen in the Sun/ Apollo battle.

Probably as important, and maybe even more important than the profit improvements, though, are the intangible rewards to the organization of being a time-based competitor. People like to believe they are winners. Growth and improvements in financial indicators clearly tell an organization and the world that they are winners. Imagine how good the employees of Wal-Mart feel when they read the annual reports and press reports about their company. There is little more motivating than to see one's accomplishments in public print.

Competitors of time-based competitors are often frustrated by their inability to match the growth and returns of their rivals. But they may misjudge the competitive factors contributing to their decline. Formica, in decorative laminates, and Overhead Door have both lost their leadership positions to time-based competitors. Both companies have responded by claiming that their industry is one where no one can make good money because of cutthroat competition by companies that do not know how to make money. On two points, they are correct: The competition is cutthroat, and it is their throats that are being cut. However, Formica's competitor, Ralph Wilson Plastics, earns very good returns and so does Atlas Door. This is the classic case of the retreating competitor not understanding the strategy and capability of the advancing competitor.

Managements should look to time-based competition not only as a source of above-average returns but also as an opportunity to make their people feel like winners.

6

◇◇◇◇

Redesigning the Organization for Time

W hat distinguishes a time-based organization from a traditional one? Basically, it has asked two simple questions. What deliverables do my customers want? And, what organization and work process inside my company will most directly provide these deliverables? With the answers to these questions in hand, the time-based firm then shapes it operations and policies.

This approach sounds fairly conventional. Winning customers is the aim of any business, and finding the best way to get them what they want seems like the right place to start in designing an organization. But the fact is that competitors can differ enormously in their level of understanding about how best to deliver value to customers. They don't always consider carefully what customers are really paying for or how a company can most directly and efficiently provide that. A company only becomes time-based by developing superior insight into what customers value and by building the company around it.

One aerospace equipment producer was surprised to learn that it was not delivering value efficiently. This company, whose customers included Boeing, McDonnell Douglas, and other major aircraft builders, was successful. It had good profits, growth, and highly regarded products and people. Its managers thought of its products by name and number and thought of its business as driven by programs. Consequently, the firm supplied whatever resources were requested by program managers. However, during one recent budgeting period, a couple of senior managers were struck by the volume of requests from the company's divisions asking for more of everything—more engineers, more contract officers, more test facilities—all needed to deal with lengthening backlogs and lead times to customers. Business was strong, but in looking at budget requirements, management discovered that every year the requests for more resources had grown across the board.

The company was budgeted by program, and top management always gave the program officers what they needed as long as results were on target. The two senior managers had been approving the budgets routinely, but after this recent evaluation, they decided to pull back to take a closer look at exactly what the company did for its customers and try to explain where all the additional resources were going. They asked the first simple question about deliverables. If you break down all these long, multistage programs into key milestones and outputs, what specifically is the customer paying for? They were able to list four separate things that customers actually want:

1. New program proposals with performance specifications complete
2. Proven design concepts, with drawings, prototypes, and field-test results
3. Physical products, both originals and spares
4. Product improvements, fully documented

The two managers then set out to explore the company's operations to see how these four deliverables were produced. The organization was a matrix of departments and programs, and it took some time to trace the path of each deliverable. Table 6–1, for example, is their summary description of what the company did to produce one typical modest proposal. Obviously, this description raised an important question. If the proposal required only 35 people performing a total of 7 days of value-added work,

TABLE 6–1 Resources to Produce Typical Proposal

Departments involved		12
People involved		35
Cycle-backs among departments		9
Signoffs		25
Functional	18	
Executive	7	
Cross-functional handoffs		16
Geographic transfers		11
Total days inside the company		91
Total value-added work days		7

why did it take 16 cross-functional handoffs, 25 signoffs, 11 transfers between locations, and 91 days to get it out the door? Of course, there were good answers to this question. People working on the proposal needed information from some of the top specialists who had tight schedules. Communication took time because the company was in several locations due to historical acquisitions. Signoffs helped control technical quality and budgets. And it took time for all this to happen because people were busy.

The two managers then asked the second simple question. What organization and work process inside the company contributes most directly to producing the proposal? After thinking about that awhile, they began to see a number of different ways. They realized that the most direct, least time-consuming way to facilitate the process would be to organize people to work directly around the proposal instead of loading the proposal onto the matrix organization, which was not geared to handle it. But this now raised some tough questions. Would such a focused organization be cost effective? Would it provide the technical and business skills needed to make good proposals that would be profitable if the company won them? Also, wouldn't the company have to learn very new ways to assign responsibility, train people, handle information, and control budgets?

With the answers to some of the questions, the two managers started a revolution in this aerospace equipment company. The firm's top management began to see the job of getting out proposals as providing "the best technical value in the shortest time."[1] The way the company approached other deliverables changed, as well. For example, after evaluating the proposal process, management rethought their method for producing proven design concepts. Longstanding engineering practices began to evolve, for example, engineers of different disciplines could work together more closely. Prototypes were attempted earlier to force managers to see all of the design issues at an earlier date. Test personnel were trained and evaluated in new ways. Each facet of processing a proven design concept through the company was affected as the goal of shortening the total cycle took hold. As a result of all this, proposals now took less than half the time they used to; and only one out of six proposals was late, instead of the previous one out of three. Lead times improved every quarter. Most importantly, proposal win rates were up.

According to the plan, the company first determined what it was selling, then streamlined its operations and the practices guiding them to facilitate production. Before, the company management had pushed its programs and products laboriously through a matrix organization. Now it focuses on four specific, physical deliverables and shapes operations and policies around them. This is what a time-based competitor does—it designs and builds delivery systems for what the customer really wants—and the customer wants a variety of products and services provided on short lead time. So the time-based company must be flexible and fast at the same time. Because this is hard to do and because the possibilities are always changing, time-based companies never stop working at it.

The characteristics of a time-based company are best explored under three headings:

- How work is structured
- How information is created and shared
- How performance is measured

HOW WORK IS STRUCTURED

Time-based companies approach work differently than do traditional ones (see Table 6–2). People in time-based—or fast-cycle—companies think of themselves as part of an integrated system, a linked chain of operations and decision-making points that continuously delivers to customers. In such organizations individuals understand how their own activities relate to the rest of the company and to the customer. They know how work is supposed to flow, how time is supposed to be used. Also, work that is not critical to delivery of value in real time is taken off-line so it doesn't slow down delivery.

In small companies, this way of thinking is usually second nature. People find it easy to stay focused on creating value because almost everyone works directly on the product or with a customer.

TABLE 6–2

Traditional Companies	Time-based Companies
Improve function-by-function	Focus on the whole system and its main sequence
Work in departments, batches	Generate a continuous flow of work
De-bottleneck to speed work	Change upstream practice to relieve downstream symptom
Invest to reduce cost	Invest to reduce time

Policies, procedures, practices, or people that interfere with getting the product out the door are easy to see and can be dealt with quickly.

As companies grow, however, the system-like nature of the value-adding process often gets hidden, and so does the customer. Distances increase as functions—such as product engineering, customer credit authorization, shipping—focus on their own needs. Support activities multiply, specialists are hired, reports replace face-to-face conversations. Before long the clear visibility of the product and the essential elements of the delivery process are lost. Instead of operating as a smoothly linked system, the company becomes a tangle of conflicting constituencies whose demands and disagreements frustrate the customer.

Fast-cycle companies—especially the big ones—have to recognize this danger and work hard continually to avoid it by heightening everyone's awareness of how, why, and where time is spent. They must make the main flow of operations from start to finish visible and comprehensible to all employees. Then they must invest in this understanding with thorough training. By highlighting the main interfaces between functions, they reveal how these affect the flow of work. Employees become aware of the way policies and procedures in one part of the company influence work in other parts. And, most important, the companies reinforce the systemic nature of the organization in their operations architecture.

The simplest illustration of the way small time-based operation structures work is probably at a McDonald's restaurant. The entire operation, including the customer, is visible to each employee. The entire work flow can be seen, and people rotate through all the jobs. The principles of the operation are communicated regularly.

Larger operations have to work a little harder for this clarity. For example, the aerospace equipment company had all the engineers involved in its value-adding process trace out by themselves the entire flow of activities and decisions in the development of a proven design concept. Then they sat down as a group with each department head and discussed the kinds of problems that accumulate as work moves through the company. Finally, select members of the group were asked to help redesign a better process.

There are two core concepts in structuring work for time compression. One is organization around the main sequence, and the other is continuous flow of work. Regardless of the size or nature of the organization, these dynamics are what drive faster cycles.

MAIN SEQUENCE

The main sequence comprises those activities that directly add customer value in real time. Everything else a company does is support, which either prepares employees to add direct value or is off-line activity that can be done anytime. Time-based companies identify direct value-adding activities, isolate them from the sea of support work, and organize them into a clear and consistent sequence. This does two valuable things. First, it moves preparation and off-line work out of the way so that all essential direct work in delivering a product or service to customers can be done in line and without wasting real time. Second, it highlights the critical connections between different parts of the company that add direct value, making possible the design policies and procedures that will make this work flow faster and better.

Most companies don't think in terms of a main sequence of value-adding activities. Instead they organize and control around departments, functions, and skill sets. Within these structures, they don't distinguish between core value-adding and support work. This traditional approach makes sense for better controlling the inputs, but it dramatically penalizes the quality and timeliness of the outputs.

Producers of heavy-duty, on-highway trucks in the U.S. are a good example of how companies can differ with respect to time compression, and of how main sequence–oriented competitors changed the whole industry. For decades, GM, Ford, Mack, and the old International Harvester had dominated this custom-order business. It took months from the time a customer went to a dealer and specified desired truck options until the vehicle was delivered. Then, in the 1980s, one competitor—Freightliner—cut weeks off the delivery time and reduced costs and prices by refocusing its operation around the main sequence. Freightliner doubled its market share in the process. Paccar, a competitor oriented to building more highly featured trucks, also started to deliver faster. It, too, gained market share, in part because of a unique product and in part because of speed. Both these companies seemed to not only deliver faster but also to handle product variety better than traditional producers could. In fact, many traditional firms gave price incentives to customers who would *limit* the custom features they ordered.

Let's explore how Freightliner and Paccar were able to produce variety and be fast at the same time. Exhibit 6–1 shows major value-adding activities, from the point of customer's initial inquiry to the

Exhibit 6–1 Time-Compressed Delivery Process of Heavy-Duty, On-Highway Truck

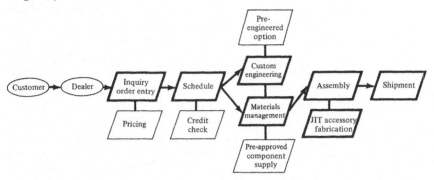

point of shipment. This main sequence is shown in bold-lined boxes and includes all the steps that can be triggered only by a customer order, that is, those activities that have to go on while the customer is waiting. The order is first recorded, then scheduled; then custom engineering begins, at which time skilled workers lay out the particular combination of engine, axles, configuration of cab interior, outside lighting, and so on, that is required. Materials management orders the outside components from suppliers, and in-house fabrication of the truck is done according to schedule. Finally, the vehicle is assembled and shipped.

Freightliner's and Paccar's main sequence takes weeks, not months. This is because the main sequence is free of the support activities, shown in thin-line boxes, that can slow down an order as it moves through the system. The order flows directly through the main sequence. Support activities are done off-line and are organizationally separate. In contrast, most producers, don't separate main and support activities—in fact they often combine them in the same organizational unit, where they compete for the same people's time. With all activities strung out on the same time line, traditional firms can't possibly compete on the basis of time.

For example, at Freightliner, customer credit checks and pricing used to hold up scheduling, because both were done on-line. Orders often waited while the finance department passed judgment. Now, scheduling and credit checks are done simultaneously, and predetermined guidelines establish prices. Only occasionally do the finance people delay an order. Also, easy-to-fabricate parts such as gas tanks are now made from just-in-time inventory, instead of in response to a forecast from held inventories. All support activities are now coordinated off-line and must be ready to service the main in-line activities when the order reaches them. Main and support work are done by separate, but closely located, groups of people.

The most important improvement in support systems has been the pre-engineering of a variety of truck combinations. Before the streamlining effort, truck assemblers had custom-engineered most of the orders after they received them. Some orders demanded more engineering than others, causing a lumpy flow of on-line work. As a result, the custom engineering was hasty, which led to errors and rework. Freightliner decided to invest heavily in pre-engineering hundreds of combinations of components and truck styles so that nearly all orders would be from a pretested menu. They were able to eliminate lumpy and hasty work, and also keep all component paperwork on file. This dramatically collapsed the processing time on the order before it got to the assembly plant.

In recent years, nearly all heavy-duty, on-highway truck producers have followed Freightliner's and Paccar's changes. Navistar, the former International Harvester, for example, has made real strides toward competing with the first movers.

This key rule—don't hold up the main sequence—is true throughout all time-compressed businesses. In product development, for example, don't delay the new product that marketing needs promptly in order to perfect a quirky new technology. Technology refinement is off-line business. Solve the problems before introducing the refinement into the final product development process. In retailing, don't wait for weeks of accumulated sales results and a new forecast before reordering the items that are selling. Reordering should be triggered by what is moving off the shelf this week. In home mortgage lending, don't hold up an individual's mortgage application to make decisions on overall lending targets and limits. These issues should be addressed off-line. Banks should take hours, not weeks, to approve mortgages.

All of this makes sense from the customer's perspective, but companies are often not well equipped to do it. Separating on-line and off-line activities breaks up long-held turf, scrambles established skill bases, confuses existing control systems, and forces the organization to rethink a system that they may believe is working. Because of these complexities, time-based companies are usually in transition, and occasionally in turmoil. Time compression requires substantive change; it cannot be gained simply through elegant thinking and new computer links.

CONTINUOUS FLOW

Once management identifies and isolates the main sequence they can concentrate on orchestrating the flow of work through it. By creating a smoother, more regular flow through the main sequence, they can reduce the cycle time of the entire delivery process, thus raising throughput capacity. Most organizations manage the cycle time of the longest or most visible part of their operations—the "bottlenecks"—but neglect the others that are less obvious or buried, like information batching or engineering data bases that take too long to access. Further, most companies allow decisions to pile up between stages and allow feedback loops that should be closed routinely to be left open. All of this interrupts the flow of useful work and stretches out elapsed time. And as a result, time is wasted and costs increase. Experience across many industries indicates that often less than 5 percent of the total elapsed time spent providing a deliverable is spent adding value.

Coming back to heavy-duty trucks, Freightliner's and Paccar's time compression required more than taking support activities off-line and parallel processing main sequence activity wherever possible. It also required redesign of both main sequence and support activities to create a continuous work flow through the main sequence. This meant smooth, sure-footed interfaces between steps so that workers can pass forward their completed product in bite-sized form with no quality problems. In addition, it meant designing upstream activities to relieve downstream stress.

Most operating problems in a business appear as work proceeds downstream from its upstream origins. New-product development, for instance, usually goes off track in the later stages as waves of engineering changes and manufacturing problems expose an earlier failure to resolve the fit between product, process, and materials. Shipping is another example. Many factories go through a mad scramble at the end of the month to assemble and ship product that should have been flowing out the door continuously. The reason is usually that upstream suppliers were late in shipping or that managers changed the scheduling for parts fabrication too often earlier in the month, so that assembly didn't have what it needed to finish the product.

Heavy-truck producers traditionally have had problems getting continuous work flow through their plants. They would start to assemble a truck but couldn't finish because the hastily custom-engineered pieces did not fit into the space provided or because purchasing took longer than usual to get a new supplier validated, and as a result, components were missing. These were common occurrences. Once the truck production flow is broken up, time not only stops, it is set back. The unit in question has to be moved into a holding pattern and other units brought forward prematurely, raising the possibility that they too will not flow continuously. This lack of continuity shows up as overhead in the form of problem solvers, rework, expediters, and dead-in-the-water inventory. The only way to avoid these problems downstream in the plant is by investment of effort upstream and, in particular, by designing systems more carefully.

For the truck producers, pre-engineering hundreds of combinations and configurations based on what you project the market will want is an investment in continuous workflow downstream. This in turn puts pressure on marketing and product planning upstream to get their story right. Another upstream investment is staff work which at Freightliner showed so few prospective customers failing to qualify for credit that it did not pay to hold up the main sequence to wait for a credit check. Generally, it costs the company as a system more to hold up the main sequence on every order than it does to pull the occasional truck from the schedule. Freightliner's third upstream investment in downstream continuity was the on-line product data base that linked the truck marketing function, custom engineering, order entry, and the dealers. Now every player in the system is up-to-date on changes in the pre-engineered menu and product codes. This way no one will be entering data codes that another function cannot later tap into because it is behind in updating its own data base.

The same upstream and downstream effects take place in all businesses. Management needs to consider carefully the impact of a new system on the downstream effort before they implement the system, however. Some Blue Cross/Blue Shield health insurance operations invested upstream in centralized data systems that promised a uniform data base to all users downstream. Management hailed the investment as high speed and cost-saving before they discovered that the policy codes and subscriber data entering the system were so incompatible that additional translation had to be done on all the data. Downstream users ended up waiting longer to get what they wanted than they had before the investment. An illusory upstream economy of scale thus became an expensive mistake.

Up-front investment in reliable and cleaner working systems as a whole distinguishes time-based competitors from companies that simply go after the bottlenecks. The key to getting functions to work together more efficiently in the company lies first in the overall organizational and system design. Time-based companies think about where to place responsibility for results and how to reposition people to close the distances that big companies can create. They think about balancing the flow of work upstream and downstream, making allowances for how a changing product mix demanded by customers will affect this balance. A time-based company will justify investments that traditional companies cannot because they don't understand the linkages throughout their systems. The pre-engineered truck combinations are a good example. The savings in overhead, inventory, and the customer goodwill more than pay for the continuing effort. And the product gets delivered faster.

HOW INFORMATION IS CREATED AND SHARED

Time-based companies create more information and share it more spontaneously. For the information technologist, information is a fluid asset, a data stream. It is an object itself, something to be carefully measured and handled. But to the manager of a business, information is something less elegant, less separate from the employees who create and carry it. Information is fuzzy and takes many forms—knowing a customer's special needs, learning what works and what doesn't, seeing where the market is heading, knowing where to go to get the answer and so on. Companies that win in business are those that keep generating new information about these concerns and share it with as many employees as possible. Companies that want to compress time have to be especially good at it.

Table 6–3 lists some clear differences between traditional and time-based competitors in how they generate, share, and use information in their everyday working patterns. A company wanting to provide fast response for its customers has to start by

TABLE 6–3

Traditional Companies	Time-based Companies
Specialists create, then share with users	Teams create and use simultaneously
Managers build information bridges across organization	Multifunctional groups build their own source of information to do everyday work
Central processing, slow feedback	Local processing, fast feedback

creating, inside the organization, fast response among employees. Work of any kind, whether it's in the laboratory or on the shipping dock, is essentially the same in terms of information processing. People process and share information for the purpose of taking actions. Then after seeing the results of those actions, they go through the cycle again. For example, the output of new product development work is information—what the product will do and how it will be made. The faster this product gets to market, the sooner feedback from customers will be available to help the designers in their next round. The value of such a fast information cycle is most clear in a money management company. The faster the portfolio manager and account rep can read the market, make a buy/sell decision, and execute the trade, the higher return they will make for their accounts.

These cycles of creating information, then acting and acting again, are the heart of business, and time-based companies push hard so that everything they do—staffing the organization, choosing technologies, making decisions—will be geared to collapsing these cycles.

THE OODA LOOP

The model to keep in mind here is that of a fighter pilot competing against another pilot in a dog fight. Given fighter planes of roughly the same capability, why do some pilots consistently win? The U.S. Air Force has studied what winning pilots do differently. The answer they found is that winning pilots compress the whole cycle of what happens in a dog fight and keep repeating it faster than their adversary until he is in a weak position and can be shot down. The cycle is called the OODA Loop—for *observation, orientation, decision,* and *action* (see Exhibit 6–2). The best pilots quickly size up the situation in any new encounter—observation—and read the opportunities and hazards that it presents—orientation. The pilot then decides what move he wants to make against his enemy—decision—and proceeds to execute the maneuver—action. Each dog fight is a highly compressed series of OODA Loops, with each pilot playing off the other's moves and trying to get into an advantaged position. The movie *Top Gun* portrayed all this very dramatically. The pilot tries to take control of the dog fight by sizing up and acting before the competitor, preempting the advantaged moves. The object is to get the enemy pilot reacting to you and eventually get him into a confused reactive spiral and a vulnerable position.

A time-compressed company does the same thing as a pilot in

Exhibit 6–2 The OODA Loop

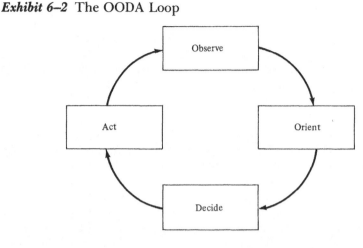

an OODA Loop. In business, the contests last longer and are played by organizations. But it's still the competitor who acts on information faster who is in the best position to win. Batterymarch, a portfolio investment management company in Boston, is a good example. The firm performs the portfolio management loop—deciding what to buy and sell and the price, executing the transaction, and crediting the customer account—up to three times faster than traditional firms and with one-fifth of the employees.

Most of the investment industry's portfolio managers follow the same path in processing portfolios. They generate paper indicating their desire to buy or sell and the price range within which they will do so, then pass it to the trading room, where traders telephone brokers to bid or offer. Once a deal is struck verbally and the transaction clears, the firm's accounting department is notified and the investor's account is changed. This can take up to 72 hours. Batterymarch does it in 24 hours, including overnight clearing. There is no paper or telephone or separate accounting department. All of this work is done on line through interactive software that links portfolio managers to brokers; the actual buying and selling decisions are automated. Batterymarch has also invested in models that calculate "what ifs" for the customer's account, comparing different trades. This accelerates the buy and sell, and pricing decisions. All this allows the customer to get into rising stocks and out of falling ones faster than before.

Surprise is also a part of the OODA Loop dynamic. It's companies that can pull all parts of the organization together quickly and act on an idea before others can who win. A pilot can surprise his opponent in a dog fight by executing a series of moves faster than the opponent thought possible. Fast-moving businesses are like dog fights. Apple's MacIntosh and Ford's Taurus and Sable had tremendous impact because their competitors did not think Apple and Ford could move new concepts through an organization to fruition that fast.

Companies that work like OODA Loops describe themselves differently. One senior manager who left a more traditionally managed organization to join a time-based management company says he could tell the difference as soon as he asked his new colleagues to describe the company over lunch. His former company used conventional organization charts with hierarchies of boxes and levels to describe itself to new employees or outsiders. The company listed its departments and buildings—its structures. In contrast, his new colleagues talked mainly about how the company works and who works with whom. They sketched out on a piece of paper a picture of the company that was basically a set of loops. The loops were small boxes representing functions connected by arrows. Some loops overlapped. Process and interaction were the main points he remembers from the discussion. And, as it turned out, the new company is faster than the old one.

It is one thing to develop a fast-cycle organization when your people know exactly what the product will be because customers keep asking the same thing from you. Henry Ford got a huge organization at River Rouge to take in iron ore and coal at one end and to turn out sheet metal on a fully assembled automobile at the other end in less than four days but limited his customers to one product. The real difficulty in designing fast-cycle organizations comes when complexity grows—different customers start to want different things, and the product line needs changing continuously. Now, fixed information channels and established lock-step routines don't work so well. Some functions in the company, especially those located farthest from the customer—such as a design engineer or a data systems specialist—do not see what is happening. They stop creating useful information, and they no longer understand the signals they are getting from others.

A company that works well is something like a communications network, with each station performing a particular role and each sending and receiving messages continuously. A room of interconnected foreign currency traders is an example. They will usually outperform a group of independent, isolated traders even on a quiet day. But on fast-moving days full of complex events, they will *always* perform better because they learn quickly from each other. As the world changes, the networked traders see more patterns and are then able to get into and out of positions faster. Variety and complexity compounds the amount of information flying around and the combination of actions that can be taken. A closely connected room of traders will sort through it and make more of the right moves than the isolated trader can.

Many companies, however, instead of allowing the network to speed information flow, take the opposite approach in trying to cope with variety and complexity. They rely less on network learning and more on additional structure, and they end up short-circuiting the network. If, for example, new technologies are emerging, they specialize their engineers by technology. If a product is getting more complex and more and more employees have to work on it as it moves through the company, they will increase the number of formal control points. And, when greater variations in the mix of orders show up as they try to increase product variety to the market, these companies will typically build more inventory and put slack capacity into the system to handle the overload.

All of this is costly and will slow the company down. The marketplace demands for variety are real and growing. But additional structure and buffers are not the answer to meeting them. The buffers break up and slow down the OODA Loop. In contrast, time-based organizations cope with variety directly, by building up their flexibility and greater capacity for creating and sharing information. One way they accomplish this is through closed-loop teams.

CLOSED-LOOP TEAMS

For years, banks have taken several days to get a decision to a personal loan applicant. The application would be passed around the various departments, traveling at its own pace. A series of supervisors, clerks, and internal mailpeople handled it. Today, aggressive banks take the application directly into a focused, co-ordinated group—a credit analyst, a collateral appraiser, and a senior personal banker—who decide and respond to the customer sometimes in thirty minutes and always inside a day. This is a small closed-loop team.

A closed-loop team includes everyone who is necessary to make the deliverable flow. The team includes all the needed functional people and decision-makers and is self-scheduling. Everyone on the team is working for the same objective—to provide the deliverable on time. The team is empowered to make decisions and to act. It has all four OODA Loop functions inside it with short lines of communication. Its leader is responsible for its overall performance and for seeing that it gets all the capability, both technical and human, it needs. All of these are essential to flexibility.

The old bank loan approval process was open loop. There was no continuity in the process, no visible standard, little learning between the principals, only occasional feedback on the process, and no one responsible for making it better. The OODA Loop was long and broken. In order for the loop to close on a process it must be tightly organized around the deliverable; the same core group must be involved in the process every day; and there must be a working leader on the team.

Naturally, small teams work better than large ones because large groups create communication problems of their own. It's best to include only essential functions and to exclude people whose job is peripheral to the deliverable. For example, the bank loan team excludes accounting and records people. However, teams have to be self-managing and empowered to act because referring decisions back up the line wastes time and often leads to poor decisions. So the team includes a bank officer because if the officer were not on the team, he or she would be prone to second-guess the group's decisions. It's better if all the questions are asked and answers are exchanged just once.

As we've said, closed-loop teams handle variety better than open-loop teams because they can create new information and flexibility. For example, one manufacturer of custom-designed jet engine parts realized that its order entry process was taking anywhere from two to ten weeks. The order-processing task is basically to record the order, to make sure it is properly specified, to order necessary materials from suppliers, and to schedule the order. Because this order entry process was the first stage in the company's main sequence, the wide variance in time required to complete it was creating problems downstream in scheduling and in setting a promise date to the customer. The company's order flow contained a variety of low- and high-complexity orders. So the company wanted to narrow this time range and make order entry more reliable.

Two core problems caused the time variance. One was that each of the six departments the order passed through had a queue of other work besides order entry waiting to be done. Order entry was a small part of each department's work so a new order would sometimes get last priority in the queue, especially when other, complex orders came through that took a lot of the department's time. In addition, the length of the queues varied depending on the function of the department and its current workload. No one could predict, therefore, how long a new order would take to clear these six queues in succession. The second problem was that departments often had different product codes, so that the information from one department was not always directly intelligible to the next; codes had to be translated as each order made its way through the departments. And this process took even longer on the more complex orders.

It was clear that the solution to shortening the order-processing time and reducing its variance would involve avoiding departmental queues and creating comparable codes across the departments. A closed-loop team of six individuals—one from each department—was established. Their first job was to unify the product codes, which took three months. Incidentally, this job had been sitting in the data systems department for a year and had died there, because the department had no strong cross-functional sponsorship. Now, a group of knowledgeable, empowered people were in charge and could actively work on the problem, so it got done.

The next step was to set aside a portion of each team member's time twice a week to perform all the order entry work for his or her department. Capacity was not taken out of the departments but effectively dedicated, and the team could function as a stable unit. To solve the variety problem, the jet engine supplier revised the procedure for processing complex orders to balance the amount of work each department did on each order; before, a complex order would typically burden some departments more than others. Also, the team tried to even the mix of complex and simple orders every time it worked on order entry. These two changes balanced the work load associated with complex orders. They no longer choked the system when they came through.

Once this system had been established and fine-tuned with one team, each team member trained two others in his or her department. Now, order entry can be done in this more managed, focused way by several different people in each department. If total orders surge, they can still be processed without delay. The overall result is that all orders are now processed in one to two weeks, instead of from two to ten weeks. This has helped downstream scheduling and makes the company's promised ship dates more reliable. Ultimately, the total amount of labor time devoted to order entry across the six departments has declined because of unified coding and because of the even flow of complex and simple orders.

The interesting point about this is that the company had been trying to solve the order entry problem for years. It had tried hand-carrying orders around. It had tried a PC-based software to keep track of them. It had tried brute force. None of these methods worked because the problem was more complex than ordinary management tools applied from *outside* the problem could address. The problem had to be broken down and reassembled by a multifunctional team empowered *within* the departments. The key was to keep all the information and the operations inside the team so they could work out the way to get flexibility. To close the loop.

Closed-loop teams work in product development as well as in production. AT&T, for example, now uses a variant of the self-managing team concept to develop new telephones, and Deere & Company does the same in designing new construction equipment. By bringing people from product engineering, manufacturing, marketing, and purchasing together throughout the development process and by giving them authority to make real technical and business decisions, these companies have cut significant time and expense out of bringing new products to market.

A warning is in order, however. Simply forming teams will not produce time compression in companies. In most businesses today, teamwork still means something less rigorous than what is described above. It usually means simply closer, better interaction among individuals and more awareness of common goals but not necessarily a structure functionally different from that of traditional firms. Many companies like to think they are working in multifunctional groups when they form special task forces that cross organizational lines. They encourage managers to wander around informally and to share observations across the company. These are useful but very limited steps. Putting together teams without changing the embedded work routines and management practices will not compress time. Time compression demands that old habits change fundamentally. For example, companies that believe in functional heads playing a strong role in day-to-day operations will have trouble truly empowering self-managing, cross-functional teams. Functional heads will find it hard to resist getting involved. Also, companies that can't resist rotating project heads every three years will never develop team leaders who are experienced enough to manage an empowered, closed-loop group. Closed-loop team leaders are principal contributors to their teams, not just administrators. Finally, a word to the wise: Companies that have a habit of lengthy project reviews in large rooms will find that time doesn't compress.

Ultimately, senior managers can make or break how well the

closed-loop concept works. Senior managers typically have good ideas to contribute to teams, and there is always a constructive way to do it. But their intervention can also carry disproportionate weight and often comes at awkward times in a project's life. Moreover, their calendars are so crowded that the more they get involved in a project, the harder it becomes to schedule meetings and to keep decisions on track. Senior executives in fast-cycle companies understand this problem and appreciate the way they can bottleneck a team and hurt motivation among junior people.

Skunk works are an example of the kind of ad hoc, closed-loop experiment that will not make a company time-based. While they can reduce the time some kinds of development projects take, skunk works bypass the organization's regular practices. They circumvent the rules rather than rewrite them so they don't do the rest of the organization much good. In fact, because many of the best people are pulled out into the skunk works, the rest of the organization further slows down. In addition, because a lot of these experiments fail, their members may come back to the regular organization highly stressed. Basically, skunk works are unsustainable organizations. In contrast, time-based companies try to raise the capability of the entire system and put people in a position to make continued improvements.

The closed-loop concept is useful not only in organizing routine operations like order processing and product development, but also in solving more diffuse, long-term problems in a company that show up as extended process-time cycles. Automobile companies, for example, all face the problem of correcting original design problems once a new model is out in the field. Some working components like brakes or suspension may begin to incur well-above-normal warranty expense. If the problem goes untreated, it costs the manufacturer dearly in lost earnings and customer goodwill. A long string of functions spread over considerable distance has to focus jointly on this problem to solve it. Dealers have to get data to the manufacturer's regional field office, which brings the problem to headquarters. Product engineers then work on the problem and issue engineering change notices to the tooling people at the plants that manufacture the redesigned parts. Finally, the service parts organization restocks its shelves. Eventually, the bad parts in the field are all replaced.

How long this cycle takes from first detection to field fix determines what the total cost to the company will be. The longer the cycle, the more cars with bad original parts will be made and the more customers will be unhappy. Yet, despite the value of fast response here, this difficult loop is one that many auto companies don't manage well. To begin with, the players—field offices, engineers, plant tooling people, and service—are far apart and in different organizations. Parts nomenclature and numbering systems are not the same in engineering as they are in service. Moreover, no one is responsible for this cycle. It is just layered over the regular lines of organization. The complete cycle is not visible to any one of the functions that are a part of it, so none are aware of how their policies and actions influence the others. This is mainly because the cycle takes so long—sometimes up to 18 months—that there is no feedback or sense of completion of any specific component's fix cycle. The cycles of different components overlap each other, with each player in the loop just doing its work and passing its product on. The whole problem becomes a serial open loop.

One company decided to try to close the loop. Their first step was to follow one component through an entire fix cycle to capture a picture of the whole, which was then shown to all players to allow them to see what actually happens and how long it takes. Although no new formal organization was developed, an able middle manager took charge of the cycle, and each player became accountable in terms of new time standards. The manager closed the major gaps in the process, such as the delay between field office recognition and engineering action. Then the firm developed software to connect the different numbering systems. Through feedback loops for sharing information about performance by component, everyone could see what was going on where.

All of this allowed the players to understand the system they were a part of, and they started to create and share better information about how it worked and what would help. The loop began to tighten over time. Eventually the customer became part of the loop—owners are now told when to expect their field repair to be made and what the benefits will be. The company has reduced the average fix cycle from 18 to 6 months.

This core concept of compressing cycle times by more carefully defining and then closing loops is implicit in a number of new approaches inside faster-moving companies today. Focused factories, for example, are emerging within some large, aging manufacturing plants that make several different product lines. The plants build each self-contained factory around one product family or one set of processes. Then someone with the powers of the old plant manager manages the focused factory, controlling all support functions as well as actual production. The idea is to create several closed loops inside a large complex to simplify management. As a result, plant cycle times have improved. Global companies are also finding faster ways to transfer a successful product innovation from one country to another. Markets and company cultures across different countries have always made transplants difficult, even when they were a good business idea. More closed-loop approaches—in which people from both the sending and receiving country's organization get involved in the other's operation well before the product transfer is attempted— usually work better than the traditional "missionary" approaches.

Closed loops don't just happen, however. They can either be cultivated over long periods or created with some architectural preparation. Japanese companies in general tend to place a high value on networking and on maintaining diverse communication channels both inside and between companies. This improves the chances of loops forming around problems and opportunities that weren't recognized before, and it may help account for the Japanese competitive success. Because of the Japanese business culture, informal, semistructured channels have long existed in Japan between suppliers, neighbors, industry associations, and of course customers. It's interesting to compare, for example, how Japanese companies decide where their headquarters should be. In the last 15 years, urban cost pressures have prompted many American headquarters' moves to suburbs or to the South. Costs are lower in these areas, but information density and networking opportunities are thinner. By contrast, Japanese companies have invariably stayed in Tokyo or Osaka. They focus on time more than on cost. The creation and flow of information move faster because these channels are in place.

HOW TO MEASURE PERFORMANCE

Time-based companies go back to basics when they decide how they are going to keep track of their performance (see Table 6–4). Time is already widely used to measure performance in business.

TABLE 6–4

Traditional Companies	Time-based Companies
Cost is the metric	Time is the metric
Look to financial results	Look first to physical results
Utilization-oriented measures	Throughput-oriented measures
Individualized or department	Team measures

Managers use terms like *lead-time, on-time delivery,* and *response time* almost instinctively in describing how well a company is serving its customers. But, time-based companies go a step further. They use time-based metrics as diagnostic tools throughout the company and set basic goals of the operation around them. In effect, they use time to help them design how the organization should work. They will often compare their own performance in time with that of their best competitors or best practices anywhere. The core view that they have on performance tracking is this: Time is the best diagnostic measure and design parameter available. If we can provide the product that customers want and still compress time, we are also going to be solving cost and quality problems in our value-delivery process. It is cost that doesn't add value that takes up most of the time in business.

How do time-based companies measure time? They follow two rules: Keep the measure physical, and measure as close to the customer as possible. Table 6–5 summarizes the mainstream indicators of time compression in the four performance areas—developing new products, making decisions, processing work along the main sequence, and servicing customers.

Overall measures, such as time to market with new products or lead time on deliveries, are good places to start, particularly if there is a competitor or a best practices standard available for comparison, which there usually is. You know many measures of competitors' time performance because customers tell you. On the other hand, some measures require that you go into your operation and learn details. Knowledge about the amount of time lost waiting for decisions is something you have to put together. It is not commonly known. The same is true for most of the pro-

TABLE 6–5 Time-based Performance Measures

New-Product Development	*Decision Making*
Time from idea to market	Decision cycle time
Rate of new-product introduction	Time lost waiting for decisions
Percent first competitor to market	
Processing and Production	*Customer Service*
Value added as percent of total elapsed time	Response time
Uptime × yield	Quoted lead time
Inventory turnover	Percent deliveries on time
Cycle time (per major phase of main sequence)	Time from customer's recognition of need to delivery

cessing and production measures, with the exception of inventory turnover.

Companies are usually surprised by what these measures reveal. For example, managers typically overestimate the portion of total elapsed time that is spent adding value that customers recognize. Another often surprising measure is uptime multiplied by yield, which tells you actual first-time throughput for any multistage process and which you can then compare to potential throughput. In any processing sequence where work goes from station to station, the actual throughput of work relative to potential is a function of how often each station is operating and manned (that is, uptime percentage) times how often the work coming out of that station is done right the first time (that is, yield percentage). These two numbers are multiplied together across all stations to give you actual throughput of good work the first time through. For example, if you have three work stations and each is up 99 percent of the time and do the job correctly 99% of the time, the overall throughput is 94 percent—six times 0.99—of potential. This measure is useful in operations like claims processing, product lines, and so on, where there are several people working in line. Companies are usually surprised at how far below 100 percent capacity actual first-time throughput is. The effect of downtime, interruption, and error at the various stations is compounded as work moves through the sequence, and it takes longer to get acceptable product out at the end. Competitors can sometimes be two to three times higher in throughput efficiency. (More on this measure in the next chapter.)

Another measure that often produces unexpected results is time lost waiting for decisions—any kind of decision, from those made by major executives to those involved in simple inventory replenishment. Most decisions could be made sooner and better, closer to the time all the information needed to make them is known. But the right channels of information haven't been created. Furthermore, the gap between when a customer discovers the need for replenishment and when you learn this is not only direct time wasted but will probably amplify forecasting errors elsewhere in the system. A critical pipeline is missing between customer and supplier. The same thing is true for regular go/no-go decisions on new product features. The right information is slow to get to the right place. This is why closed-loop architecture is important to time-based companies.

Time-compressed companies measure the cycle times and lead times of all important activities. Cycle time is their staple measurement. They start with cycle times of major activities like developing a new product or moving material through a plant. They analyze this big picture, then start breaking it down into smaller pictures and more specialized time measures.

Time is a more useful management tool than cost. Cost is by and large a lagging indicator, a symptom, a set of control accounts after the fact. Cost is tracked through a set of accounts corresponding to what money is spent on—payroll, amortization of fixed assets, holding inventory, and so on. Cost is a financial calculation that includes some arbitrary allocations and deferrals. There are price level adjustments and variances of several kinds. It is sometimes hard to say what cost is really measuring—better real performance or just better utilization of sunk costs?

Also, some costs add value for customers, while others detract from value. Adding cost in the form of better raw materials or hand-finishing a portion of the product adds value. But many overhead items like factory rework or the cost of idle assets add cost but no value. In fact, a lot of cost is incurred because the operation is out of sync. It is very difficult to look at cost analyses in most companies and tell which cost reductions added customer value and which took it away.

Managing time, on the other hand, opens up the company for analysis. Time is an objectively measurable current flow, not a calculation shaped by accounting conventions. A manager can measure and quantify the flow of activities directly and ask with respect to each whether it is adding real value. For example, inventories are idle materials, just as in-baskets contain idle information. Reworking is doing something twice. Holding up a decision because the necessary data is late in arriving is response time lost. Time is a common, direct measure.

Time's major advantage as a management tool is that it forces analysis down to a physical level. Putting together a time line of activity—a chart that says what happened every hour or every day to an order, or to a project, or to whatever you want to track—tells you what actually goes on in your company. Once physical activity is laid bare, the right questions can be asked: Why do we do this step twice? Why are these tasks done serially and not in parallel? Why does this process work only half the time? Why do we invest to speed this up and then let its output sit and wait for the next process? Answers to these questions lead managers to where the cost and quality problems of the company actually are.

This physical way of looking at the business gives managers more insight and power in looking for ways to improve results than cost analysis typically can. Once a bank, for example, lays out what happens during the three weeks it takes just to approve a credit application, the first steps of the solution become obvious. When a heavy duty truck executive looks and sees lots of rework of custom-engineered features and production hold-ups in the plant, he can begin to place some value on an upstream investment like pre-engineering that could eliminate this downstream waste of time and source of overhead cost. Once a manager sees a layout of where time goes, he or she can start to translate it into cost reduction opportunities. But looking at cost analyses first doesn't often tell anyone where to save time.

Nevertheless, time and cost are strongly related in the product development process. Time-based companies insist that a schedule-driven development program will lower cost without sacrificing anything. One project manager puts it this way: "No matter how elaborate the support systems and services provided to a design team, it is simply not possible to spend as much development money in two years as it is in four years. If you work to a tight schedule, the budget takes care of itself."[2] Exhibit 6–3 summarizes results of a survey of U.S. companies on their R&D policies and results, conducted in 1988 by The Boston Consulting Group and the *Wall Street Journal.* Managers felt that to the extent that firms wasted their R&D budget, they were slower to market with new products. So time and cost are closely linked in R&D managers' minds. The best way to get development costs down is to contain the time available.

As consumers, we get conditioned to paying a premium for speed. We pay more for rush orders or for getting laundry back fast in hotels. Yet, in most businesses, the less time it takes, the less

Exhibit 6–3 Time to Market and R&D Waste *Survey Results from 70 Companies in U.S. (1988)*

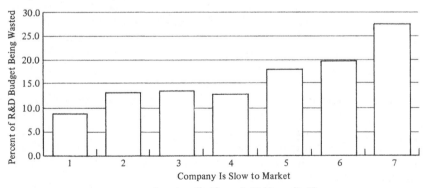

1—not applicable   7—highly applicable

SOURCE: Boston Consulting Group and Wall Street Journal survey of R&D practices, "Missed Opportunities: Americans Hold the Lead in Research, But Let Foreigners Develop the Products," *Wall Street Journal,* November 14, 1988, p. R-21.

it should cost. Time-based companies reduce cost indirectly through compressing time. When a company attacks time directly, the first benefits to show up are usually shorter cycle times and faster inventory turns. Lower overhead costs usually follow, as the costs of dealing with breakdowns and delays begin to disappear from the system. So, when a company goes after time reduction in the right way, it tends to get both time and cost out.

The reverse is not always so. Companies that focus on getting costs out can impose delays on an organization. Cutting work-in-process inventory will work until the slack is gone, but once shortages start to occur, shipments will slow down. Downsizing staff in the wrong places will create bottlenecks in the organization. And doing away with those costly project review meetings is not such a good idea if reviews are the only place problems seem to get uncovered. Companies that need a lot of extra staff and review meetings in order to function cannot just cut them and avoid paying somewhere else. Companies that first change the way they operate first find it easier to pull costs out.

Of course, all time-based companies use both cost and time measures. Cost is key to knowing financial performance and to controlling the expenditure of resources. However, managers have to be careful that they don't just add new time-based measures to the cost-based goals and controls that have always existed, because these can conflict and send mixed messages. One company, for example, convinced itself that its lead time to customers, that is, days from order to shipment, should come down. Once it did, its backlog did too. Shorter lead times automatically reduced the days of backlog in the system, and the false backlog of customers who ordered because lead times were long began to disappear. But backlog had always made the company feel secure, and when it went down, some managers were uncomfortable. So the chief financial officer persuaded senior management to keep high backlog as a goal and urged marketing to build it back up. A lot of confusion was generated. In another instance, a plant manager was told to reduce his cycle time and increase his inventory turns and at the same time to continue to maximize utilization of his equipment and minimize direct labor content. These latter goals kept him from shortening his production runs and from transferring existing indirect labor functions to direct labor employees. As a result, he was not able to reduce cycle times very much.

Unlike time and cost measures, time and quality measures usually reinforce one another, rather than conflict. Pure quality measures like error rate, yield, rework, and so on are directly connected to overall cycle time. Once again, time is a manager's way to locate quality problems—the more central to the value delivery and the closer to the critical path of the business, the more a quality problem will slow down the delivery process. In some managers' eyes, a time focus is better than overall quality audits because it identifies more quickly the most critical quality issues and raises awareness about them. All quality programs must work at the grassroots level, but some programs start so low and move so slowly that big opportunities for earlier, high impact results are lost. A time-based diagnosis—to determine where time is wasted—will usually uncover the quality problems faster.

CHAPTER

7

◇◇◇◇

Becoming a Time-based Organization

B ecoming a time-based company requires a sustained, focused effort, and that's hard to make. There is a lot going on in any good company today beyond getting product out the door. Any number of different themes and visions—quality, globalization, innovation—are competing for share of a manager's mind. And some of these themes seem, especially to a CEO, more concrete and more manageable than time compression. Also, time compression may sound as if it can be delegated to operating heads.

But even among operating heads, it's easy for time to get passed over—not ignored, just undermanaged. Managers deal with time every day in an episodic manner—delivery dates, lead times, moving up product launches, and so on. But they rarely stand back and consider time systematically or as a key to competitive position. Two facts of organizational life explain why time is so easily overlooked and undermanaged.

First, decision options are rarely presented to managers in terms of the effect they would have on time. A proposal for a new production process may highlight cost savings and capacity but neglect to mention that the larger economic batch size will slow the whole organization down. Proponents of a new headquarters building will talk about space and amenities but fail to point out that the floor plan separates marketing from engineering and thus will lengthen the new product development process. In short, it takes a special effort for executives to focus routinely on system time as something to be managed.

Second, and more problematic, most people in organizations, including senior managers, like to have stability in their working procedures and social patterns. Serious efforts at cycle time reduction disrupt both. Multifunctional teams break up existing departments and routines. Compressing cycle time sweeps away longstanding crutches, such as quality inspections and redundant data entry, which exist only because work isn't designed or done right the first time. Some valued specialists are exposed as the cause of bottlenecks, while others become completely unnecessary. You don't need sophisticated short-term adjustments to market forecasts, for example, if you can respond immediately to any change in the level of demand.

Even if management does get excited about time compression as a manageable source of competitive advantage, it is difficult to keep people throughout the company focused on it for very long. Management themes come and go in American companies, and unless senior people stick with a few philosophies and implement them consistently, the organization will take the attitude "this too shall pass." When employees see a strong theme coming down that they can't relate directly to their work, they discount it. Strategic planning and value-based purchasing concepts have died in many companies because management really didn't mean what it said.

Strong as these internal forces inhibiting time management are, however, the compelling external fact that speed wins can override them. And speed is tangible. It is also easy for employees to relate time compression to other things they are concerned about, such as cost and quality. Looking for where time is wasted will lead to the sources of quality and cost problems in the company. Moreover, getting to the market sooner means something personal to many employees. To a product engineer, it means that maybe management is now serious about removing unnecessary reviews that slow down her work. To a market researcher, it promises that he can be a core member of a new-product development team. He can observe directly how his readings of the market influence decisions, as opposed to filing reports from a distance and waiting for the next request. To a mortgage lending officer, it means getting an answer back to a loan applicant before she gets impatient and runs off to another bank.

An organization goes through three phases in becoming a time-based competitor. During the first, a company discovers the opportunity and decides to go for it. We call this *vision and decision.*

The second phase is changing the basic ways the company works—an alternately uncomfortable and exhilarating period in which new solutions and practices are developed. Straightforwardly enough, this phase is called *making the change.* The third phase, *sustaining improvement,* lasts indefinitely. Time compression, like any really worthwhile management idea, is a journey, not a program. It's a rough road because every major advance in responsiveness and speed means overturning some accepted assumption or practice. And, inevitably, as more competitors compress time, changes may be forced on you faster than you had planned.

No two companies' paths through the three phases are the same. Some move through the first quickly into successful fundamental change, while others stumble in the first phase and have to restart several times. A hasty, shallow vision that doesn't acknowledge the hard work needed to break bad habits means a near certain derailment in the second phase. And some companies get good results for six months or so, then lose steam. But, by and large, companies that work at it do find it possible to compress time radically. What follows reflects what these companies have learned in the course of getting it done.

VISION AND DECISION

This first phase is really a process of moving from awareness to commitment, especially among the key managers who must prepare to drive the rest of the organization. The aim here is to convince key people that a great opportunity—or looming problems—lies ahead and that radical thinking around a new paradigm is necessary to make real progress. All the work a company does during this phase—reckoning where it stands competitively on time-based performance, building a vision, and deciding how to proceed—is preparation for the big moves to follow. Some changes in how the company works occur naturally in this phase—good analysis always produces some early obvious action steps. But the real purpose of this phase is to build commitment to a new way of looking at the competitive game and how the managers must play it.

Reckoning where the company stands includes looking hard at its own current performance and direction in relation to what the best companies are doing and what the near future will surely bring. So the process has both an internal and an external analytic component. The internal part involves putting together moving pictures of how the company actually works in time—how it processes information, manages projects, moves materials, engages customers, and so on, and how all this is influenced by the firm's beliefs, practices, policies, and systems. The external part involves describing what customers want now and how they would be served ideally, and piecing together moving pictures of how the best time-based competitors operate. Together these two parts allow management to self-discover in concrete fashion the new time-based paradigm and the capabilities the company must build to gain control of it.

MAPPING

The internal component works best if the key value-adding work cycles of the company are identified first and each one is explored separately. Examples of such cycles are developing new products, processing customer orders, making engineering changes in the field, and transplanting a successful new product overseas. To give you an idea of what system-wide coordination demands are placed on your employees, a first-cut cross-functional map helps. Exhibit 7–1 is a simplified version of a new product development map, showing how field offices, marketing, engineering, and manufacturing interact over time to take the company all the way from customer feedback on current products through final design and production of a new product.

Once the system-wide functional relationships have been identified, laying out the process with the key players across the

Exhibit 7–1 Cross-Functional Work in New Product Development

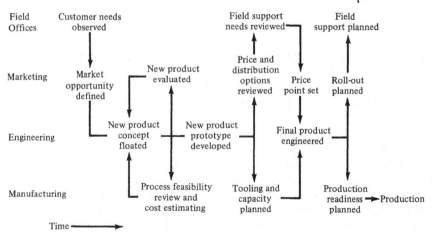

company on one axis and time on the other allows managers to start asking the right questions: What players are involved in the process and how often? What should each player know about other players' work? Where are decisions made and what do the decision makers need from other players to make better decisions? Where is time lost in the process, either directly because of delays or indirectly because inadequate thought and data lead to an adverse surprise that later causes work to back up?

Several realities have become clear in the course of exploring complex work cycles inside large companies. First, rarely do managers know the interaction map of the company. They know the organization chart and the critical path of projects, especially review dates. In other words, they know how long it takes and who's involved, but they don't know how to approach fixing it. The interactions are a maze, and the only learning about them is episodic, when there's a crisis. Second, the maze remains impenetrable because when managers ask their staffs to map it, they usually get back an engineering systems flow chart made up of hundreds of stocks, flows, and decision points that could cover a wall. What management needs, instead, is a report that boils the process down to the few essential, sensitive interactions that make or break it, so that a manager can assimilate and interpret the map. Third, system maps to be valuable have to emphasize the actual behavior of the system, not just the players' individual roles. Organizations aren't machines, they are societies. The critical links are cross-functional, but each function has its own values, rules, practices, and loyalties. A good map of how an organization is functioning must capture the influence of these factors on how the work gets done. This is first-degree learning that managers need if they are serious about time-based competition.

Exhibit 7–2 is a map showing that managers can understand not only how the system works but why it works that way. While oversimplified, it tells the core story of the operating cycle from customer order to shipment for a leading manufacturer of a big-ticket customized industrial component that customers use in their production processes.

This company was having a problem with the length of the lead times it had to quote to customers. Promised delivery dates were long—24 weeks on average—and also ranged widely, from 4 to 36 weeks. Worse, shipments were often late. The company's product reputation was excellent, but the long and unreliable lead times were undermining it. The company had a real opportunity to dominate this $400 million business if it could get its cycle times under control. The sum of actual value-adding time from sales-

Exhibit 7–2 Mapping the Operating System *Major Causes of Problems*

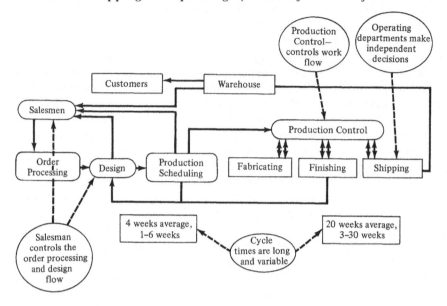

people cultivating orders to end-product shipment was only one or two weeks. So the company set out to identify where time was spent and where the process bogged down.

Exhibit 7–2 tracks the basic information flow. Customers talk to salespeople who record orders and technical product specifications and then send them to order processing, custom design engineers, and Production Scheduling. Salespeople also assign priorities to the orders. Production Scheduling releases orders to Production Control, which coordinates the three plant activities— fabricating, finishing, and shipping. The finished product is sent to a local warehouse for delivery to the customer, after which the salesperson is notified. The whole process can be visualized as two consecutive cycles—an ordering cycle of 4 weeks on average and a production cycle of 20 weeks average.

In this case, mapping helps explain the long, variable cycles. Exhibit 7–2 highlights the company's structure and policies that taken together produce the following particular system behavior:

- Salespeople, by policy, place orders and assign scheduling priorities. They closely monitor current factory lead times to determine when to place orders and how to assign priorities. The idea is to give the best service to top customers. The system effect of these policies, however, is to cause confusion downstream in production as lower priorities get set aside. Also, current high lead times encourage salespeople to place speculative orders to "get in line." These orders further extend lead times.

- Preliminary product specifications are passed along to Design when the order is placed, and salespeople continue to feed additional technical information to Design as it arrives. The idea is to capture the order early, then complete it when the customer is ready. Design is structurally driven by this information flow. The effect, however, is to cause both Design and Production Scheduling to lose control of their cycles. Design will begin work on an order for which all information is complete with the idea of finishing it and clearing it to the factory, but partial information needed to finish a high-priority order will come in and interrupt the flow. Information dribbles in and work is stop-start, so even the high-priority order is effectively slowed down. Schedules change daily, requiring costly, constant negotiations between Sales and Production Scheduling. Promised delivery dates become meaningless and Design's interrupted work flow means that some low-priority orders are designed more than once.

- Production Control breaks each order into three separate departmental work orders—fabricating, finishing, and shipping—so that it can control each department separately and move late or high-priority orders ahead of others between these three stages. The system result, however, is an unbalanced work flow. Downstream departments cannot anticipate future workload. Capacity planning is difficult. Control over lot size is lost. Total factory cycle time for any given order becomes unpredictable, causing late shipments and complicating lead time quotes at the head of the whole process. The system's imbalances feed on themselves.

This system mapping explained several contradictions about the company that were plaguing management. One, the very policies aimed at giving better customer service undermined it. The behavior stimulated by the company's policies and structure here was counterproductive—everything got slowed down. Two, the desire for greater microcontrol, especially by salespeople and Production Control, actually resulted in less. Even high-priority orders had trouble fighting through. Third, attempts to compress time by eliminating steps, such as filing interim order status reports, backfired because critical rescheduling information was lost.

A system that's out of control needs more and more information to keep it from collapsing.

Before the system was explored and explained in this way, no consensus across the company's various management posts had been possible. Functional managers had a limited view, and the actions each took to try to get control of their work usually compounded a problem elsewhere. For example, Design decided not to pass orders on to Production Scheduling until a minimum of specification data was in hand. But this just reduced the visibility of high-priority orders in the system, causing even more urgent scrambling later. Function heads cannot be expected to understand and commit to a system they don't help design and revise. Yet managers above function heads, preoccupied with critical technology and personnel issues, felt that operations were the function heads' responsibility. Before system mapping, technology was thought to be the only cutting edge of competition and the responsibility of upper management. Afterward, the problem of time compression belonged to both levels of management.

The shape and format of a good system map depend on the problem that it is being used to diagnose. This component manufacturer was at least able to easily identify its main sequence, which was fairly straightforward. In contrast, large insurance companies offering a wide variety of policies often have difficulty even with this initial step. Everyday tasks such as establishing a price on a new policy or processing a claim can take very different routes through the organization, depending on the policy's characteristics. An insurance company's main interaction patterns and cycle times can often appear to be random. In this case, the first step in mapping is some early categorization of transactions into high- versus low-intensity processing, followed by statistical analysis of large numbers of transactions to develop clusters of similarity. A series of main sequences then begins to emerge, giving the manager a useful description of his company's operations and a place to start thinking.

In another instance, mapping the decision-making mechanics of a consumer products company was particularly useful in evaluating the competitive effectiveness of the firm's brand manager system. The company developed very good products and had strong relations with retailers, but was increasingly late to market with new products and slow in executing its promotions. Mapping the company's management interaction patterns revealed that the brand managers' ability to act quickly had been eroded over time by the addition of a new specialist, a new dimension in the organization's management matrix, and a new round of market tests. The product manager's communications with both product development and the field operation, once direct and rapid, were now indirect and circuitous. The company had put itself into a position where it was making technically good but competitively bad decisions by taking away from its managers the ability to act quickly.

METRICS

Time is relatively straightforward to measure inside a company once management begins to focus on it. Time is captured explicitly in measures of elapsed time—lead time, cycle time, and so on—and implicitly in metrics normally used in engineering and finance—machine uptime, product yield, inventory turnover, and the like. When all these time-related measures are brought together with maps showing the organization's main flows and interaction patterns, a powerful picture of the company's problems and opportunities comes into view.

For example, two metrics in particular were influential in convincing top management of the custom industrial component company described above that there must be a better way to run the company. One was how salespeople spent their time. Management had thought that salespeople spent the majority of their time talking to customers, but in fact they spent more talking to Production Scheduling and Design, trying to manage work flow. The other measure was a comparison of the actual time each production lot spent in the factory with the standard time. Exhibit 7–3 shows actual versus standard time in plant for three of the company's products over one year's worth of production lots. The standard plant cycle time for Product A is three days, and that was the actual average, but the range of actuals went from seven days to one day. The standard for Product B was 7 days, but only 1 lot out of 16 achieved this standard. Most lots spent 10 or more days in the plant, and one spent 20 days. The story for Product C is similar. Any system where actual is so far off-standard and variance is so high is out of control. You cannot do reliable scheduling or capacity planning in a company like this.

It's noteworthy that the indicators top management normally looked at here were current quoted lead time, backlog, and percent late shipments. The problem is that lead time and backlog were determined both by strength of order flow on the demand side and actual average cycle time on the supply side. To senior management, rising backlog meant rising demand. Moreover, the percentage of late shipments didn't reflect the length of actual cycle times for each lot because Production Scheduling would

Exhibit 7–3 Actual Versus Standard Factory Cycle Times Per Lot

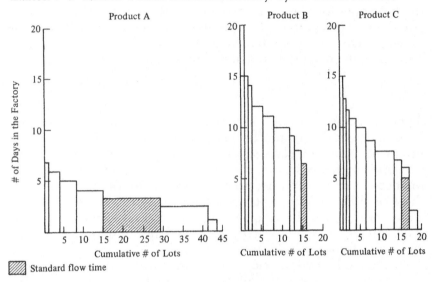

juggle orders and salespeople would simply quote longer lead times. This instance reinforces the point made earlier—it is important to look at physical measures of operations performance.

A good summary measure of time compression is a simple cumulative elapsed time bar. Just lay out a bar from left to right, its length representing a total cycle, say, for a new-product test program that took two months. Each day is one slice of the bar. Color in each slice depending on whether value was added that day, with green for value and white for delays, queues, rework, and other avoidable downtime. Results usually show a little green in an essentially white bar. For example, in one company, new-product test programs were routinely scheduled for two months by the test center, and new-product project managers built that into their time budgets. Yet analysis showed that two-thirds of this cycle time was easily avoidable—the arrival of all necessary information wasn't planned to coincide; the sequential tests were scheduled independently while they could have been arranged in tandem; one division in the company had bumping rights over others because product launch dates were crucial in its business. One look at the mostly white time bar changed all of this; test programs now take three weeks. If your data aren't ready, you lose your turn. And there are no bumping rights because three weeks meets everyone's needs. The bumping was simply the result of an unmanaged cycle. There are many such cycles inside companies.

An excellent measure of time compression in processes with several tightly linked sequential steps is called cumulative uptime times yield. Each station in a sequential set of operations—whether processing material in a factory or information in an office—is either operating or not (that is, percent uptime) and is turning out good product the first time through or not (that is, percent yield). If every station had 100 percent uptime and 100 percent yield, the process would be running on its best possible cycle time. But in most processes, there are some stations that are usually down, and others that are not turning out work up to specification. Consequently either the whole line shuts down or buffer inventories and queues are placed between stations. Either way, the cycle time of the total product is lengthened.

Exhibit 7–4 shows the 19-step manufacturing process involved in making a light fixture. This manufacturer, which had rarely thought of the business in terms of process cycles, was successful and looking for ways to expand capacity and add more product variety without having to add more equipment and people in proportion. The company laid out its process and calculated its uptime times yield at each station, then multiplied the results across all 19 steps to come up with a cumulative uptime times yield for the whole. The results were astonishing. No one station had noticeably poor uptime or yield, but each had some small problems. Neither uptime nor yield was at 100 percent for any station.

Exhibit 7–4 Cycle Time and Process Reliability *Cumulative Uptime and Yield in Manufacturing of a Light Fixture*

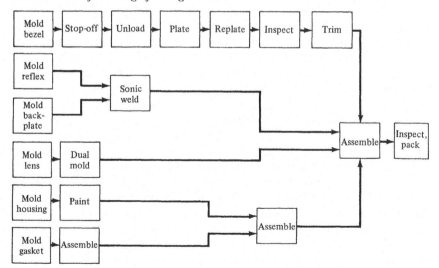

This mapping and measurement of the process showed that if each station's yield and uptime were just 1 percent better than current performance, they would raise the effective capacity of the whole process by more than one-third. (Remember the 1 percent improvement is compounded 38—19×2—times.) In other words, the way to get higher and more flexible capacity was to control the existing process more rigorously. This would reduce the cycle time—increase throughput—for existing product volume so that there would be time to run additional products. It would also help reduce the cost of variety, because the faster the cycle time, the sooner a new product variant could be set up and run through the process and shipped to a customer.

For this company, the investment with the greatest leverage was not more capital equipment or people but better process control. Sequential processes are one place where time compression, quality, and cost all meet in the same place, and powerfully. Product quality is yield here, and downtime translates into maintenance and resetup overhead cost. The best way for this company to reach its goals was to better understand and control each step of its process cycle, redesigning it if necessary. The cycle time for a finished lot—in effect the inverse of uptime times yield—was the best single indicator of how well operations were running.

This same uptime times yield perspective can apply in the office as well as in the factory. Many large information-processing organizations—insurance companies, banks, government licensing bureaus, and the like—have a main sequence of operations that is broken up into departments, because management regards volume as too large or some steps as too complex to risk structuring the activity as a continuous line. For example, processing licensing applications might involve reading applications, coding, checking references, peer review, pricing, selecting limits, documentation, and review with the applicant. When this repetitive sequence is broken into departments, cycle times lengthen. Visibility of the whole is lost, and with it the potential for designing into the process direct connections that would force uptime and yield to be managed. Once a sequence is broken up, departments go their own ways with rules, hardware, and formats that make no sense elsewhere. Managers' shortsighted fascination with scale and specialization can break the natural continuity of work, and in so doing submerge the powerful multiplicative relationship of cumulative uptime and yield that is the key to fast cycles.

There is no one fixed set of time metrics managers should use to appraise time-based performance. Those discussed here— standard versus actual cycle times, an elapsed time bar, and uptime times yield—simply illustrate what can be done depending on the situation. The list of generic measures in Exhibit 6–3 is a good place to start.

EXTERNAL BENCHMARKING

Examining how your best time-based competitors operate and manage can help get the attention of your key people. Nearly every industry today has one company that is time-compressed enough to provide a valuable data point—so fast and profitable that it must be doing things differently. The object company need not be a competitor. Any excellent company that has the same general kind of operation, customer groups, information flow, or decision cycle can be useful. The important thing is not only to record the better performance numbers but also to observe, model, or otherwise learn how the reference company has achieved its success.

It is sometimes easier to study competitors than your own company because it's easier to be objective. But it's important not to assume that in those areas where information can't be found, competitors are just like you. In fact, it's more useful to assume they aren't and force yourself to imagine how they might approach this or that differently. Figuring out a competitor's superior performance is like solving a jigsaw puzzle or like Sherlock Holmes solving a crime. You can always work around a missing piece or clue as long as you don't close your mind and assume what it must look like. The object of the search is the integrating pattern, not just the pieces. Time-based companies do lots of things differently, and it's important to keep looking for the new paradigm or insight that will govern what the pieces must be. You can't discover new paradigms by grounding yourself in old assumptions.

Keys to Good Competitor Benchmarking
- Look for unusual practices. Ask how they could make sense. View them hypothetically as missing links, not anomalies.
- Talk to customers he sells but you can't.
- Imagine him to be one-tenth your actual size. Ask how work then would be organized and managed.
- Imagine his ideal information flow. Figure how many material flow problems would then disappear.
- Study his distribution—frequency, composition of lots, channels, customer selection, and so forth—as clues to inside workings.

A good time-based competitive analysis will investigate market-ing concepts, behavior patterns, and systems in place, as well as per-formance measures. A good illustration of how all these can produce a compelling picture that promotes learning is the dy-namic view of Toyota's core auto activities in Exhibits 7–5 and 7–6. Not too long ago Toyota was seen as a great marketing company, a JIT manufacturer, a tough value-based organizer of suppliers, and an exemplar of consensus management. These separate im-pressions didn't reveal much about Toyota's operation as a whole, however. Exhibit 7–5 is an attempt to present an integrated system-wide view of Toyota for one Western automaker.

This automaker termed Exhibit 7–5 the "Toyota Racetrack." It was put together entirely from public sources and from suppliers any major auto company would have access to. It was the fresh par-adigm of looking at the whole of Toyota as a series of intercon-nected time cycles that got management's attention, not the individual pieces of the puzzle. At Toyota, self-managing, multi-functional teams take charge of product development, focusing on a particular model series. In rapid response to demand patterns, they develop products and manufacturing processes simulta-neously to collapse time and to ensure better "manufacturability." The teams are responsible for managing continuing styling, per-formance, and cost decisions, and they control their own schedules and reviews. They also select and manage suppliers, who are brought into the design process early. The result is an ever-faster development cycle—three years on average now—frequent new-product introductions, and a constant flow of major and minor in-novations on existing models.

The production cycle begins as soon as a customer orders a car from a dealer. Dealers in Japan are connected on-line to the fac-

Exhibit 7–5 Toyota Performs Critical Operations Faster . . .

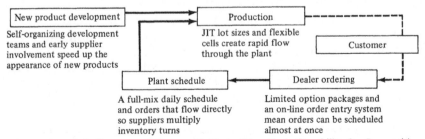

SOURCE: Joseph L. Bower and Thomas M. Hout, "Fast Cycle Capability for Competitive Power," *Harvard Business Review*, November-December 1988, p. 112. Copyright © 1988 by the President and Fellows of Harvard College.

Exhibit 7–6 ... So It Cuts Time at Every Turn

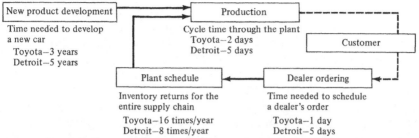

New product development		Production		
Time needed to develop a new car		Cycle time through the plant	Customer	
Toyota—3 years Detroit—5 years		Toyota—2 days Detroit—5 days		

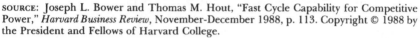

	Plant schedule		Dealer ordering	
	Inventory returns for the entire supply chain		Time needed to schedule a dealer's order	
	Toyota—16 times/year Detroit—8 times/year		Toyota—1 day Detroit—5 days	

SOURCE: Joseph L. Bower and Thomas M. Hout, "Fast Cycle Capability for Competitive Power," *Harvard Business Review*, November-December 1988, p. 113. Copyright © 1988 by the President and Fellows of Harvard College.

tory scheduling system, so that an order, complete with specifications and the customer's option package, can be entered and slotted into the factory schedule right away. Toyota schedules its plants to minimize sharp fluctuations in daily volume and to turn out a full mix of models every day. Customers get on-the-spot confirmation of their expected delivery date. Suppliers are automatically notified of the new order electronically and given a stable production schedule, so that they won't deliver the wrong components on the day of final assembly.

Actual production is executed in small lots by flexible manufacturing cells that can accommodate a mixed flow of units with little changeover time. Plants are managed to maintain high uptime and yield. The results are a fast-paced production cycle, which squeezes out all the overhead except what's needed to get work done right the first time through, and a reliable, continuous manufacturing process.

All Toyota's activities share a paradigm or vision, but current practices in each were put in place at different times and will continue to change incrementally. Competitive analysis shouldn't aim to snap a picture of "the answer," rather it should build a picture around common themes but allow for changing parts. For example, Toyota is now allowing more option-package flexibility as it advances its data systems. But the core competitive story remains the same. By coming up with new products faster, it puts competitors on the marketing defensive. By translating a customer's order into a finished product delivered faster, it captures large numbers of time-sensitive buyers and puts cost and inventory pressure on competitors. By continuously bringing out a variety of fresh products and observing what consumers buy or don't buy, it stays current with their changing needs and gives product development an edge that market research cannot match.

Good competitive benchmarking shows performance numbers and how they're achieved, and tells a story. The numbers should cover not just time but cost and quality as well. All these core organizational qualities are closely related. The story, like Toyota's above, should disclose the leverage by which the competitor controls the business. The purpose of benchmarking is to discover and confirm paradigms, not necessarily to set your own performance targets. The benchmarked company's level of performance may be inappropriately low or alternatively may be well past your foreseeable level of capability. What matters is to get outside your company's own assumptions and habits to see how system-wide time compression really works.

VISION AND COMMITMENT

Henry Mintzberg, professor of management at McGill University and a long-time student of strategy, has observed that the big question about making major change is not so much how to do it, but when. Making a big effort when everyone finally sees the new paradigm but after the game is over is too late, but trying to do it before senior management is ready and can support it is too soon. The top people have to prepare any large organization for a change of the kind we are talking about.

A convincing vision has to be put together before commitment can follow. A vision is not just a target; it should also tell a story. A good time-based vision will start with a clear picture of where the company is today—its performance with customers, its capabilities, and its problems—and where the company needs to go to gain (or retain) competitive control of its business. How fast and how often should we develop new products? What product variety do we need? How soon should customers receive shipment on their orders? How fast should we be able to transplant a new product that has been successful in Europe to the United States? The vision should clearly link these time-based objectives to the characteristics and capabilities the company will need to have in order to meet them. These characteristics should be expressed using the concepts and language of the previous chapter, describing how work will be organized, how information will be created and shared, how the organization will manage projects, how it will communicate with customers, and so on. Terms like *continuous flow of work* and *closed-loop group* are appropriate. The company's capabilities—what it can actually do for customers—should be described at roughly the same level that Toyota is described above. The vision needs to be concrete enough to engage employees, but the vision should not try to spell out these capabilities in detail—that is the work of the next phase, *making the change.* Senior management shouldn't try to do that anyway. It doesn't know enough to do it properly, and it's the proper job of middle managers and key employees.

The kinds of visions that companies put together in their strategic planning process are often premature and thin. A solid, timely vision has to be built on evaluation results, such as those derived from the internal mapping and measuring and the external benchmarking just described. Senior management has to know enough to make a good judgment about what the change process will entail for the organization. It has to decide what its people are capable of in the short term and in the long term, and therefore how far they can go and how fast. It has to decide whether the current key managers are the right ones to lead the organization into a new strategy. It has to project how much time and money will be needed. and what kind of change in values, measures, and management style will be required. These are the questions leaders ask before taking their organizations down a path of fundamental change.

Doing the internal and external analysis before the vision is the first major step in the learning process, and it must be led and actively managed by key line and functional managers. Sometimes large companies make a mistake here. They allow these key managers to delegate the actual work to task forces of senior staff and middle managers. When the critical managers simply review but don't lead and do the work, they fail to discover what they need to in order to lead their organization forward. Nor are they adequately tested as peers. Part of the reason for their involvement should be to reveal who among them are capable of grasping new paradigms and working together in new ways. Too many large companies stop putting senior people into situations where they have to perform on their own without their staffs.

The more practical reason for requiring key managers to do the work is that they will have to lead the organization through the change. If they don't believe the vision, others certainly won't. Our experience with new visions and the plans they spawn is that employees need to hear them again and again. This takes rounds and rounds of communication. And if the message doesn't clearly state the current reality and specific challenges ahead, the "great opportunity" portion of the message will be heavily discounted. The company's key managers have to have done their homework.

MAKING THE CHANGE

Once top executives and key managers develop a vision and decide their company is going to become a time-based competitor, two questions face them: (1) How do we overcome the organization's natural barriers to change? (2) How do we engage the organization to develop the solutions—the new ways of doing things—that we want? Fundamental change is exhilarating but also difficult. For some people it's a great release of energy, for others it's a threat. It is manageable if senior people are candid about what the problems are and persistent in communicating the market opportunities. Let's first address barriers to change, by differentiating between the two kinds and talking about how they are ultimately overcome.

One group of barriers to becoming a time-based company stems from the actions and policies of senior management. There may be a lack of imagination that starts right at the top. The organization's structure may undermine time compression—too many departments that break up the main sequence or functional lines of authority that are too strong. Measurements and rewards may be counterproductive. Old mythologies of the company—such as, our products are better so customers will wait for ours to come out—will confuse employees unless laid to rest. Inadequate leadership and, in particular, weak people in managers' roles, who are seen as not being able to solve the problems and make the changes they're talking about, will set any time-based effort back. All of these barriers are senior management's job to eliminate. The company can't ignore them and then talk about teamwork and fast cycles and expect much to happen.

The change from cost-based to time-based competition is fundamental and places new, sometimes conflicting demands on the company's managers, a factor that top management may underestimate at first. Profit-center managers can find the time-based message appealing but still take comfort in rising backlogs and greater use of fixed assets. Functional heads who got promoted on the strength of protecting the company from costly mistakes may find multifunctional approaches hard to accept. Data processing managers may be excellent at keeping the old systems running but see PC-centered networks and electronic data interchange with suppliers as threats to the firm's data integrity. Top executives have to be clear on what the new expectations are and help their managers through the transition.

The absolutely first step in senior management's design of the change process should be to assess the capability of managers at least three levels down. The most capable should be given strong roles in managing the task groups that remove the company-imposed barriers and design the new solution. The currently less able managers should be encouraged but left off the critical path, at least early on. The least able should be removed. Senior management has to tackle the barriers under its control right away.

The second group of barriers to change comprises the beliefs, habits, and concerns of employees that are ultimately under the control of employees themselves. There is a wide range of legitimate problems here. Many employees fear operations will collapse if serious changes are made. Some will see the concept but not the payoff. A large number will simply not know how to make the change and work under a new set of rules; the new paradigms will frighten them. Others will see the new rules as a loss of turf or status or as a downgrading of their skills. And some will simply be immobilized by grief over the end of a way of working with colleagues that they loved.

Although some of these problems must take time to heal or require individual counseling, most employees will respond to positive involvement in the change process and to clear, consistent communication from those they recognize as leaders. Fears and skepticism or disbelief for most employees simply indicate that they haven't *seen* a different approach in practice or that they haven't heard their immediate leaders endorse it. It's easy for management to underestimae how many exposures to the new message and to early pilot successes employees need. The reason is that there are a lot of countermessages—years of doing it the old way, short-timers who say it isn't worth it, concerns that certain job classifications and specialists will be gone, and so on. We have found that management has to communicate to all levels between three and five times more often than it may have thought necessary at the start.

It's a good idea for management to address doubts about the time-based concept directly. Employees, especially long-term people, have strong beliefs about how the business works, and unless these are specifically challenged they can undermine everything you're trying to do. Many employees will find the time-based vision runs counter to the facts. For example, they will believe that better service will mean more inventory. It always has in the past. It is not intuitive to most people the first time they hear it that synchronized, continuous flow operations can shorten cycle times, which in turn reduces the lead time needed to give customers what they want. Others will believe that yours is a commodity business where no one makes good returns. To counter this perspective, the idea of time-sensitive segments where higher prices and profits are available will have to be laid out in detail and examples shown.

Another firmly rooted belief may be that while the company "wastes a little time," it is impossible to reduce by one half or more the time it takes to service orders or to develop new products. Such prospects are unbelievable. In response to this opinion, management needs to shift employees from thinking about wasting time in an efficiency expert's sense to compressing time in a strategic sense. This takes a lot of explaining. Pictures and flow charts with boxes and arrows help.

The second question posed at the beginning of this section was how do we engage the organization to develop solutions that we want? This question brings us to the heart of the change process. There are lots of ways, and in every successful case that we know of, management used several. In some parts of the company, experiments and pilots that can generate solutions spontaneously down in the organization should get started right away. In others, especially where complex cross-functional issues are involved, a more deliberate process of bringing people from various parts of the organization together to design solutions is the right approach. And, nothing concentrates the mind of the company more effectively than focusing a cross-functional group on customers: What do they want, and how can we better serve them?

Focusing a group on how to create more value for customers should produce new insights. The aim is to locate the best customers, those who will reward you for taking time and uncertainty out of their businesses. One approach here is to ask the question: What difference would it make to customer X if we could customize our product for him in a particular way or deliver to him in one-half the time it now takes? For example, if we are a magazine publisher, what is it worth to our largest advertiser if we develop a new variant of an existing magazine whose content and format are targeted directly to a particularly important customer group? This line of thought gets you into your customer's imagination and what he or she could do with the right product or channel. It allows you to hypothetically manipulate revenue streams and capture rates, and figure out what would radically change the customer's business. Then you can more readily help him or her do that. It's likely that if you become a big link in the revolutionizing of that business, the first move was yours, not theirs. It's hard to find a more win/win situation than showing your customers a way to higher profits via your help.

A case in point is a building materials producer who sells to distributors, who in turn sell to several customer groups. The distributors' two largest customer groups are large contractors and small prefab manufacturers. Since these two customer groups provide the distributors' volume base load, distributors pay most attention to them. The building materials producer assigned two people—one from marketing, the other from production—to do a time-based segmentation of distributors' customers. By going to distributors and watching various customer groups' lead time and product mix demands, they found a group—small contractors on upscale jobs—who demanded exactly what the building materials producer's new flexible plant could produce and who were willing to pay 20–30 percent more to get small quantities of what they needed the same day. The two people brought this to the attention of selected distributors, and together they set up an ordering and delivery channel to service this segment. It's now the most profitable customer group for both the manufacturer and distributor.

Learning to think in terms of small segments is part of becoming a time-based competitor. Think about how more speed might change your best customers' fortunes and then figure out how to do it. It helps to have the stretch goal in a concrete form with a well-considered dollar value attached. Organizations respond to this better than to abstract targets.

PILOTS AND BREAKTHROUGH TEAMS

Pilots are a good way to energize those parts of the organization where good people are ready to go and where local trial-and-error experimentation is the right way to get solutions. It's important to keep the rest of the company out of the pilot undertaking. This means buffering it physically and politically. If necessary, build up a temporary stock of materials or data between the pilot unit and those with which it interacts. Keep senior people with turf issues out of the pilot itself and put them on a group at the end that interprets the pilots' results. Let specialists into the pilots only at the request of the operators.

Examples. Six salespeople in a field office decide that they need to spend more time with customers and less in administration. They come up with a plan, which includes new data links and better software for field reporting, and review it with the regional head. One company information system specialist of their choosing is included in the pilot, and together they rig up prototype data links and buy the closest off-the-shelf software. Only after they demonstrate that it works and get other sales offices excited do they bring in the information systems department and the controller to start to budget and build something, based on the pilot concept, suitable for the whole company. Experiment before specifying, and involve small groups before large groups.

A construction equipment company decides it needs to take half the time out of its new product development process. There are at least seven key functions—product marketing, product engineering, research center, manufacturing engineering, tooling, purchasing, and test engineering—involved. This product line manager had earlier tried to reduce development time but had failed. His process had involved all seven heads at once and had gotten bogged down in complexity; in addition, two heads—test and tooling—had opposed any change in procedure. This time the line manager took three heads committed to change—marketing, product engineering, and manufacturing engineering—and told them to simply begin developing a new product around some basic time-based principles and to shape the process as they went. They were given permission to go outside the organization to buy any services they wanted if internal functions weren't flexible. The three did just that when tooling and test people said what they wanted couldn't or shouldn't be done. The pilot was a success, vindicating the product-line manager's hard ball approach. Tooling and testing have managed to change. A set of old chestnuts has been broken.

Pilots work best when demonstration is the right first step and when a local manager already has a pretty good broad idea of the change he or she wants and knows it can get done if not exactly how. Having the critical pilot drivers in place, in this case the three function heads, is a prerequisite.

There are, however, other cross-functional situations where issues are harder to define, where no one has a general solution in mind, and where there is no natural champion to whom everyone involved reports. Here breakthrough teams can be useful. They are select groups of usually four to six leading middle managers chartered for a few months to think through new, radical solutions. A typical large company might have several breakthrough teams operating in the early stages of a time-based transition. Following are some typical charters:

- How to cut the customer order-to-shipment cycle in half
- How to accelerate cost estimating for new products and engineering changes
- How to establish an around-the-clock global short-term money management function in the company

- How to ensure that all suppliers get the same order and schedule information at the same time the company does
- How to accelerate the transfer of a successful product from one country's organization to another inside a multinational company

These teams are one-time solution-finding teams, not permanent working teams. Their members are the most capable middle managers from the parts of the organization involved in the cycle, so they know the problems and the difference between paper and real solutions. Part of the breakthrough team experience is to get them talking without day-to-day problems grinding at them, to get them to see the whole system. Their charter is to drop assumptions about how the company works and to come up with a better way. The aim is not a highly polished, no-loose-ends presentation, but rather the core workings of a way to do things that is dramatically better and faster.

Experience suggests that these teams must be given radical goals, like collapsing time in half. Otherwise, assumptions aren't challenged. The whole premise is using bottlenecks, breakdowns, and unmet customer needs as opportunities to learn. The teams use a variety of techniques—root-cause analysis, scenario building, pursuing conflict between two people until the real problem crystalizes, and old-fashioned imagination. Between regular meetings, research into technical or other problems is done. There are no formal reports to the team members' superiors. The teams report to a senior steering group that is responsible for all the breakthrough teams operating. This steering group is responsible for managing change under the time-based vision that the management team has decided to pursue.

One example is a breakthrough team that was chartered to compress the cost-estimating cycle for new parts inside an automobile company. Formerly, the cycle took two to three weeks as each function added its step serially and passed the work package on. Exhibit 7–7 shows this. Product engineering prepared the blueprints, manufacturing engineering developed routings, industrial engineering added labor standards, purchasing quoted purchased parts, finance added burden rates, and sales priced the part. This cost-estimating cycle had the classic earmarks of a loosely managed serial process. No one was accountable for the cycle; it was buried among many others. There were numerous handoffs, with each function playing a limited role. Because decision rules were formal and timely interaction was difficult, it was hard to catch inappropriate numbers until late in the process.

Exhibit 7–7 Cost Estimating Procedure—Before and After
Breakthrough Team

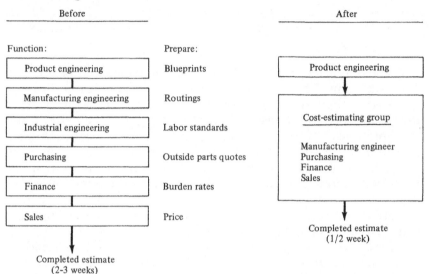

And it slowed down the whole process of quoting prices for new parts.

A breakthrough team representing these functions developed a solution over a set of five meetings. Looking at several case histories, the team determined that new parts fell into a few classes, and that parts within a class had similar costing characteristics. The team developed a set of procedures and rules, including notes on how to identify problems. It had interviewed all users of the cost estimates and their functional department heads, so it knew the real issues.

The team's recommendation was a standing closed-loop cost-estimating cell of four members that met twice a week to process all of product engineering's new blueprints. All the work was done in one room, with no formal handoffs. Difficult cases were researched off-line and settled at the next meeting. The group had a chairman. Once the cell was up and running, the members rotated off every six months in staggered fashion. The average cycle time dropped to one-half week, and the quality of work improved.

Each problem breakthrough teams address is different, but here are some common principles of solutions applied in time-based companies:

• Align organizations, authority, data collection, scheduling, etc., with the main sequence.

- Pass the best information upstream fast.
- Continuously measure performance and performance improvements.
- Make debottlenecking investments in people and in equipment.
- Do not allow a support activity to gate the main sequence. Either eliminate it, carry deliberate excess capacity, or take it off-line.
- Work out a triage among required processes and tasks, and realign work flow.
- Use parallel processing as much as possible.
- Reduce batch sizes, and execute each batch more frequently.
- Synchronize operations; especially, balance the cycle time across different mix loads so that downstream activities are not held up by mix variations.
- Do not allow incomplete work to be passed on.
- Eliminate causes of rework at the source.
- Understand the process and where its performance leverage points are before you prescribe changes.
- Do not compromise the above principles for the sake of keeping peace among team members.

Breakthrough teams, taken together, redesign the work of the company. Each charter has to be sufficiently large and cross-functional to make a real difference in time compression that customers can see and that strategists can exploit. Cost estimating in the example above was a modest-sized charter and took only five weeks to design and be up and running. Designing new simultaneous information systems for suppliers, in contrast, can take several months to crack and involve twice as many people. The steering group that charters and integrates the breakthroughs becomes the principal orchestrator of the change. The number of teams is important. Setting up too many teams will fragment the problem and fail to confront the real issues of organizational complexity and distance. Too few teams will overwhelm each team with an impossible charter. Breakthrough teams should be set up to succeed.

Breakthrough teams, or something comparable, are especially useful for making organizationally complex changes, where analysis should precede action. Analysis is needed because the solution isn't obvious and different parts of the company have to be involved. These teams are the backbone of a company's move toward time compression and can be mobilized quickly. Teams can shape recommendations early and draw reaction. Once a solution takes shape, it can be refined during implementation. Breakthrough teams lose effectiveness if they stand too long.

In this way, the change process is neither top down nor bottom up, but really driven from the middle and coordinated at the top by those who settled on the vision. The able middle managers are in the best position to do the cutting-edge learning that will reshape the company's practices. They are junior enough to know the particulars of what will work and what won't, and senior enough to grasp the larger picture. Equally important, they will be among those implementing the new systems that they design, positioning them to continue learning. Companies don't become time-based in one shot, and it's the capacity to compound learning—the learning to learn—that distinguishes successful time-based companies. Keeping the best middle managers in the learning loop from design through implementation gives them the feedback they need to come up with the next round of improvements.

REORGANIZATION EMERGES

The best approach to becoming time-based is to structure the company around the flow of work that customers value and to depend more on the middle of the organization to discover this flow and reshape the company's operations accordingly. This method rests on the belief that senior management can only create visions and motivate change; it cannot prescribe the solutions and reorganize operations from the top. Scholars and practitioners often observe that American companies are stronger on control than on coordination, and that Japanese companies look more to management process and sources of leverage than to tidy structure. Time-based companies build coordination and process strength. Companies whose first instinct when trying to improve performance is to reorganize or restructure operations will usually compromise their opportunities.

Reorganizing or restructuring operations should generally follow, not precede, pilots and breakthrough teams. These exploratory mechanisms help management decide such questions as—What should departments have in them? Where should authority and responsibility rest? How many layers are necessary? Operations are organisms, not mechanisms; no one can correctly design them at much of a distance. The right organizational structure should emerge after operating managers have wrestled with meeting radical time-based goals. Becoming time based is more of a creative and less of a formal process than is a one-time management event like overhead value analysis. It happens in an irregular series of big and little steps. Improving a big step at the wrong time—like installing an expensive new information system or organizing too many product-based profit centers that share a main sequence—can be expensive.

At the same time, the process of becoming a time-based company requires strong senior management leadership and steering. It involves several senior actions—developing a vision, assessing managers several levels down, chartering pilots and breakthrough teams, reading their results, and modifying the whole process as it proceeds. Senior management must also resolve major tensions that surface along the way. For example, radical prescriptions will usually challenge the prerogatives of some decentralized line managers or senior function heads. At this point, these people have to be reminded that decentralization of operations doesn't preclude rethinking, or mean that some operations cannot occasionally be centralized.

And senior managers who begin to move their organizations toward time compression face an inescapable dilemma: How do we achieve faster cycles in the long run without being badly damaged by work interruptions in the short term? Most organizations cover their delays and errors with slack resources and loosely fitting interfaces. But when a company begins to compress its cycles, the delays and errors can rarely be fixed as quickly as the slack is taken away. Temporary breakdowns occur, and fast response to customers—the whole objective—is undermined. Every management must find its own pace and mechanisms to walk this tightrope. More pilots can be done. Dynamic computer simulations can help predict problems. More temporary buffers can be added. But what's critical is that managers keep pushing the change process and not suspend their efforts when the inevitable problems arise.

SUSTAINING IMPROVEMENT

The foregoing prescription for becoming a time-based competitor—radical vision, breakthrough teams, with top management involved and leading the way—is the jump-start. A large organization at any given time is invested in a way of doing business that carries with it a set of expectations and implied standards for what is good. The slower the industry rate of change, the more is invested. Even successful organizations experience inertia. The companies that over a period of years dramatically compress time start by overcoming inertia: They set new goals, discard old routines, and celebrate new approaches that work better. Leaders get this done by mobilizing the best people in their organization. This is the jump-start, and it is always a radical, stressful period. It is also eventually highly satisfying.

This high energy start-up does change measurable performance in the short term, but its main function is to overcome inertia by establishing the new paradigm and by building momentum in new directions. It puts more energy into the organization than will show up early in improved numbers. But the short-term improvement can still be significant. Table 7–1 shows what several companies accomplished during their jump-start periods, which ranged from five to ten months. Most were able to halve the cycle time of the activities they targeted, and they got measurable benefits in the market, ranging from better price realization to share gains.

The early momentum is by no means self-sustaining, however. Early successes are often achieved in those parts of the company where thoughtful people knew big improvements could be made (although not exactly how), and they are the work of the company's more able, motivated employees. But momentum can be blunted if tough problems go unsolved or if hastily convened teams compromise their solutions for easy, incremental gains that leave the company basically unchanged. If key managers stop driving the process, if the old measures are still the ones that really matter, and if problem people aren't taken off the critical path, progress will grind to a halt. The same thing may happen if time-compression efforts grow mainly out of an earnings shortfall. Once the market comes back, the effort will probably die.

Sustaining the effort requires institutionalizing the basics of the process:

- Monitoring progress against the vision, and emphasizing the gap that still exists

- Continuing to benchmark the best time-based performers (They won't stand still; they'll get better.)

- Involving key managers in driving the next set of pilots and breakthrough teams and making sure that goals are not compromised

- Taking people from early teams that completed their work successfully and seeding new teams that are attacking difficult

TABLE 7–1 Examples of Successful Jump-Starts

Industry	Early Time-based Focus	Early Benefits	Time Frame (Months)
Auto components	Order processing; plant operations	Cycle time reduced 50%; market share slide arrested	8
Telephone equipment	New product development	Cycle time cut 40%; new product introductions up 55%	9
Insurance	New policy applications; claims processing	Cycle time reduced 45%; productivity up 15%	10
Specialty paper	Total system, from order to distribution to customer	Cycle time reduced 30%; price realization up 10%; reversed market share slide	8
Commercial bank	Consumer loan approvals	Cycle time reduced 70%; new applications up 25%	7
Packaged food product	Transplanting successful products to global markets	Cycle time reduced 65%; preempt growth segment in Europe, profits up 25%	5

problems with them, demonstrating that the company values the process, not just the first results

- Following up by formally instituting a new set of measures and rewards, and phasing out the old ones
- Granting capital spending authorizations for proposals that promote time compression, like distributed information networking; and denying proposals for new plant and equipment that won't be necessary if cycle times are reduced
- Communicating the principles and objectives to all constituencies again and again, including employees, suppliers, customers, union leaders, and others

The real benefits come from sustained effort over years, not months. This applies not just to the numbers, but to the learning as well. Companies learn how to learn by having a group make a difficult change, by thinking and talking about what the group did that made the difference, then by continuing to use elsewhere the practices that made the difference. The dramatic time-based improvements made by major divisions of big companies—the consumer products division of AT&T, the copier business at Xerox, and the construction equipment division of Deere—worked just this way. These businesses are different now because their people *expect* each other to continue to entertain changes and therefore to make continuous improvements. Once this expectation is lost, continuous improvement will stop.

Good companies have always made continuous improvement. It's implicit in the experience curve institutionalized in many companies' thinking in the 1970s. The experience curve traced the rate of decline in real costs per unit for aggressive competitors in an industry and found costs continued to decline as experience in the business accumulated. The best operations, like Hillenbrand Industries, which dominates in hospital beds and coffins, or ICI in chemical fertilizers, maintain their rate of improvement over years and years. It happens in low-tech as well as in high-tech industries, and in low-growth as well as in high-growth markets. Continuous improvement is a function of management—not of technologies or growth rates.

The experience curve applies to time as well as to cost. For example, the automobile company shown in Table 7–1 cut its cost-estimating cycle from two or three weeks to one-half week by moving from loosely managed functional specialists working independently to a closed-loop cell. The next move was to automate some of the information flow and to reduce the team by one member. Some team members had become multifunctional enough to allow this. This reduced cycle time even more. Future time compressions will probably involve simplifying and standardizing the information that comes from the engineers upstream. Eventually, the whole cost-estimating function may be folded into the organization and disappear as a discrete cycle.

Where continuous improvement will come from in the future is not always clear. In fact, if companies knew what the next changes had to be, they would make them. But there is a tool that can help, especially with processes that can be studied, such as production or distribution. Root-cause diagrams can help lay out a continuous improvement agenda for the future. Exhibit

7–8 shows such a diagram for a typical machine setup in a high-variety plant. Each step going from left to right takes the problem back further into root causes. The exhibit shows causes four levels down, and each level compounds the number of things to get done. Such a chart can organize the relevant challenges for coordinating the efforts of a machine cell crew.

Institutionalizing the management process that gets time compression started is the first condition for sustaining time improvement. But to keep time-based learning going, a company needs rapid feedback loops in all its activities. Learning slows and dissipates when the results of decisions or actions are late reaching the people directly involved.

Here are some examples of rapid feedback loops:

- Implement early prototyping in everything from new-product development to competitive intelligence research projects. Force participants to put together preliminary product early, even when major issues are still unresolved.

Exhibit 7–8 Root Cause Analysis Showing Path of Continuing Improvement for a Factory Set-up

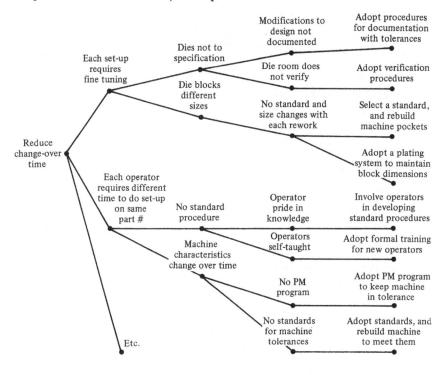

This gives everyone involved the big picture and shows where the holes are.

- Apply continuous market research at low levels of intensity using people from various functions, as opposed to conducting episodic big studies. With the latter, too much is missed and attitudes harden in between. At Du Pont, even production workers, not just salespeople and product engineers, visit key customers to learn their needs firsthand.

- Organize colocation of as many parts of a business as possible.

- Require a continuous flow of proposed engineering changes to supervisors, with no dollar value minimum on submitted changes. One engineering supervisor told his engineers to concentrate on major changes, so no small ones were forthcoming. Competitors were hurting the company badly in the market with a stream of small but useful changes.

- Monitor new-product launches early, tracking not just sales and customer satisfaction, but engineering, packaging, and other aspects of performance. The sooner the company can learn which product versions and sales approaches are working best, the more it can emphasize them and the faster it can build volume. This is true regardless of how long the market conversion is projected to take.

- Shorten the economic lives of equipment. Many companies bias their purchases toward longer-lived equipment, citing lower depreciation costs. But shorter-lived equipment may force more frequent process reviews among key departments, opening opportunities for improvement.

- Conduct frequent performance evaluations, both between supervisor and subordinate and among peer team members.

- Develop in-house proprietary techniques, such as engineering design algorithms, performance evaluation forms, and market research segmentation descripters. Using mainly off-the-shelf techniques simply perpetuates someone else's view of the problem and prevents the company's employees' light bulbs from switching on.

There is one other condition for continuous improvement, and that is growth of the business. Market share is nice and in many businesses it's a major advantage, but growth is essential. Vital organizations grow regardless of the industry's growth rate. Growth forces you to get new customers and new problems. Growth makes your people change the way they spend their day. Growth makes your company create new segments or cross existing boundaries to encounter new competitors. The longer you grow, the longer you can put off the day when your business is "mature" and your organization is "settled." If that day comes, you have a real management problem on your hands.

CHAPTER

8

◇◇◇◇

Using Time to Help Your Customers and Suppliers Compete

B uying a car in Hungary can be puzzling: a used car often costs more than the same car brand new. We're not talking about an antique but a garden variety used car that will cost more to repair and that has a shorter life ahead than does the new model just coming off the assembly line. The reason for this price inversion is simple—time. A used car in Hungary is available any time you want it. A new car, on the other hand, can take up to two years for delivery. And the people who have enough money to buy a car want it now.

This problem, which highly structured socialist economies usually have, can be thought of as a supply chain problem. In the automobile business, the sequence of activities that precedes assembling a vehicle—raising capital, obtaining raw materials, building steel capacity, getting delivery from component suppliers—is the supply chain that really determines how successful the car industry will be and how fast it can grow. Under any economic system, each of these levels in the chain depends on the others. In a typical socialist economy, though, each level in the chain is also controlled by a different ministry with its own agenda, which doesn't fully overlap any of the others. As a result, the chain easily gets bogged down in shortages and in bureaucratic gridlock. For example, auto demand may be high but steel capacity lagging because of a capital shortage. Or two ministers may be fighting.

Regardless of the cause, car production slows down, and customers look for alternatives, in this case used cars and repair shops. For used cars, the supply chain is very short and market driven—a current owner simply decides to sell to a buyer when the price is high enough. But for new cars, the supply chain is long and driven by conflicting forces unconnected to the market.

In capitalist economies, the supply chain works much better for producers. Higher prices trigger new capacity. Suppliers are held to schedules. If a customer is unhappy with one supplier, he or she can get another. The market system we live under nearly always gives us options. As producers, we can pick the customers and suppliers with whom we want to do business, and picking the right ones can be an important factor in how successful we are in our business.

SUPPLY CHAIN LEADERS

Today, creative producers are taking this a step further by making supply chains work even more closely with them. These companies are actually helping their suppliers and customers to compete more effectively at their own levels and in doing so are helping the whole chain compete more effectively. For example, some years ago J.C. Penney, always strong in soft goods, was looking for a new hardware product that could build traffic in that area of the store. The retailer worked closely with an automotive battery supplier to come up with the first mass market long-life battery. Both companies succeeded in expanding their markets through this collaborative R&D effort. Another firm, Milliken, directly impacts the speed of the supply chain to help its customers compete. Milliken, the best large textile company in America, helps U.S. apparel manufacturers compete against lower-priced imports by shortening the time an apparel retailer has to wait to have its order filled and on the store shelf. Imported apparel has long lead times, so in higher-priced seasonal or fashion product lines, the retailer can afford to pay higher prices to a manufacturer who delivers much faster. Milliken organizes the whole supply chain from yarn to garment maker for faster response than imports, and thereby helps defend its own business as well as the U.S. apparel makers'.

It is now more important than ever for a company to think of itself as one player in an interdependent chain of companies competing against other chains for the ultimate customer at the end. One reason is technology. More end products, from personal computers to automobiles, depend on a delicate design match between the end product and components purchased from suppliers. The Japanese technology-based firms have demonstrated the value of picking one or two suppliers and developing the relationship. Another reason is time. Customers want to hold down inventories and so insist on shorter lead times from suppliers. This pressure on lead time travels up and down the supply chain. The best way to shorten the lead time for delivery of the final product is to collapse the time that all players in the chain spend waiting for each other. If one of your key, trusted suppliers is regularly making others in the chain wait for him, every company in the chain is jeopardized.

You can think of the supply side of the U.S. economy as many interlocking supply chains, and in most of these there are customer and supplier relationships that last for years. So there is a lot of opportunity to talk about what each could do differently to compress time in the chain as a whole. Many customer–supplier pairs share general information about upcoming new products and about short-run demand forecasts. Most suppliers use this information to work on anticipating a good customer's order pattern and special needs, so that they can respond quickly to a sudden request. In fact, some have moved to just-in-time delivery patterns. But, still, relatively few have gone beyond these items of obvious common interest into issues that very much affect how effective the chain can be but that traditionally have not been talked about between companies.

Here we're talking about the specific ways in which a company determines how much inventory it is going to hold, or how a customer decides what amount of product it needs from its key suppliers and when. Few companies when they redesign their internal information systems think about including key customers and/or suppliers into their systems. Yet these supply chain factors have major effects on market success. Clearly, companies that buy and sell from each other will do better as an overall chain if they set inventory policies together, not separately. Cost and time can be drained from the chain if suppliers know immediately the customer's rate of usage of their products rather than having to wait to receive orders from the purchasing department. And information systems that are built together by the chain of companies around the needs of users will help these firms outperform competitors.

Throughout this book, we have been highlighting the current performance difference between traditional cost-focused companies and their time-based competitors. The same comparison can be made between supply chains. The longer and more complex the chain, the greater will be the difference in performance. Take retailing, for example. Each retailer stands at the top of a chain that links at least four tiers of companies—raw material suppliers that sell to intermediate product makers that in turn sell to final product manufacturers that finally sell to the retailer. Today's best retailers don't just carefully pick a final product supplier and hope all goes well back through the supply chain. Today's best are involved throughout the chain, managing the removal of time and cost at and between any levels they can. Today's stand-out retailers—The Limited, Wal-Mart, Toys "R" Us, and others—are time-based chain managers, and that's a major reason they are on top.

Just as retailers like The Limited are leaders in supply chain management, so are manufacturers like Milliken and Ford. These companies lead by working to make the companies with which they do business more aware of opportunities, by bringing them together, and showing them time-based concepts and technology, and by rewarding with more business those who act accordingly. Every chain needs a leader—a powerful player who steps forward and organizes the effort. In autos, it's Ford. In apparel, it's Milliken. Supply chains are like any group that works together over a long period. They can bump along with business as usual and make improvements one at a time. Or they can get together and agree that they could do a whole lot better if they reassessed how they work together and challenged some old practices. A more traditional company might only feel comfortable challenging its direct suppliers. Supply chain leaders challenge the whole group.

All of these leaders are interested in the same thing—overcoming the inertia of longstanding relationships in order to compress the time it takes the chain to do its normal work and to increase the variety-carrying capacity of the chain. Toy store shelves, automobile showrooms, and apparel shops all offer more product variety today. The problem that all these businesses face is how to serve consumers who want that variety available all the time without keeping their suppliers swimming in inventory at every level. This is the big issue that keeps store managers and suppliers awake at night.

Supply chain leaders intent on time compression work with their chains on three fronts: first, they work to provide each company in the chain with better and more timely information about orders, new products, and special needs; second, they help members of the chain, including themselves, to shorten work cycles by removing the obstacles to compression that one company often unwittingly imposes on another; third, they synchronize lead times and capacities among the levels or among tiers of the supply chain so that more work can flow in a coordinated fashion up and down the chain. Each of these three fronts is demanding, and it takes a big effort to get the various companies in the chain cooperating in all these areas. But the results are worth it.

BETTER AND FRESHER INFORMATION

Every supply chain can be visualized as a vertical system made up of several companies, one on top of the other, which are regularly sending and receiving information and products between one layer and the next. The information exchanged between levels in a chain is of many different types—new product specification, new orders from customer to supplier, forthcoming product introductions from supplier to customer, suggestions about how to solve problems and so forth. The products can be anything from raw materials to finished products that are made at one level and then sold to the next value-adding level.

Exhibit 8–1 is a very simple chain, but it will demonstrate the value of timely information. The top level is a retailer, the second level is an apparel maker, the third is a fabric maker, and the fourth is a yarn maker. The regular day-to-day business of this chain is moving orders down the chain and moving products back

Exhibit 8–1 A Simple Supply Chain

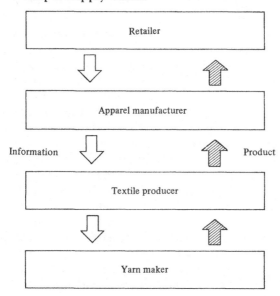

up. That is, a retailer places orders, say for blue jeans, to a blue jean maker, which in turn places orders to a denim fabric maker, which orders from a yarn maker. Shipments go in the reverse order—yarn is shipped to fabric makers, which ship to jean makers, which ship to retailers. All of these activities go on continuously, driven by the following forces: demand in the market, inventory levels at each of the four tiers in the chain, and the rules governing production lot sizes that each player uses to run its business.

Let's see how this simple system reacts to changes in the volume of information that one level sends to another. Let's assume retail demand has been drifting slowly down during the past year. Each level has been gradually reducing the amount it orders from its suppliers and, in turn, each supplier has been producing and shipping just a little less each month. Inventories are also drifting down. Suddenly, there's an unforeseen surge in retail demand for blue jeans as the fashion cycle turns. The retailer has been slowly liquidating inventory that she considered too high and sees this surge as welcome. She doesn't reverse her gradually declining monthly order to the blue jean maker because she believes the surge may be random and short-lived. Instead she draws on inventory for two months. After the third month of the surge, the retailer becomes convinced demand will stay strong and raises her monthly order.

The retailer now realizes that she not only needs higher regular inventory levels than before to support a higher level of sales but also needs to start replenishing inventory lost during the two-month surge. So her new order to the jean maker is larger than the rise in sales she's been experiencing. The jean maker meanwhile has been gradually liquidating his denim inventory all the while retail demand was rising, because the retailer's signals to the jean maker—declining monthly orders during the first two months of surge—were downward. Now, the blue jeans maker is hit with a sudden large order. He reads the retail press saying blue jean sales are up, but he is filled up with late orders on other apparel this month and cannot change production schedules for a month. Besides he wants to see if the retailers' monthly order will be high again next month before he sets up for blue jean production and steps up his denim orders.

But the next month, the fourth month of the surge, the retailer's order stays high—because she's still replenishing inventory lost during the surge—and the blue jean maker places an order to the denim maker that's even larger than the retailer's order to him. The blue jean maker suddenly realizes that he needs to replenish his inventories and fill the retailer's order and move his regular inventories to higher levels than before to cope with the rise in demand.

Of course the denim maker has also been liquidating inventory and must do a radical about-face. The jean maker's order is so large that the denim maker will have to run his machines all month to fill it. Because the jean maker is one of his biggest and best customers, he will have to bump off the production schedule other customers' orders. He will have to somehow deal with these customers. And of course, he will now be very low on raw materials, which will prompt a huge order to his cotton yarn suppliers—and so it goes.

This story is frequently repeated in business. Consumer demand month-to-month varies and cycles. The changes may be up or down 10–15 percent. But back in the supply chain, the changes in orders get larger and larger as each supplier further down the chain struggles to catch up from the last ripple in the demand curve. Weeks or months may pass between the first sign of a retail demand rise and the time a low-level supplier finally hears about it in the form of an order that's up, say, 30–35 percent over the last order. This is called amplification of order changes and is a continuing source of late orders, excessive inventories, and high overheads in industry.

The root problem here is the timeliness of information. Most companies, like our retailer and blue jean maker, still use traditional procedures to determine how much and when to reorder from suppliers and still have little regular contact with suppliers beyond the order channel. In our blue jeans example, the retailer provided no information to her supply chain about the rise in sales for nearly three months, then sent a discontinuously large order, which represented a mixture of greater demand and replenishment of depleted inventory. The blue jean maker, while he has read that there's a general sales rise for blue jeans, doesn't know about this particular retail customer's increased sales for nearly three months. And when the large order arrives, he doesn't know how much of the order volume represents a sales increase and how much represents a one-time inventory replenishment. So the blue jean maker gets information that's both late and hard to interpret.

Then the blue jean maker compounds the lateness of information and amplifications of the order when he passes it on to his supplier. He waits a month to reorder because he has been liquidating inventory and has been in a contraction mindset. So it takes him a month to reverse his expectations, and then he acts by amplifying the order yet again to cover for the month of unexpected inventory depletion that he's experienced. Meanwhile, the denim maker still has no information about the tidal wave heading his way, and because he is further from the blue jean market and makes many other fabrics, he is the least prepared to be deluged by the sudden order. The only way he can cope is to delay some of his other customers' shipments.

To compensate for these perverse dynamics in supply chains, companies carry buffer inventories and extra overhead in the form of expediters and schedulers to handle sudden demands as well as extra capacity. Each tier or level in the supply chain carries additional inventory, and as product variety increases, this means more and more grades, sizes, colors, and so on of inventory. Each level learns to delay nonpriority orders to make way for those that are late or that are critical to fill on time. Every time production schedules change to move critical orders ahead, all the work-in-process associated with the end product that's being moved aside represents capacity that has been wasted and lead time that has been lost forever. The capacity is wasted because it was used to make work-in-process that now just sits, instead of to make the product that's now being expedited.

And all of this rescheduling and coping with amplification takes management. More people are needed to monitor and manage the disjointed flows and to deal with the customers and suppliers who are being pushed around.

The underlying problem here is that once information ages, it loses value. This causes the supply system to lose time and money. Once order information flowing through the chain loses any resemblance to the real end-product demand, the actions taken on the basis of that information have more and more costs and unintended side effects. In our example, the old data caused amplifications, delay, and overhead. They are inevitable once the data ages. And huge buffer inventories to "smooth" all these sudden shifts just cover up the core problem. The only way out of this disjointed supply system between companies is to compress information time so that the information circulating through the system is fresh and meaningful.

An example of one evolving solution to this problem of distorted information and costly side effects is that of a supply chain in health care products. This chain has four key tiers—hospitals, distributors, end product manufacturers, and raw material suppliers. It was suffering classic symptoms of a disjointed supply chain: lengthening lead times, higher overheads, and more inventory at each tier. The companies finally got fed up with this and got together to study the problem. They discovered that the root causes were late and distorted information flows starting from the top of the chain, the hospitals. To deal with these, the chain made some dramatic changes in the way it created and managed information:

- The frequency of orders from one level to the next was increased from monthly or biweekly to weekly and in some cases daily.

- For products where demand varied sharply across the variety range, hospitals gave their actual product usage data to distributors on a daily basis.

- Distributors were able to analyze these usage data to discern trends, which they promptly communicated to manufacturers to help them plan their scheduling. In effect, an information channel beyond simply placing orders was established.

- In order to limit the amplification, a size limit was placed on the change in orders so that orders from one week to the next could not go up or down by more than a fixed amount. This made it easier for suppliers down the chain to fill all orders on time and with a minimum of disruption to their operations. It also forced customers to be sensitive to emerging trends and to translate changes in their sales into changes in orders to suppliers quickly. The problem of the blue jean retailer who waited over two months to signal her suppliers of a demand rise is avoided.

- Electronic data interchange was installed between the levels so that information could be received with no delay. The simple presence of this new channel also stimulated new ideas about using it to produce new kinds of information.

The distributor's analysis of the hospital's usage data has shown that the hospital's weekly patient mix mainly determines the mix of products actually used and reordered. In other words, knowing the patient intake can help the hospital predict its next week's usage and order. The distributor now uses this information in forecasts and orders. This, plus the electronic data interchange, gives manufacturers earlier and better information on the mix they should be scheduling in their plant. And finally, for the first time in 15 years, overhead as a percent of sales, is declining.

These changes were developed and phased in over an 18-month period, and the supply chain is now working far more smoothly. All the symptoms have been reduced, which is no accident because they were all related in the first place. Lead times had been long because the size of orders varied so much that the distributor and manufacturers could not fill them from normal inventories and production schedules. This also meant that inventories would be high one month and low the next as large orders with an unpredictable mix crashed through the system periodically. Moreover, as additional people were hired to cope with all this, overhead had grown.

Now the amplification of orders through the system has subsided because of more frequent orders and limits on period-to-period changes. So the inventories, both finished and work-in-process, that are needed to keep the system going are about one-third of what they were. Lead time is now only 40 percent of what it was, and as lead times come down, the need to place big, speculative orders has diminished. Therefore, more frequent and stable orders and shorter and reliable lead times reinforce each other.

The lessons from this experience are clear. Accelerate the flow of good, current demand-based information, and get bad information out of the system. Late, reactive, amplified, and batched information is bad. Develop a lead time number that customers can live with if it is met reliably, then stick to it. Develop a set of rules about frequency and about change limits of orders and stick with them. This health care products supply chain has done these things, and life is a whole lot easier.

COLLAPSING CHAIN-CYCLE TIMES

A supply chain has compressed its collective cycle when the top company in the chain—the retailer or the end manufacturer—can deliver the product to its customer with short lead times and without carrying excessive inventory at every level. Benetton, for example, revolutionized the fashion sport and casual wear business in the mid-1980s by creating the ability of its U.S. retailers to replenish their shelves with a made-to-order garment from Italy in three weeks. Before this, imported sportswear replenishment times had been about three months. Benetton did a great job of collapsing cycle time by getting order information back to Italy quickly and organizing the cut-and-sew and dye houses to work in fast-turnaround, small-lot cycles. So Benetton could keep its retail shelves full of the colors and styles that were currently selling without carrying piles of inventory in its pipeline.

To compress a whole chain's cycle time, companies have to coordinate in new ways. The system's total time problem will not be solved by each company working independently to compress its own cycle. There are also too many reasons why a company won't spontaneously make the changes needed to help the whole cycle. Actions have to be taken together by pairs or groups of companies.

The clearest opportunity to compress chain time is probably in the area of duplicate buffer stocks. Each customer usually holds buffer inventory in incoming goods in the very same form that its supplier holds inventory in its outgoing area. For example, a refrigerator manufacturer will hold a safety stock of compressors received from its supplier, who in turn will hold some units for the refrigerator manufacturer that have not yet been ordered. Both hold them against the same contingencies—a sudden demand surge, a mix change, or a supplier breakdown. However, both usually calculate how many to hold in this buffer status as if the other party held none at all. The redundancy costs time and money. The problem is that the customer doesn't want to rely totally on the supplier, and the supplier doesn't want to run the risk of shutting down the customer's production line. So because they can't get together, buffer inventory is doubled.

Another opportunity exists when the customer and supplier work in series when they could be working in parallel. For example, the compressor manufacturer traditionally makes engineering improvements on his product, then notifies the refrigerator manufacturer of them once they are complete. Then the refrigerator producer makes any design changes in his product that are necessary to accommodate the improved compressor. The rationale for this protocol is a logical one. The compressor maker retains commercial security for its product until it's launched, and the refrigerator maker avoids the need to make any changes in its product before the compressor's improvements are all proven and available to ship. The group in each company responsible for a trouble-free handoff of new compressors to refrigerator engineers believes it is optimizing for its company. Yet the process is suboptimal from the standpoint of the chain. Both manufacturers could have their new products in appliance showrooms months sooner if the two sets of engineers collaborated on changes earlier.

These are everyday problems in chain suboptimization that most companies experience. They result from policies and habits that keep good employees' sights trained on correct but narrow targets. And until principals from the two companies meet and put together a picture of what time compression across the chain would be worth to each company, these problems will not be overcome.

The automotive seat business is a good example of what can happen when companies in a chain start looking at an opportunity together. This chain has four levels of interest to us here:

1. An automotive assembly plant that assembles finished seats into an automobile
2. An auto seat maker, who buys a seat frame, foam cushions, and seat cover fabric and manufactures the complete seat
3. A seat cover fabric maker
4. A yarn supplier who sells to the fabric maker

The challenge for this chain is to keep up with the ever-changing needs of the auto assembly plant. Car buyers have a choice of color, fabric, and mechanical seat type, so the variety of different finished seats the chain must produce is large. In fact, the number of combinations is several hundred. Moreover, auto assembly plants in the United States sometimes change the assembly schedule, hence the mix of seats needed; so the chain has to be flexible.

Exhibit 8–2 shows a cumulative elapsed time bar for these four companies. It was put together by a team of people representing the four companies whose mission was to measure the chain's cycle and to recommend ways of compressing it. Their first finding surprised them: the four levels together used 71 days to provide and assemble a finished seat. This was the sum of all days in the system—whether spent adding value to product, moving product in transit, or having product wait in queues or sit in inventory. Of these 71 days, only 19 were spent adding value or moving product

Exhibit 8–2 Supply Chain for Automotive Seat Covers

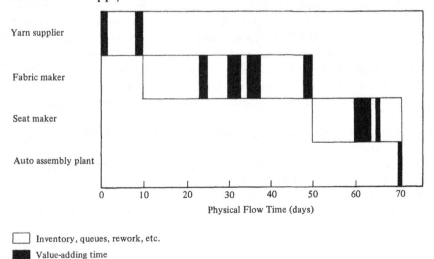

in transit, represented by dark slices in the exhibit. The other 52 days, represented in the exhibit as white spaces, were spent in inventories or queues.

The team went to work exploring these 71 days, first the white spaces and then the dark. It was found that 18 days worth of dyed and finished fabric were in inventory. In part this was because fabric makers were not coordinating safety stock with seat makers and so had more than enough between them to cover schedule changes and supply breakdowns. However, there was a real need to keep finished fabric stocks because the assembly plant often gave the seat maker very short notice of changes in the assembly schedule. The team also found 20 days of yarn inventory in the system, again in part because of duplicated buffers between the yarn house and fabric maker, but also because both the yarn- and fabric-making processes had long set-up times and very long economic production run lengths.

The team dug deeper into these 38 days of fabric and yarn inventory. Before addressing cycle time, the team decided that it must get better information about the assembly plant's production schedule. The auto company had three assembly schedules— a long-term view two months out, a medium-term schedule two weeks out, and a near-term schedule covering the next week. The seat supplier had access to only the long and short schedules, but not to the medium schedule. The short-term schedule often contained significant changes from the long-term schedule, and the fabric maker received these changes at such short notice that he did not have time to adjust production to meet the changes. Unfortunately, while the medium-term schedule reflected most of these changes, its distribution was limited to departments inside the auto company. So the team arranged for both the seat manufacturer and fabric maker to receive the two-week schedule simultaneously, the day it was issued. This allowed them to see most schedule changes further in advance, reducing the safety stock needs.

The team project also gave the chain an opportunity to eliminate the duplicate buffers. Using the two-week lead time provided by the new schedule information, the team took the first step to shorter cycle times for the chain. The main reason for carrying fabric inventory in dyed and finished form was that the old short-term schedule did not provide enough lead time—one week—to dye and finish fabric in the colors and quantities called for by the schedule. So the fabric inventory had to contain all the combinations, making for a huge inventory. Now, however, there was two weeks notice. The fabric maker and the seat maker determined that the two-week window would just allow the fabric maker to hold all inventory in undyed form, because it took only two weeks to dye and finish fabric, ship it to the seat maker, and assemble a seat.

Not only did this extra lead time allow the suppliers to reduce inventory, but it enabled the chain to, in effect, dye fabric and assemble seats to order. With fabric inventory in an intermediate and more flexible form, the cycle time of the process became less than its lead time so that "making to order" could replace inventory as a way of meeting the customer demand.

The second step toward cycle time compression involves reducing the cycle time of the major value-adding steps themselves—spinning the yarn, weaving and dyeing the fabric, making the seat, and so on. There are two benefits to bringing these times down. One is the direct elapsed-time savings decreasing the length of the dark slices in the bars. In this example, the time needed to assemble seats has been reduced, and since this is the last production step before the product is shipped to the auto assembly plant, the reduction has directly improved the chain's cycle time.

But the second and more powerful benefit of reducing processing time is that it can allow a breakthrough in the scheduling practices and inventory needs of the chain. If, for example, the yarn maker can reduce its set-up and production run lengths, then the yarn supplier's cycle time can be cut, and less finished yarn inventory would be necessary. Or, if the fabric maker could weave the fabrics as well as dye and finish inside the new medium-term schedule's two-week window, then the chain could carry almost no fabric inventory at all. All fabric, from weave to finish, could be made to order from yarn inventory. The only inventory needed would be yarn.

In general, the shorter the process cycle time, the more a chain can let its production schedules be driven by actual demand, in this case, the final assembly schedule. The more making-to-order the chain can do and still meet lead time, the shorter the overall chain cycle time.

The auto seat business team has successfully completed the first two steps described above and is now working through the third. They have already taken more than 28 days out of the original 71 and, in another year, hope to take out another 10 days. They are on a continuous improvement track and now see an eventual goal of a 20-day chain.

This team is succeeding only because two key executives in companies involved decided to make time compression of the chain a number one priority. It's always an interesting moment to watch management announce "number one" priorities because some mean it and others don't. When a number one priority is set forth with commitment, other goals, programs, and long-held beliefs will be ignored or set back in order to make fundamental changes in the system. Sometimes, managers say "number one" but don't expect the implementers to knock anything over or create stresses in the company. Such priorities are fake, and the efforts associated with them die early. But these two executives were quite seriuos about helping the team overcome several obstacles inside the four companies.

These obstacles were the same kind of legitimate, everyday concerns common to many large corporations. First of all, two of the companies were skeptical about collapsing redundant buffer inventories; they had done this before, and suppliers had failed them, costing them millions. This concern turned out to be constructive because it forced much higher standards on suppliers that had to be met before redundant inventories could be liquidated. A second obstacle was that the yarn supplier had several customers outside his chain that were not so concerned about time compression and didn't require much product variety. The other customers were more concerned about lower cost, so until he began to work closely with the auto chain, the yarn supplier found it difficult to justify spending more on capital equipment and tooling to make his processes flexible. Within the auto chain, though, the payoff in short cycle time justified paying the yarn supplier the small cost of greater equipment flexibility. When the yarn supplier considered only the customer focused on the cost of a single-grade yarn, the logic wasn't there. But fortunately, the chain's volume was large enough to justify dedicated equipment.

Without leadership, these obstacles, which are components of the significant inertia in any large organization, would have sunk the time compression effort. An incremental six or seven days might have been taken out, and the project would have been declared "a good step forward." Instead, a far more substantial process reform emerged and is continuing to evolve.

SYNCHRONIZING LEAD TIMES AND CAPACITIES

Once a supply chain has more timely information flowing through it and gets the cycle times of its various processes down, the chain can work in a tighter cycle and operate with fewer surprises. It can quote shorter lead times to customers and will need less inventory to meet these lead times.

But as product variety keeps growing, supply chains must open up another frontier of improvement to avoid being swamped by the planning and scheduling complexity that greater product variety brings with it. Remember what kitchen toasters used to be like—there were three or four models to choose from. They were all vertical, chrome on the outside, and all took regular sliced bread. Today, any one toaster manufacturer may make dozens of toaster models—vertical or oven type, chrome or plastic bodies, even some for toasting something other than sliced bread. All of this creates a problem for the toaster chain. There are now more processes and routings in the plant, more purchased parts from more suppliers, and more variation in the month-to-month sales of particular models. As a result, there is a lot more going on inside the chain, more planning to do, and more things that can go wrong or get out of balance.

Let's explore what happens to the toaster supply chain when product variety grows. One effect is that different models will take different amounts of time to move through the chain. If chrome plating takes more time than plastic forming, or if suppliers of the new electronic controls used in oven-type toasters have longer lead times than are required for old, conventional controls, a manufacturer no longer has only one simple chain to manage. When a product has only a few versions, you can count on it taking about the same time to move through the chain each time you make it. But different versions need varying amounts of custom engineering time, supplier lead time, assembly time, and so on. Because of increased variety, most companies in chains today are faced with an explosion of varying cycle times.

This effect leads directly to another. If cycle times vary with the particular version ordered, so does capacity needed to make it. If an oven-type toaster needs twice the assembly time as a conventional one, it will use twice as much of the manufacturer's assembly capacity. In particular, if oven-type models with electronic controls are selling unusually well this season, the controls supplier may become a bottleneck. Each chain has levels that are unusually sensitive to shifts in the demand mix. And these bottlenecks will appear at different locations in the chain as demand changes from month to month.

A good example of a high-variety chain that struggles with these problems is the home furniture industry. Furniture makers are notorious for long lead times and for shipping incomplete sets. In part, this is because customers often mix colors and sets when ordering bedroom or living room pieces, so there is no consistent match between chairs and tables. Often, too, the chair and table suppliers are two different companies, with different lead times. While a simple chair's legs and seats may have similar plant cycle times, a high-styled chair may have leg machining and finishing times that are longer than those for seats by a factor of four. Moreover, the shape and number of individually cut pieces of fabric needed to upholster the chair will vary with the chair style. Finally, the quality of the wood entering the sawing operation will vary from week to week, and the yield will depend in part on the product mix being cut. All of this is a planning and capacity scheduling nightmare. It's no wonder it takes months to get the set of furniture you ordered. Yet there are actually just a few days of work in building the set.

The only way for a chain like this to escape long lead times and high inventories is to design flexibility into its operations by synchronizing lead times across the mix, balancing capacity between levels of the chain, and thus simplifying the planning mechanisms. This is a heavy agenda for a chain, especially if its companies have traditionally run pretty independently.

Synchronizing lead times across the mix simply means that each company works hard to bring its cycle time for the most time-consuming product down close to the cycle time for the least time-consuming product. The idea here is that the customer company in the chain can count on the supplier's providing its product (or process) at the same time as the other products in the same purchase order, regardless of which version of the final product is being made by the chain. If each level in the chain could synchronize its lead times in this way, the chain could count on each level meeting a consistent schedule, regardless of the mix going through. In other words, the toaster retailer could count on getting his entire toaster order in, say, four weeks regardless of the mix of toasters he ordered.

The home furniture industry is making some strides here. For example, one furniture producer has standardized his different finishes so that each finish takes the same time to apply and to cure. Before the standardization, finishing cycle time varied widely. This improvement means that the effective capacity of the finishing operation is now independent of the mix of finishes going through it, which simplifies planning throughout the chain. It allows this company to schedule batches of product through finishing without having to worry about the mix of finishes. So on this dimension of variety, the chain no longer needs to implement separate planning and balancing. The company can use the same lead time for all finishing.

Synchronizing lead times also means that parallel activities taking place at different suppliers can carry consistent lead times, so that planning can be done with confidence. For example, tables are made by manufacturers that may have different cycle times than those of manufacturers making chairs. Before synchronization, a retailer who ordered a set would receive the tables and chairs on a random schedule. The retailer would wait for both to arrive, then ship them to the customers. But a retailer can now manage the chain more aggressively, because a chair or table manufacturer can schedule its assembly mix so that its lead time for a particular model can be specified within a narrow range. The retailer can then schedule receipt of the tables and chairs for a particular date and quote a lead time to the customer. There is no reason for the head of the chain to wait for random arrivals and have to expedite the late-arriving piece. This requires costly overhead and annoys the customer.

Balancing capacity between levels in a chain is difficult when product variety is high, but it is necessary if a chain is going to control lead times and meet promise dates for shipment to the end customer. Each level's capacity had to be flexible enough to accommodate a product mix shift and still produce at its advertised capacity. If any level in a chain gets bottlenecked when the mix changes, product that was flowing through the chain gets trapped and accumulates behind the bottlenecked point. And throughput capacity of the chain as a whole is lost. Good chain leaders look for imbalances in capacity among the levels and help the level with troubled capacity resolve its problem with production cells and other closed-loop solutions.

Capacity balancing is not just a matter of fixing the bottleneck, however. Real capacity balancing requires cooperation from the rest of the system, especially the seller of the end product. Once again information is the key. When orders get down to all suppliers earlier, suppliers have more time to plan and use their capacity effectively. Most bottlenecks occur because the company was working on the wrong things last week and didn't find out until too late what it needed to finish by this week. Capacity balance through the chain is largely a matter of using capacity in a timely manner, not building more capacity. And simplifying the management of the chain helps everyone cope with variety. This sounds easy, but it is not easy for large companies to break down old planning routines and build new ones. Simplifying planning usually takes a counterintuitive step away from accepted practice. An example from the furniture industry illustrates this.

Chair manufacturers for years have used particular methods to cut the seat and back pieces out of long rolls of fabric. These pieces are used to upholster the chairs. Most methods concentrate on minimizing the fabric waste. It turns out that with limited chair variety, the best way to get the most out of a roll of fabric is to cut all the seats at once, then all the backs. This meant that seat pieces and back pieces would be held in inventory, but this was all right because analysts of furniture companies have shown that with this method the inventory costs are less than the savings in material. The alternative would be to cut the pieces for each chair—the seat, back, arms, and so on—all at once.

The analysts were right as long as the chair product mix didn't change much. The fabric cutters, inventory handlers, and production schedulers could all manage two or three stacks of seat cuts and two or three stacks of back cuts. But now there are dozens of chair designs, each with a different seat and back. There are stacks of seats and backs everywhere, and it's difficult to keep track of them. The alternative of simply cutting the fabric for the chair you are now making is far superior because the overhead and inventory savings far outweigh the fabric losses. This just-in-time alternative also eliminates stockouts of cut fabric, which interrupt production when product variety is high and the demand mix shifts.

This simpler way of planning fabric cutting reduces the chain cycle time by eliminating inventory and substituting a quick cutting process for a long, large batch-cutting process. It also makes the lead time more reliable by doing away with stockouts. And it makes life easier on the fabric maker who no longer gets emergency calls from the furniture maker saying that he has the right fabric but it has been cut into the wrong pieces.

Yet relatively few furniture makers have adopted this simpler way to plan cutting and to plan fabric inventories. The reason they haven't is that it makes sense only when you think about the furniture-making process and the entire chain in the context of time—maintaining a steady flow of product through different stages with stable and predictable lead times. If you approach the planning of this chain from a traditional cost perspective, as most furniture makers still do, you build a different system.

YOU NEED DEMANDING CUSTOMERS

The plant manager of a large Eastern European truck manufacturer recently explained why his company cannot sell trucks in Western European markets. He said it has nothing to do with politics or economics. Rather, the problem is that his main customer is the Soviet Union. This customer has ordered the same truck for years and has told the manufacturer that no changes are to be made. He wants the same chassis and same components, because he doesn't want to have to stock any more spare parts or teach his repair people any new procedures. The plant manager believes this is the worst kind of customer you can have, because you cannot get better as a supplier unless the customer demands improvements.

Supply chains face the same issue. They need the lead customer to demand time compression and coordinate the actions that provide better information, reduce cycle times, and synchronize capacity. Without this, the supply chain's overall progress is limited to improvements that companies can see and then make by themselves. And they don't take the chain very far against its competitors. As we have seen, most of the actions that can dramatically upgrade the chain's performance as a system and cut its lead times and inventories need to be agreed on between companies. These actions are usually the opposite of what a single company operating alone would do. So a leader needs to drive a vision and some guidelines down through the chain.

Time-based chains do these things differently:

- Send current order information for end products down through the entire chain. In contrast, companies that do not think in terms of chains will send order information only to their direct suppliers.

- Limit the percentage change in the size of successive orders to suppliers to avoid amplification of inventory adjustments among suppliers down the line. Conventional practice is that companies place whatever size order will adjust their inventory this month to the level they want.

- Take out duplicate safety stocks that simply raise carrying costs and hide the problems the chain should be working on. Normal practice of companies acting alone is to keep safety stocks, regardless what suppliers and customers do.

- Reduce the cycle time of levels in the chain to allow faster throughput and flexibility of the entire chain. Conventional practice is to determine cycle times based on the local cost and inventory economics in the company.

- Use capacity to add value to work in process only when your customer needs it. Normal practice is to fill equipment to avoid poor utilization and to ensure product is ready just in case the customer needs it.

- Synchronize lead times and capacity across the product mix so that each level in the chain can plan production schedules consistently without regard to normal changes in mix. Conventional practice is to quote longer lead times on different product mixes, which complicates planning and lead time quotations to the end customer.

One major chain that broke conventional rules and rose to prominence is the Japanese steel industry. Its low cost, high speed position internationally in the 1970s and early 1980s was built on a compressed supply chain. During this period, American steel buyers often remarked that the lead time from Japanese mills was less than from domestic U.S. mills. Japanese mills were equipped with continuous casting to eliminate intermediate product stages. The mills were built at modern port locations to accommodate imported iron ore and coal transported in specially designed carriers and to avoid inland transport and queuing. Mills sought to maintain near constant operating rates, which often meant loading finished export steel on ships headed for the U.S. before the steel was sold. Trading companies' offices in the U.S. sometimes took orders from American customers while the ship was enroute and negotiated price to make sure all the steel was sold by the time of its arrival.

The Japanese chain included the mines and transport carriers, the mill and port facilities, and the trading company. The chain broke many of the conventional steel industry rules in the early 1970s, for example: Build plants near raw materials or markets. Continuous casting does not yield an adequate return on investment. Accept orders and produce only when price exceeds cost.

Supply chains reflect the values of their leaders. The Limited, for example, has been working with American and foreign suppliers for years to compress time. It has taught suppliers to compress time in every aspect of dealing with The Limited—submitting prototypes for proposed new products, notifying of any coming delivery problem, sending invoices, and of course filling orders. Most suppliers in the chain have been able to respond. In addition, The Limited has put new apparel makers in business in those few cases where current suppliers could not make the adjustment. In this way, strongly managed chains develop new discipline and a new set of expectations.

In contrast, it is not so surprising that American military procurement chains perform badly. For the most part, lead times are long and overheads are high among American defense contractors. Defense purchasing has some of the most outdated ordering patterns, highest in-process inventories, and slowest closing loops inside the chain among all U.S. industries. Most of the problem lies with the ultimate customer, the government. The government has multiple and conflicting decision makers and an ever changing agenda in defense procurement, and the chains underneath reflect this.

Some of the more aggressive supply chain leaders today in the U.S., Europe, and Asia are global competitors. Global competitors increasingly design, manufacture, purchase, and sell products all over the world, mixing value added from many different locations. Caterpillar or IBM cannot afford to quote one lead time to a customer for a wholly U.S.-made product and a longer lead time for the accessory product made overseas for the same customer. The design and engineering for a new product goes on in several different locations, but product introduction dates can't be held up for that. Global companies are in effect laying down one common standard of responsiveness and time compression around the world. Otherwise, their supply chains could not be of the mixed nationality which their economics now demand. The product line variety is such today that no global company can afford to secure all of the value added for a product locally. The broad reach of time compression efforts around the world today is the result of global competitors at the head of their supply chains.

9

◇◇◇◇

Time-based Strategy

The creation of value by using time as a competitive weapon requires strategies to lock up the most attractive customers and to keep competitors at bay. Strategy choice at most companies means choosing from among three principal options:

- Seeking coexistence with competitors. This choice is seldom stable since competitors are not likely to stay put.
- Retreating. Many companies, today, are doing just this. The pages of the *Wall Street Journal* are filled with accounts of companies that are retreating—by consolidating plants, focusing their operations, divesting businesses, pulling out of markets, or going "upscale."
- Attacking, either directly or indirectly. The direct attack in business is typified by the classic cut-price-and-add-capacity strategy. It is head-on competition. Indirect attacks require strategies of surprise so that either competitors do not understand them, or they do understand but cannot respond because the attack is happening so quickly.

Of the three options, attack is the only choice for growth. The direct attack requires superior resources over competitors to be successful. Strategies of direct attack are therefore expensive and potentially catastrophic if not successful, since almost all resources are committed to the attack. Strategies of indirect attack gain the most for the least cost.

The attractiveness of the indirect over the direct attack has been best established in the history of armed conflict. Liddell Hart, the well-regarded war historian, observes that the history of 25 centuries of armed conflict shows that:

[A] high proportion of history's decisive campaigns, the
significance of which is enhanced by the comparative rarity of
the direct approach, enforces the conclusion that the indirect
attack is by far the most hopeful and economic form of
strategy.
    Can we draw even more specific deductions from history?
The most consistently successful commanders when faced by
an enemy in a position that was strong naturally or mate-
rially, have hardly ever attacked it in a direct way. And
when, under pressure of circumstances, they have risked a
direct attack, the result has commonly been to blot their
record with a failure.[1]

Because of the expense, executives are naturally cautious about
attacking directly and will usually seek increased share and profitability with strategies of indirect attack. The "tools" available to
support indirect attacks include: resegmentation of the market,
repackaging of goods and services, differential channel strategies,
and others. However, none of the tools are broadly applicable.
When used, these tools have a limited effect on the operations or
on customer base and are difficult to defend in the face of determined competitors.

Time provides the means for indirect strategies of attack. Providing value—delivering new products and services, filling orders,
providing service to customers faster than competitors can—is
destabilizing to the competition. The possibility of establishing a
time-based advantage opens new avenues for constructing winning competitive strategies. As well as creating value for the customer and the company, time-based strategies are often opaque to
competitors—causing confusion within their executive suites. Few
time-based competitors have experienced serious or effective
counterattacks from their cost-based competitors.

AN ANATOMY OF AN INDIRECT ATTACK

In early 1982, the board of directors of the Mad River Company*
met to consider the fate of the company. Mad River had not made
money in years and the prospects for the future were not any
better. Something had to be done.

Mad River was an anachronism in the world of office supplies
manufacturers. Mad River was one of the few remaining small,

* Mad River is a fictional name to protect the strategy of the actual company.

technically out-of-date plants in the industry. Many other plants like it had been closed or converted to purely custom products over the last 20 years, as larger competitors replaced small-scale, slow production processes with the larger-scale and faster processes that were becoming the industry standard. The small plants had virtually the same strategy options the board of Mad River now considered:

- The old machines could be replaced with a new machine
- The plant could be sold for "a song" to a competitor whose management would then cut the wages of the employees
- The plant could be closed

These were not attractive options to the board. First, a new plant would spew out far more product than Mad River currently could sell. Besides, a new process and plant cost more money than the company had or could borrow. Second, the competitor was not buying, since they were already straining to turn around other plants recently acquired. Closing the plant was the choice of last resort since the plant had been in the family since its beginning and the town depended on it as a source of employment.

Another option existed. The new president had a plan that might save the company. He had been surprised to learn shortly after he arrived that Mad River had a very high market share in St. Louis compared to its share in other metropolitan areas. The response of the vice president of sales when asked about the anomaly by the new president frustrated him. The vice president of sales insisted that the high share in St. Louis was the result of a very special personal relationship the Mad River salesman had with the distributor in that market. If the share was indeed the result of a strong personal relationship between the distributor and the local salesman, the new president could not expect much to happen quickly in the other Mad River markets.

While at an industry convention, the new president ran into the St. Louis distributor. Taking advantage of the opportunity, the new president asked the distributor what it was about the Mad River salesman that made their relationship so special. The new president was shocked by the distributor's answer, "Sure we have a special relationship. I tell Joe (the salesman) all the time that as long as he ships me daily the products I order we're friends. When he stops doing that, we will no longer be friends."

On the flight back to Mad River the president thought about the distributor's response. Could there be an opportunity for Mad River to become profitable by emphasizing service to the distributors rather than simply the price of its office supplies? If so, what level of service needed to be provided, what would the company have to do differently, and what prices should it charge? How would the competition react?

The president surveyed some of the Mad River distributors to determine the levels of service they were currently getting from the competition. He was surprised and pleased at the results. The competitors provided fairly poor service. The distributor had to wait four to six days from the time he called in his order to the time the order was placed on the competitor's truck. The competitor's truck came to the distributor only three times a week. When the distributor checked his order he often found that 50 percent of the order was missing and was on back-order, which not only cost the distributor potential sales but forced him to keep track of what had been ordered, not delivered, and not paid for.

The response of the competitors to the distributor's desires for specialty products was so poor that the distributor had to carry extra inventory to meet his customer's needs. The inventory turns for the distributor's stock of specialty products was only 4 to 5 times a year compared with 10 to 12 times for his standard-product inventories. If the distributor wanted a special order manufactured, the competitors forced him to wait 5 to 6 weeks and to buy a large minimum order. The wait of 5 to 6 weeks corresponded to the competitors' plant scheduling cycle, and the minimum-size order was a truck load quantity. To the president, the only good thing the distributor could expect from the competitors was low price. They certainly were not easy to deal with.

The president was intrigued by another aspect of the emerging service strategy. Over the last 20 years, the competitors had shut down all the plants they had that were like Mad River. The managements of the competitors had done so in a race to become the lowest-cost producer in the industry. If a service strategy could be made to work, the competitors might not be able to respond or might even think that not responding was the right thing to do if it meant higher costs. A service strategy for Mad River might enable the company to coexist with the competition!

But what level of service? After some careful thought and discussion with his people, it was decided what the service objectives should be. Instead of making the distributor wait 4 to 6 days from the time he called in his order to the time the order was placed on the truck, Mad River would promise one-day order turnaround. Mad River's trucks would be sent to the distributor's market daily rather than only twice a week. Mad River would do what it had to do to make sure that the distributor's order would be at least 96 percent complete.

Mad River would emphasize specialty, lower-volume products. The minimum order size would be much smaller than the competitors' and would be supplied to the distributor in less than 2 weeks. Mad River would price its specialty products at the same price as the competitors'—35 percent more than standard product typically—but would price its standard product 20 percent higher than the competition, so that over time the distributor would de-emphasize Mad River standards for its specials. The competitors could have the high-volume standard products, Mad River the specials, and everyone would be happy.

Before such a strategy could be successful, Mad River management had to make a few changes to the company's value delivery system. These changes were planned and taken to the board where they were approved. Although the board was wary of the service strategy they recognized that Mad River had no other alternative but to shut down.

The first change was in the production process. The machines had to be made flexible so that the minimum order size could be manufactured for reasonable costs. These machines are notoriously inflexible beasts. Because of the high speeds of the machines great volumes of waste come off the end of a machine during a change from one product version to another before the process can be brought under control. The key to economical changeovers is computerized process controls that enable the process to be brought in "spec" quickly. The industry practice had been to use computerized process controls only on the newest, best, and fastest machines where vast amounts of waste can be generated very quickly during a changeover. Despite this, the large machines are still expensive to change from one product to another.

After the products are manufactured, they are transferred to the finishing and packaging department. This department, like the production process itself, has been very cost sensitive to variety. Generally, only the large-volume products were finished and packaged on the high-speed machines and the low-volume products were run over slower, more labor-intensive pieces of equipment. Investments were made in automated finishing and packaging equipment that could be changed from one style to another very quickly. Also, extra machines were purchased, so that plenty of capacity would be available. Finishing and packaging were not to be time bottlenecks in the overall process.

The investments in the reduction of changeover costs at the Mad River plant enabled management to schedule more product variety than in the past. Management planned an increase in the number of products offered to customers to 175 distinct versions. The most offered by any competitor was 65 choices.

The next portion of Mad River's value delivery system needing attention was order entry. Orders had to be received and turned around fast enough to meet the one-day commitment to the customer. Mad River's order entry system was as complex and time consuming as the system of the central office switchgear manufacturer described in earlier chapters. Mad River's system was streamlined and then computerized (rather than computerized and then streamlined after the computerization failed to have an impact).

As the speed of Mad River's order-entry system was being addressed, management's attention shifted to logistics. Mad River had a fleet of trucks to carry its products to its distributors in many cities. The logistics function was as cost-effective as any in the industry. However, when the metric is time, an analysis of its consumption in the logistics function revealed:

- The desire to ship truckload quantities so as to minimize costs added days of delay to most distributor orders.
- When a region's distributors ordered product in great volume the available capacity of trucks would be exhausted and the customer would experience delays as the shipping backlogs increased.
- When the truck had to traverse more than 400 miles to a customer its driver would stop and sleep for 8 hours as required by law.

For Mad River to implement a service strategy, logistics needed attention. The full-truckload practice was suspended. Keeping the promise of "daily trucks into your market" would be more important than whether or not the truck was full. Schedules were set and, as needed, additional trucks were leased and tandem drivers were used.

Implementing the service strategy with the distributor should not have been difficult except for one problem. Traditionally, distributors and producers in this industry have exclusive relationships. For those product lines manufactured by the plant the distributor agrees to sell only the manufacturer's products and not those of other manufacturers. In return, the manufacturer agrees not sell its products to competing distributors. Mad River could not afford to send trucks daily into a market if the trucks were going to only one distributor. The shipping costs would be prohibitive. Therefore, Mad River needed to sell to more than one distributor in each market, thereby breaking the long industry practice of exclusive relationships.

Nobody liked this. Of course the distributor was not going to want his competitor to get the same products as he was getting if he was not going to get anything more for his pain. The Mad River salesmen did not relish the thought of having to go to their longstanding and exclusive customers to tell them they were no longer exclusive. The pain was heightened because after they had told their old customers they would no longer be treated exclusively, they had to go across town and call on a *new* customer—one they had been comfortably ignoring for all those years. The president had to force this aspect of the program through and accept the risks that some distributors might be so upset that they would abandon Mad River.

The Mad River salesmen did have something positive to tell their customers. The distributors who went along with the program would have much faster inventory turns. Because Mad River trucks would be coming to the distributor's markets daily, the distributor could place his order much closer to the time he sold it. Thus his inventory turns would increase, thereby increasing his return on inventory investment. Mad River could promise the distributor inventory turns of 15 times a year and the aggressive distributor could do even better by reordering very frequently.

The president faced additional implementation resistance. The director of logistics could not bring himself to release trucks if the trucks were not full. After all, throughout his professional career his goal had been to reduce shipping costs and full trucks meant lower shipping costs. No matter what the president said, the director would revert to his old ways and hold trucks up, thereby damaging service. After a few months of trying, the president moved the director out of his job to be replaced by another who would see that the service promises were kept.

Some resistance was met from the finance department. Finance was holding approval of the capital requests for the extra, automated finishing and packaging equipment. The concern was that given the precarious financial condition of the company, what was the logic of extra equipment that would be underused except when demands on the finishing and package department were at their peak? The president emphasized that if the equipment in the finishing and packaging department were sized to meet average demand so that overall utilization could be high, customers would not get the service promised as delivery time varied with the backlog in the department. After much debate, the president was forced to order the representatives of finance to sign off on the paper work.

After eleven months of intensive effort, the service strategy was in place. Management knew that the organization could set up the machines quickly, that trucks could make it to the key markets twice a day, that the fill rate for orders could meet or exceed 96 percent, and that specials could be handled. At that point, the merchants were promised service that exceeded anyone else's service in the industry.

The results have been phenomenal. Demand is surging. In key markets, the market share has more than doubled in 24 months. The mix of product is shifting towards the more profitable specialty versions although the volume of standard product did not decrease as was expected because of the higher price. Indeed, distributors are still ordering standard products because of the convenience of Mad River's service rather than its price.

The success of Mad River's service strategy has surprised competitors. The company has come from being on the brink of closing to turning in record earnings. It has come from not being able to sell out all its capacity to being constrained by capacity. All are amazed at just how large is the demand for specialty versions when they are supplied with good service compared to the demand before there was good service.

So far the competitors have not reacted to Mad River's service strategy. Mad River is selling many specialty products, the very same products these companies had been discouraging the distributors from buying with high prices, large minimum order quantities, and long delivery times. These companies are content selling the core items in the product line at the price their low-cost manufacturing facilities will allow them to and still make enough money to meet their budgets. Everyone is happy.

LESSONS FROM MAD RIVER

A number of key lessons can be gleaned from the Mad River experience. They include:

- The competitively effective level of timeliness and choice exploited by a time-based competitor may be very alien to the traditional industry participants.
- The plan to become a time-based competitor must encompass the value-delivery system from end to end.
- Getting people to change the ways they think about their jobs

and how success is evaluated can be as difficult as deciding what the new state of the organization will be, or even more so.

- When the enhanced system is unleashed on the market the response can be very swift.
- Always surprise your competitors and give them a way out.

The competitively effective level of timeliness and choice conceived by the president of Mad River is very alien to the traditional industry participants. Mad River did not simply offer better service, it offered significantly better service. Mad River did not resist variety, it embraced it. This makes Mad River stand out among competitors, which not only draws customer attentions to the company but confuses the competitors who are struggling with the perceived tradeoff of better service and variety versus higher costs.

Mad River's plan to become a time-based competitor encompassed the value-delivery system from end to end. The setup reduction investments and the investments in excess capacity in the finishing and packaging department enabled the plant to be run closer to the time of the sale of product rather than relying on large amounts of inventory. The costs added in this department were more than offset by the overall reduction in system inventories. Trying to save money by cutting the number of trucks to a market or by holding the trucks until they are full risks destroying the entire service concept. It is important to give all employees a sense of the end-to-end game plan and why it is crucial to avoid optimizing a segment of the value-delivery system at the expense of the system as a whole.

The time and energy required to conceive and detail Mad River's service strategy was much less than the time and energy expended by the president and senior management to convince their subordinates to act. The alterations to an organization's belief structure, patterns of working, and measurement and reward systems required to become a time-based competitor are significant. The task cannot be *delegated*. Further, the management of Mad River had a luxury that the managements of many other organizations who want to become or should become time-based competitors do not usually have. Mad River had run out of options. The service strategy was the company's last chance. Other options did not exist. Thus, a decision by an employee not to cooperate—not to find ways around blockages, not to come up with creative ideas for increasing flexibility and reducing time, not to accept a change in role, measurements, and rewards—was a decision to go out of business and lose a job. The employees of most other companies do not face such a limited choice of options while their management tries to transform their company into a time-based competitor. The management of a company that wants to become a time-based competitor must have a crisis, create a crisis, or generate a credible vision of tremendous opportunity, so the troops will not pause for long to question why they are being sent into battle.

When the enhanced system is unleashed on the market the response can be very swift. Customers are surprisingly sensitive to service and choice even if before the fact they may indicate otherwise. The buildup of the frustrations generated by long and unreliable lead times and limited choice from traditional suppliers is subtle so that when given an alternative that works, customers seldom hesitate to switch—even at a price premium.

Always surprise your competitors and, if possible, give them a way out. It does one no good to tell the world and, therefore, your competitors that the company is becoming a time-based competitor before one has to. To do so risks the chance that the management of the competitor will also want to get aggressive in time. The consequence, at worst, is that the competitor accomplishes the transformation first. At best, the transformation is faster than that of the competitor, but still the window of opportunity is narrowed. A draw may occur when all the competitors transform at the same time. Then, only the customer wins as competitors give away their service advantage to keep the customer who can choose from more than one high-service supplier.

The window of opportunity being exploited by a time-based competitor must be made as large as is possible. The journey to becoming time-based can be a long one. Therefore, the longer the competitors wait to respond the better. Obviously, not telling the world what is being attempted is good. But the window can be kept larger by either employing strategies of deception or by offering the competitors a way out. Strategies of deception use information to mislead the competitor into taking the wrong action or no action. For example, the executives of a manufacturer of building products that is well along in transforming itself into a time-based competitor have told the trade press that they have been able to speed deliveries from 22 weeks to 4 weeks by holding large amounts of finished goods inventories and by working longer hours. The hope is that the competitors will either ignore the company or will increase their inventories and work harder. So far the competition has not disappointed the management of the time-based competitor.

As one becomes time-based, the alternative to deception is to find an out for competitors. The best time-based strategies not only surprise competitors but make the competitors think that they are winning as well. Mad River has locked up the service-sensitive distributors who need specialty product. These are the same distributors who are buying competitively priced standard product from the less service-oriented suppliers. These suppliers do not want to be bothered with too many products anyway so they see this new segmentation as being OK for them. Because Mad River's return on assets are buried in overall corporate results, they don't see that they are twice the industry average.

When pursuing a time-based strategy either allow for a way out for the competition that fits with their traditional view of how their business works or plan to go as far and as fast as is humanly possible. Competition can be most intense when an opponent is cornered. Cornered opponents have no choice but to fight to the bitter end draining profits dramatically for all involved.

For some businesses, there is no way out for the slower competition. Management of slower companies must respond or be destroyed. The participants in the world automobile industry have no choice but to move towards time-based competition as the leaders in their industry do. In a private conversation about the differences between Mazda and Toyota, a managing director of Mazda observed, "We can never be as good [at fast manufacturing] as Toyota-san. Toyota-san started much sooner than we did. We have to try as hard as we can though, because if we do not try we can not stay in this business."

THE FUTURE BELONGS TO THE TIME-BASED COMPETITOR

The mass markets for goods and services are disappearing. Marketeers lament the fragmentation of demand. Consider this statement by Carl J. Johnson, director of product management of Johnson & Johnson Baby Products:

> The consumer package goods industry has evolved through the steady proliferation of brands and escalation of advertising. Both are growing faster than underlying product demand. Escalations in branding and variety regularly cannibalize more than they contribute. We have two choices: we can stop playing the game or we have to adjust our business and information strategies to the fragmenting world.[2]

Mr. Johnson's frustration is typical among the executives of consumer products companies. Their customers seem to want more and more specific variations of the products and services they buy. While it is certainly true that customers are demanding more choice and wanting faster delivery, competitors are *providing* more choice and faster delivery. Sometimes it is difficult to know who is leading whom.

From the perspective of the customer, more and faster is better. The demographics are driving this. As America grays, another part of the population matures. The fastest-growing segment of all the population is the population between the ages of 45 and 60 years. This is the group that traditionally accounts for a large portion of discretionary spending. This segment of the population will increase from 45 million people at the midpoint of this decade to over 60 million people by the year 2000. Combined with an almost equal expansion of the 35-to-44-year age group, these people will have the increased sophistication of tastes and desire for diversity expected of people with large disposable incomes. And they will be satisfied.

It seems that no matter where one looks one sees an explosion of choice and an expansion of fast service. The number of Chinese restaurants in Orange County, California, has exploded in the last 18 years from 4 to over 78, and the diversity has intensified. The number of stock-keeping units has tripled since 1974 in the average U.S. retailer. Increases in choice are even being mandated by local government bodies. In 1984, the governments of the Chicago area suburbs of Carol Stream and Buffalo Grove passed "anti-monotony" laws to force developers to make the houses in their projects look different even if they were not different on the inside. In 1988, in the neighboring Bartlette Village, the village board members passed an ordinance requiring that any four homes in a row have to look different from each other. The village board members "like the amount of variety (they) saw in the custom homes being built. The community is looking to have more of a custom flavor."[3]

In 1988, Panasonic, an operating unit of the Japanese appliance and electronics giant Matsushita, introduced the Panasonic Individual Custom System (PICS). Panasonic guarantees that anyone can walk into a PICS dealer in the United States, be fitted for a made-to-measure bicycle, choose a color and paint scheme, and pick up a newly manufactured almost one-of-a-kind bicycle in three weeks or less. The consumer has a choice of 4 models, 41 frame sizes, and 35 color schemes, for a total of 11,655 combinations.

The consumer's alternative is to order his semicustom or custom bicycle from the myriad of custom bicycle manufacturers in the United States. Panasonic prices its bikes about the same as the semicustom offerings of the competition and significantly lower than the custom offerings. The variety choices of the PICS offering are greater than the standard offerings of the competitors and, since the PICS is a semicustom product, choice against custom offerings is difficult to compare. The major difference for the PICS offerings is that the consumer can have his bike in three weeks or less compared to the much longer delivery times for the competitor's custom offerings and not much faster delivery times for the competitor's standard offerings.

Panasonic manufactures the bikes in Japan. The frames are constructed on regular production lines using flexible manufacturing techniques. The factory has virtually no inventory and the bike is constructed within eight days from the time the consumer places his order. Another six days are consumed by the air freight; this time will be substantially reduced when a factory is opened in the United States.

The factory in the United States should be expected. In one year, the volume of semicustom bikes delivered by Panasonic gave the company the number two position in the U.S. The head of sales in the U.S. said, "Fast delivery is the entire future of the high-end bike market"[4] and in so saying is not taking much risk. The fast delivery semicustom bike business of Panasonic in Japan is probably two years more developed than in the U.S.! Delivery is in two weeks in Japan rather than the three weeks required in the U.S.

In a review of Matsushita's PICS offering, Scott Martin of *Bicycling* observed, "They're not trying to make it a totally custom fit. If that is what you want the option is to go to a custom frame builder and wait perhaps a year. PICS represents a good way for somebody to get a professional frame the way they want it without the wait."[5]

Today, consumers do not have to seek out mortgage originators who will give them rapid loan commitments. Citicorp has been joined by Prudential, First Wachovia, and others in offering quick decisions. The only consumers who are not interested in this rapid service are those having the most credit risk or who are unaware that such a service is available.

Even in deal making, differences in the speed of decision making of the managements of competing companies can make the difference between winning or losing. Such speed was credited as the reason the Bass Group beat the Ford Motor Company in the bidding for the American Savings and Loan Association in 1988:

> Another big advantage for the Bass Group stemmed from the simple fact that it is controlled by one man, who makes decisions quickly based on advice from a few advisors. In contrast, negotiations for Ford were handled by executives in its San Francisco-based First Nationwide Bank unit who had to clear key decisions with Ford executives in Dearborn, Michigan.
>
> "The structure of the Bass Group is that the decisions are being made at the top," said E. Garth Plank of Shearson Lehman Hutton in San Francisco. "It's much easier than through a multitiered organization."[6]

DECIDE TO BE IN OR OUT OF THE GAME —BUT DECIDE

Management must decide whether it wants to watch the transformation of its industry by a time-based competitor from the sidelines or to lead its customers and competitors by being first in transforming its company into a time-based competitor. One thing is certain, watching this transformation from the sidelines will be hazardous to the health of the company. No examples yet exist in which an early time-based leader has been upset by a follower unless the leader stumbles. Managements that choose not to lead or even to follow are condemned to trying to make money in commodity-like competition. Meanwhile, until an antidote is found, time-based strategies appear to be very hard to overcome.

The source of this great strength is people and the way they work together. The organizations of time-based competitors are the company's competitive proprietary advantage. The managements of their competitors must respond by changing their people and the ways their organizations work together. This is more difficult than, say, buying the largest, most efficient airliner to be cost competitive the day the airliner is put in service.

Thus, leading the transformation is the only option. As discussed in earlier chapters, by leading the transformation, management can:

- Design and execute better basic strategies
- Invigorate mature markets
- Protect and strengthen the home market advantage

- Managing the supply chain and even the global system as a competitive weapon

The internal and external benefits of becoming a time-based competitor are very attractive. The benefits include lower costs and increased effectiveness, higher prices and increased customer dependency, faster and more effective expansion and refreshment of the product line, enhanced financial performance, and competitive supply chains.

Of all these benefits, the one having the most powerful impact on a company, its customers, and its competition is the ability of a time-based competitor to conceive, develop, and introduce new products and services faster than competitors can. When a company can establish a time advantage in the process of conceiving, developing, and executing new product/service concepts, many good things happen. Costs can be reduced quickly. New technologies can be brought to customers rapidly. The freshness of the product/service line can be maintained, resulting in higher margins.

The experience to date strongly suggests that if a company's new-product development cycle is substantially longer than that of key competitors then the company is terminally ill. Nowhere is this more apparent than in the competition to capture the demand of the U.S. automobile purchaser. In 1989, the U.S. purchaser of automobiles can choose from among 600 models of vehicles offered by 40 manufacturers! This is more choice than is available to purchasers of household appliances and TV sets and is approaching the standard of choice set by many fashion products.

As shown in earlier chapters, managements of fashion businesses succeed when they push winners and can back away from losers in a timely fashion. In the automobile business the analogy is the speed at which new designs can be brought to market. With the possible exception of the Ford Motor Company, no Western automobile manufacturer of significance is yet capable of competing in a fashion business. The product development cycles of the Western companies are just far too long to withstand the effects of the blistering pace the Japanese are setting.

The luxury divisions of Ford, General Motors, and the luxury European producers are most likely to be affected by the success of the Japanese at the higher price points. These organizations will have to field automobiles of comparable value or face being forced out of the premium car segment. Ford, GM, and the Europeans can ill afford to let this happen. GM, in particular, must respond. The company faces intense competition in the low and moderate price points from Ford and the Japanese. In the last decade, GM's position in the prestige segment was diminished by the Europeans. In the late 1970s and early 1980s, GM sold half of all the prestige luxury automobiles in the United States. At the end of the decade, GM's share had shrunk to one-sixth. GM is caught in a big squeeze.

The early returns are not encouraging for the luxury divisions of the Western producers. The sales of Honda's Acura in the United States now out-pace the sales of Mercedes-Benz, Volvo, BMW, and Saab and are encroaching on the greater volumes of Cadillac and Lincoln. The success of Acura has attracted Toyota and Nissan into fielding cars priced over $25,000. In the trade press, the reaction of many executives of the Western luxury automobile producers has been to "wait-and-see" how the Japanese do, since few believe that producers of inexpensive automobiles can successfully migrate into the luxury market, where image and ego appeal prevail.

A strategy of "let's-wait-and-see" is very dependent on being able to perceive the nature of the threat/opportunity, decide what action is appropriate, and execute the concept. Product design cycles at Western luxury automobile producers are still too long to enable a "wait-and-see" strategy to succeed. The speed at which General Motors can respond is crucial to the company's fending off further loss of market share in the higher price offerings in its product line as has happened in the mid- and low-priced segments of demand. The long product design cycles of four to five years are a problem for GM and the Europeans because their principal competitors are much faster. Ford is believed to need about three years. The average design cycle for all the Japanese manufacturers is about four years. Toyota claims that it has driven its time down to two and a half years, and Honda may be around two years. These Japanese automobile companies are the ones challenging GM and the Europeans for a share of the luxury car demand in the United States.

Many executives of Western automobile companies are aware of their shortfall in the speed of new product development. This slow reaction frustrates many in and out of the industry. The most striking frustrated executive was H. Ross Perot, who said: "It takes five years to develop a new car in this country. Heck, we won World War II in four years. We are spending billions to develop new cars. This isn't a moon shot, it's just a car."[7]

The magnitude of the forfeiture being made by the managements of General Motors and the Europeans is almost too great to imagine. Try to imagine the internal challenge for these companies now that the Toyota, Nissan, and Honda premium cars are selling and taking away the customers of Cadillac, Oldsmobile, Mercedes, and BMW. After what will likely be a two-year debate, the decision will be made to field products that are comparable to the Japanese premium offering. Four to five years will then be required to develop these models. The Japanese will have been in this segment virtually unchallenged by the Western luxury producers for more than five years. Few businesses exist today without government protection that can survive such a headstart by the competition.

The frame of mind needing changing can be found in slow response to the Japanese threat in the premium segments by such companies as BMW. The intensity of the competition in the $20,000–$30,000 range has stimulated BMW to retreat into higher-priced vehicles and to hide behind beliefs like this:

> The image of being a luxury producer is hard to achieve for somebody who produces millions of cars, sniffed Gunter Kramer, the chairman of BMW of North America. "We're looking for qualitative growth, not quantitative growth."[8]

To obtain "qualitative" growth the European manufacturers have raised prices heavily in the last four years and the "quantitative" growth has been negative growth as volumes have shrunk 20 to 35 percent from the highs of 1986. The prospect of such a retreat is terrible overcapacity in the luxury car segment. Instead of standing and fighting, the European manufacturers are pursuing strategies of segment retreat that can only take them to the same place such strategies have taken European manufacturers of motorcycles, consumer electronics, cameras, and the like. They become fringe players.

TIME-BASED STRATEGIES

Today the leading edge of competition is the combination of fast response and increasing variety. Companies without these advantages are slipping into commodity-like competition, where customers buy mainly on price. The European luxury car producers, for example, had until now enjoyed a safe retreat away from price competition—the brand conscious, strong-road performance segment of the U.S. car market where long model lives were actually part of the cachet. But Japan's new premium cars are dating that strategy. As Japanese producers' more frequent product upgrades close the product performance gap and the brand distinction starts to erode, the Europeans will lose control over price. If the Europeans then fall behind in the rate of new product upgrades—as their longer development periods suggest they will—prices will fall.

This is a global phenomenon. The price-sensitive low end of markets has always been the low-feature, low-service offering— the econobox automobile, the distress shipment of imported steel, and the no-help discount retailer. We pay lower prices for these. Aging models of anything have always sold at a discount too. But now a competitor that develops new products significantly faster than you will control the aging and hence pricing of your middle market and even upscale products. Before it was up to you how often you brought out new generations. Unless you have genuine product advantages over a faster competitor, the market for your older product will be increasingly driven by price. As product improvements come out faster, the brand premium shifts away from the established toward the current. Prices slide, as in a fashion business. This is what happened to Sears apparel in the U.S.

All of which forces us to revise our thinking about the basic ingredients of competitiveness. Many American companies have been concerned about their competitiveness for much of the 1980s, largely in response to Japanese competition and the revolution that's occurred in manufacturing philosophies. In fact, the typical well-established manufacturing company has probably been through something like the following self-assessment during the last five years. My cost structure and manufacturing approaches became uncompetitive, but my brand name and distribution are still pretty good. So my main priorities right now have to be driving a quality program through the company and restructuring my operations to get cost out. Once I'm cost-competitive—and the weaker dollar will help here—my product line and established position in the market will make me competitive again.

The emphasis on restructuring in the 1980s has been appropriate. Many U.S. producers found themselves managing with too many layers, manufacturing too many low-value components in high-burden-rate factories, and paying the cost of product line complexity in the form of high inventories and overheads. And they were not close enough to their customers. So these companies went to work—they collapsed their staffs, outsourced where appropriate, and began to take waste out of their operations. They got engineering and manufacturing talking together when developing new products. Competitiveness or near competitiveness was restored to many companies during the last five years as a result—20 to 30 percent reductions in total costs and customers saying they're happier with the product. A lot of U.S. brand names from Chrysler to Zenith have been shored up.

Badly needed as this restructuring was, it is just the price of admission for competing in the 1990s. In the 1980s, U.S. companies reduced costs to restore profit margins. Now they will have to compress product development cycles to keep prices and margins from eroding. The sources of competitive advantage keep changing, depending on how the leading-edge competitors find new ways to create customer value. The power to take market share and price realization away from others now lies with competitors who innovate faster. In the 1980s, chief executive officers made names for themselves and saved their companies by getting rid of overheads and getting back to basics. But once most companies get this done, the earning power goes out of them. In the 1990s, chief executive officers will distinguish their companies by compressing time and going beyond basics. Roger Milliken of Milliken & Co. and Leslie Wexner of The Limited have already distinguished themselves in this way.

Restructuring and time compression are different kinds of transformations. Restructuring is essentially a reductive process, a sorting down of businesses and procedures, a compression of activities around fewer people. The road to faster cycle times is a more integrative process. Time compression gets started by making more connections and seeing more of the whole. New working systems and organizations emerge out of this process. Eventually, time-based companies often reverse some of the reductions characteristic of restructured companies. For example, time-based companies make themselves what they once outsourced because they couldn't handle it. Harley-Davidson and Hitachi are doing this. Also, successful time-based competitors go into new, unrelated businesses because they now have a superior organizational process they want to exploit. The corporate development dictum about staying out of unrelated businesses is true only if commonality and familiarity are the main strengths of the company. But the more effective organizations, like Canon and Hewlett-Packard, can go further afield.

American companies have the same opportunity to compress time as Japanese or European companies. Time is an equal-opportunity advantage. Unlike wage rates, trade barriers, size of markets, and currency rates, time presents the same issues to every company and country. In fact, the U.S. could have some advantage. It is a rich, complex market with many leading-edge market segments. Incomes are high. Service industries like specialty retailing, finance, and computer services are ahead of Japan's. The deregulated information infrastructure and private network opportunities are richer in the U.S. than in Japan. U.S. customers are used to paying more for superior products. For example, U.S. steel users still pay more for fewer impurities in steel while the Japanese don't. There are more price gradients in electronics components in the U.S. Although Japanese companies are among the time-based pioneers which this book has referenced, there are equal numbers of U.S. pioneers—Milliken, Sun Microsystems, The Limited, Hewlett-Packard. Good U.S. organizations have the same potential, the same fertility for time-based ideas as Japanese organizations.

In fact, the Japanese can help U.S. companies become time-based competitors. Japanese-owned companies and subsidiaries operating in the U.S. are a part of U.S. supply chains, and good ones can help improve the competitiveness of the chain as a whole. A strong Japanese auto component supplier in Tennessee is helping a U.S. auto assembler in Detroit compete more effectively. The diffusion of business ideas and the customer-supplier links that are formed out there in the market do not observe national lines or origins. The more global and sophisticated U.S. and Japanese corporations become, the more influence the best of each country's companies will have on the others and the more supply chains will be mixed. How much of a Ford small car or Boeing jetliner is American today? These two leaders are better off today than five years ago because their materials inputs and management processes are of mixed origins.

OWNING THE CUSTOMER

The ultimate purpose of the time-based competitor is not maximizing speed and variety, but owning the customer. Speed and variety are just tools allowing one to do more for the customer, to solve his problems, to reduce his costs—in short, to help him compete and make money.

The way to secure a company's position within its industry is to find the most demanding customers, determine their needs, and serve them better than competitors do. Time-based concepts will lead to the cutting edge of better service, and better service will generate system cost savings between supplier and customer. For example, Procter & Gamble and Wal-Mart are rewriting the book on how a consumer packaged goods producer and a large retail chain do business with each other. The cost savings will come from changes in information exchange, scheduling, pricing, logistics, and product packages. Wal-Mart is a powerful, tough customer and may preempt most of the savings—but not all. P&G will learn new ways of operating that will not only save money and secure more business from Wal-Mart but also put P&G way ahead in dealing with other, less demanding customers. A company doesn't want all its customers to be tough, but it needs some tough core customers.

A time-based competitor develops the high degree of internal responsiveness and coordination among different parts of the company that allows it to discern differences among key customers and customize the products and services delivered to each. Among magazine publishers, R. R. Donnelley is a leader in selective binding. A subscriber to one of its magazines will get a different version—different editorial content as well as different advertisements—depending on what Donnelley knows about his demographics, purchasing pattern, and interests. The more customized the magazine's content, the more likely the reader will renew the subscription and respond to the ads. Donnelley also runs a catalogue business. Its telephone operators are trained to suggest items one might be interested in based on what one has bought previously and how one's needs may have changed. All of this is simple in concept—it requires several data bases, a customization-driven business logic, and an organization capable of making it work every day and regularly innovating—but it's not easy to do. Such a company needs to be a network of interactive pieces with short feedback loops. Intelligence and action must be everywhere, but actions have to be coordinated. This is neither traditional hierarchy nor chaos nor many small, independent strategic business units operating on their own. This company must have the internal responsiveness and clear, cross-functional communication lines of a time-based competitor.

The world is moving in the direction of Segment of One: The competitors who successfully differentiate products and services delivered to individual customers will grow and be profitable. Computers are not giving us the standardized, regimented society predicted by sociologists 20 years ago. Instead, computers and time-based organizations have found each other. The customer is being heard. Business bureaucracies are being melted down by competition from faster, leaner companies. The prognosis for the health of a business organization that wants to compete is excellent.

Notes

CHAPTER 1
The Dawn of a New Competitive Age

1. Bruce D. Henderson, *The Logic of Business Strategy* (Cambridge, MA: Abt/Ballinger Publications, 1984), pp. 10–11.
2. Henderson, *Logic of Business Strategy*, p.11.
3. Henderson, *Logic of Business Strategy*, pp. 96–99.

CHAPTER 2
Time and Business

1. Taiichi Ohno, *Toyota Production System—Aiming at an Off-Scale Management* (Tokyo: Diamond Co., 1978), p. 2.
2. Translated from *Nihon Keizai*, February 23, 1983.
3. Jay W. Forrester, "Industrial Dynamics: A Major Breakthrough for Decision Makers," *Harvard Business Review,* July-August 1958.
4. "Toyota Tries to Apply its Kanban System of Purchasing to Retail Procedures," translated from *Nikkei Communications,* February 23, 1987, pp. 2, 23.
5. George Stalk, Jr., "Rules of Response," *Perspectives* series, The Boston Consulting Group, Inc., 1987.

CHAPTER 3
Time and Customers

1. "Trends, Consumer Attitudes and the Supermarket," *1988 Survey of Consumer Attitudes and the Supermarket* (Washington, D.C.: The Food Marketing Institute, 1988), pp. 3, 7.
2. *The Future of Wholesale Banking* (Rolling Meadows, IL: The Bank Administration Institute, 1986), pp. 66–67.
3. Joe Girard with Stanley H. Brown, *How to Sell Anything to Anybody* (New York: Warner Books, 1977).

4. Robert Guenther, "Citicorp Shakes Up the Mortgage Market," *Wall Street Journal,* November 13, 1988, p. B1.
5. "Mortgage Lenders Lavish New Attention on Real Estate Agents," *Savings Institutions,* February 1988, p. 82.
6. "Mortgage Lenders," p. 83.
7. "Mortgage Lenders," p. 82.
8. George Stalk, Jr.'s interview with an anonymous realtor.
9. Guenther, "Citicorp."
10. "Mortgage Lenders."
11. Anita Willis-Boyland, "1988 Outlook for Private Commercial Conduits Is Dim," *Real Estate Finance Today,* February 19, 1988, p. 6.
12. Personal interview, February 1988.
13. Guenther, "Citicorp."

CHAPTER 4
Time and Innovation

1. "Nissan Tries to Turn the Corner," *Forbes,* November 3, 1986, p. 51.
2. "Will Toys 'B' Great?" *Forbes,* February 22, 1988, pp. 37–39.
3. R. E. Gomory and R. W. Schmitt, "Science and Product," *Science,* May 27, 1988, p. 1132.
4. Gomory and Schmitt, "Science and Product," p. 1204.
5. Clarence L. "Kelly" Johnson with Maggie Smith, Kelly: *More Than My Share of It All* (Washington, D.C., and London: Smithsonian Institution Press, 1987), p. 97.
6. Johnson with Smith, p. 160.
7. Johnson with Smith, pp. 160 and 163.
8. Translated from *Nihon Keizai,* February 23, 1983.
9. "Sun's Sizzling Race to the Top," *Fortune,* August 17, 1987, p. 89.
10. "The Maturing of the Workstation Wunderkind," *Electronic Business,* March 15, 1987, p. 58.
11. "Sun's Sizzling Race," p. 90.
12. "Domain of Apollo Under Siege," *Electronic Business News,* May 23, 1988, p. 24.
13. Sun Microsystems annual report, 1988, p. 7.
14. "Domain of Apollo."
15. "Domain of Apollo."
16. "May I Use Your Laboratory?" *The Economist,* June 18, 1988, p. 78.
17. "Japanese Firms Build Consumer Interest by Flooding the Market with Tiny TVs," *Wall Street Journal,* October 8, 1987, p. 29.
18. "Black and Decker Wows Industry with New Items," *The Sun,* September 11, 1988, pp. C1, C6.
19. "From Fuji to Mt. Everest," *Forbes,* May 2, 1988, pp. 35, 36.

CHAPTER 5
Time and Money

1. Henry Ford, *Today and Tomorrow,* reprint (Cambridge, MA: Productivity Press, 1988), pp. 112, 113, 114, 118. Originally published by Doubleday, 1926.
2. "Hewlett-Packard Agrees to Acquire Apollo Computer," *Wall Street Journal,* April 13, 1989, p. A3.

CHAPTER 6
Redesigning the Organization for Time

1. The new motto "the best technical value in the shortest time" was coined by the president of the company after reviewing the findings of his two senior managers' study.
2. Excerpted from letter to *Wall Street Journal,* published December 22, 1988, from David E. Lundstrom, a development engineer and then marketing manager in the computer industry for 30 years in Minneapolis.

CHAPTER 9
Time-based Strategy

1. B. H. Liddell Hart, *Strategy,* 2nd rev. ed. (New York: Signet, 1967), p. 145.
2. Philip Evans, The Boston Consulting Group, personal interview with Carl Johnson, Fall 1985.
3. "Suburbs Tackle Ticky-Tacky," *Chicago Tribune,* October 22, 1988, p. 3-1.
4. Personal interview, October 1988.
5. Scott Martin, "Take Your 'PICS'," *Bicycling,* September 1988, p. 107.
6. "Bass Group's Readiness Gives an Edge in Thrift Rescue," *Wall Street Journal,* April 25, 1988, p. 6.
7. "Now on the Inside, Ross Perot Tells GM and Its Rivals How They Must Change," *Wall Street Journal,* July 22, 1986, p. 4.
8. "BMW, Porsche Set Price Increase for 1988 Autos," *Wall Street Journal,* December 3, 1987, p. 14.

Index

Made in United States
North Haven, CT
14 May 2023

36573165R00178